CORE BIBLICAL STUDIES

THE PENTATEUCH

General Editors
Core Biblical Studies

Louis Stulman, *Old Testament*
Warren Carter, *New Testament*

Other Books in the Core Biblical Studies Series

The Apocrypha by David A. deSilva
The Dead Sea Scrolls by Peter Flint
Apocalyptic Literature in the New Testament by Greg Carey
God in the New Testament by Warren Carter
Christology in the New Testament by David L. Bartlett
The Holy Spirit in the New Testament by John T. Carroll

CORE BIBLICAL STUDIES

THE PENTATEUCH

MARVIN A. SWEENEY

Abingdon Press
Nashville

THE PENTATEUCH

This book is printed on acid-free paper.

Library of Congress Cataloging-in-Publication Data has been requested.

ISBN 978-1-4267-6503-2

Scripture quotations are the author's own translation.

17 18 19 20 21 22 23 24 25 26—10 9 8 7 6 5 4 3 2 1
MANUFACTURED IN THE UNITED STATES OF AMERICA

for Antony F. Campbell, SJ

Contents

General Preface

"All beginnings are hard," muses David Lurie in Chaim Potok's novel *In the Beginning*. "The midrash says, 'All beginnings are hard.' You cannot swallow all the world at one time."[1] Whether learning to ride a bike or play an instrument, start a new job or embark on a course of study, beginnings bristle with challenges and opportunities. The Core Biblical Studies series (CBS) is designed as a starting point for those engaged in Old Testament study. Its brief though substantive volumes are user-friendly introductions to core subjects and themes in biblical studies. Each book in the series helps students navigate the complex terrain of historical, social, literary, and theological issues and methods that are central to the Old Testament.

One of the distinctive contributions of CBS is its underlying commitment to bring together our most respected scholars/teachers with students in the early stages of their learning. "Drawing on the best scholarship, written with the need of students in mind, and addressed to learners in a variety of contexts, these books will provide foundational concepts and contextualized information for those who wish to acquaint themselves ... with a broad scope of issues, perspectives, trends, and subject matter in key areas of interest."

One might think that such an arrangement is commonplace but this is not always the case. Take, for example, introductory classes at many of our largest universities. Rarely are 101 classes taught by our most experienced instructors. This standard practice is in part a cost saving measure, but at the same time it misses a unique opportunity. CBS addresses this common oversight by entrusting students' beginnings to mentors who will prepare them for subsequent inquiry.

The books in this series not only serve to introduce beginners to biblical texts; they also aim to meet the needs of teachers who are well aware of the complexities of interpreting meaning. The process of meaning making of Old Testament texts is framed and influenced by a range of factors including the workings behind the text (diachronic), within the text (synchronic), and after the text by subsequent reading communities (the so-called Nachleben). This dynamic process is refracted through the lens of scholarly methodologies as well as the social location of the reader. No text is an island and no interpreter stands outside of their own particular time and place. An understanding of this amalgam, especially the diversity of interpretive approaches, is rich with possibilities and crucial to informed readings; but at the same time, it can be almost unwieldy in light of time constraints and other limitations. CBS volumes seek to help teachers navigate this complicated terrain in the classroom and so are "unapologetically pedagogical."

The goal of each volume is to help readers encounter the biblical text for themselves, become more informed interpreters, and set them on a joy-filled trajectory of life-long learning.

Louis Stulman
General Editor

Acknowledgments

It is my pleasure to thank those who gave support and encouragement during the course of writing this volume.

First, I thank Professor Louis Stulman, Hebrew Bible/Old Testament editor of the Core Biblical Studies series, for his invitation to contribute to this volume. Like me, he is known primarily for his work in the prophetic literature but well understands the interrelationships between pentateuchal and prophetic texts and the need to bring multiple perspectives together in the interpretation of biblical literature.

Second, I thank the Claremont School of Theology, particularly President Jeffrey Kah-Jin Kuan, Dean Sheryl Kujawa-Holbrook, and the CST Board of Trustees, for granting me a Spring 2015 sabbatical, which provided the opportunity to complete most of this manuscript. CST understands the importance of scholarship for the development of both faculty and students and consistently strives to promote such work in keeping with its Methodist ethos.

Third, I thank my colleagues and students at the Claremont School of Theology and the Academy for Jewish Religion California for their engagement and support in relation to the many courses which ultimately led to the writing of this volume.

Fourth, I thank Chang Jung Christian University, particularly Vice President Po Ho Huang, Dean Yatang Chuang, Professor Hye Kyung Park, and the faculty and students of the School of Theology, for their collegiality and hospitality during the term of my appointment as visiting scholar, June 2015. In addition to discussions concerning institutional cooperation and a series of lectures, I was able to complete the draft of the chapter on Numbers while in residence at CJCU.

Fifth, I thank my Research Assistant, Pamela J. W. Nourse, MD, for her meticulous reading of this manuscript. She has saved me from many errors. Any that remain are my own.

Sixth, I thank my family: my wife, Muna; our daughter, Leah; our son-in-law, Brian; and our baby granddaughter, Scarlet, for the love and support they give at all times. Without them, I could never complete work like this.

Finally, I thank Father Antony F. Campbell, SJ, Professor Emeritus of Old Testament at the Jesuit Theological College, Melbourne, Australia. I first met Tony as a beginning PhD student at Claremont when he spent a sabbatical teaching a course on Samuel while beginning work on his FOTL Samuel volumes. I learned much from him about the Deuteronomistic History at that time and in the years since have learned much from his expertise in pentateuchal studies as well. This volume is dedicated to him with gratitude and admiration.

San Dimas, California
December 16, 2016
16 Kislev, 5777

Abbreviations

AB. . . . . Anchor Bible

ABD . . . . D. N. Freedman et al., eds., *Anchor Bible Dictionary*, 5 vols. (Garden City, NY: Doubleday, 1992).

AnBib . . . . Analecta Biblica

ANEP . . . . J. B. Pritchard, ed., *The Ancient Near East in Pictures*, 3rd ed. (Princeton: Princeton University Press, 1969).

ANET . . . . J. B. Pritchard, ed., *Ancient Near Eastern Texts Relating to the Old Testament*, 3rd ed. (Princeton: Princeton University, 1969).

ATANT. . . . . Abhandlungen zur Theologie des Alten und Neuen Testaments

BASOR . . . . *Bulletin of the American Schools of Oriental Research*

BJS . . . . Brown Judaic Studies

BWANT . . . . Beiträge zur Wissenschaft vom Alten und Neuen Testament

BZAW. . . . . Beihefte zur Zeitschrift für die alttestamentliche Wissenschaft

CBQ . . . . *Catholic Biblical Quarterly*

CR:BS . . . . *Currents in Research: Biblical Studies*

EBib . . . . Études bibliques

EBR. . . . . H.-J. Klauck et al., eds., *The Encyclopedia of the Bible and Its Reception* (Berlin and New York: Walter de Gruyter, 2009ff).

EncJud. . . . . Cecil Roth, ed., *Encyclopedia Judaica* (Jerusalem and New York: Keter and MacMillan, 1971–1972).

FAT. . . . . Forschungen zum Altes Testament

FOTL . . . . Forms of the Old Testament Literature

FRLANT . . . . Forschungen zur Religion und Literatur des Alten und Neuen Testaments

HALOT. . . . . L. Koehler and W. Baumgartner, eds., *Hebrew and Aramaic Lexicon of the Old Testament*, 5 vols. (Leiden: Brill, 1994–2000).

HKAT. . . . . Hand-Kommentar zum Alten Testament

HSM. . . . . Harvard Semitic Monographs

HSS . . . . Harvard Semitic Series

IEJ. . . . . *Israel Exploration Journal*

JAOS. . . . . *Journal of the American Oriental Society*

JBL . . . . *Journal of Biblical Literature*

JCS . . . . *Journal of Cuneiform Studies*

JPS . . . . Jewish Publication Society

JSOT. . . . . *Journal for the Study of the Old Testament*

JSOTSup. . . . . Journal for the Study of the Old Testament Supplement Series

LHBOTS . . . . Library of Hebrew Bible/Old Testament Studies

NCeB . . . . New Century Bible Commentary

NEAEHL . . . . E. Stern, ed., *New Encyclopedia of Archaeological Excavations in the Holy Land*, 4 vols. (Jerusalem: Carta, 1993).

OTL . . . . Old Testament Library

SBL . . . . Society of Biblical Literature

SBLDS . . . . Society of Biblical Literature Dissertation Series

SBLResBS . . . . Society of Biblical Literature Resources for Biblical Study

SBLSym . . . . Society of Biblical Literature Symposium Series

SBT . . . . Studies in Biblical Theology

WBC . . . . Word Biblical Commentary

WMANT . . . . Wissenschaftliche Monographien zum Alten und Neuen Testament

Introduction

The Torah is the foundational sacred scripture for Jewish identity from ancient Israelite and Judean times through the present. The Hebrew noun *Torah* (*tora*) is derived from the verb root, *yrh*, which means "guidance" or "instruction." It is often mistranslated as "law," based especially on Paul's use of the Greek term *nomos*, "law," in the New Testament Epistles to characterize Jewish practice as fixed and unbending and therefore unnecessary for Christians. The term *Pentateuch*, derived from the Hellenistic Greek, *pentateuchos* ("five vessels," or "scrolls") refers to the five books of Moses: Genesis, Exodus, Leviticus, Numbers, and Deuteronomy. In Hebrew, each of the books is named for the first key term of the book: *Bere'shit* ("in the beginning"), *Shemot* ("names"), *Vayiqra'* ("and he called"), *Bemidbar* ("in the wilderness"), and *Devarim* ("words"). The English titles for the books are derived from Greek: Genesis ("origin, creation"), Exodus ("departure, going out"), Leviticus ("pertaining to the Levites"), Numbers (from Greek, *arithmoi*), and Deuteronomy ("second law").

The Torah is a narrative account of the origins of the nation Israel, beginning with the creation of the world and humanity at large (Gen 1–11); the early history of Israel's ancestors and their covenant with YHWH, the creator of Israel and the world (Gen 11–50); and the formative experiences of Israel under the leadership of Moses, including the exodus from Egypt (Exod 1–18), the revelation of divine Torah at Sinai (Exod 19–40; Lev; Num 1–10), and the wilderness journey that would take Israel from Sinai to the borders of the promised land of Israel (Num 11–36; Deut). The Torah therefore provides the foundations for Israelite identity as a nation in eternal covenant with YHWH, the creator of the universe and all humanity, who revealed to Israel divine instruction that would provide the basis for Israel to create a just and holy society among the nations of the world. Israel would thereby serve as a witness to the nations of the world of YHWH's role as the true G-d of all creation and humanity.

The modern historical-critical study of the Torah emerged in the age of Enlightenment in part as a result of the debates between Jews, Christians, and Muslims to define the true meaning of the Torah. Jews had recognized very early that Moses could not have written the entire Torah; the Babylonian Talmud states that Joshua must have written the account of Moses's death in Deut 34 (b. Baba Batra 14b–15a).

Medieval interpreters such as R. Saadia Gaon, Rashi, Radak, R. Abraham Ibn Ezra, and others likewise advanced the use of rational philosophy and philological study of the Torah text while remaining true to their traditional Jewish identities in order to defend Judaism against the challenges posed by Christianity and Islam.

With the eighteenth-century Enlightenment, human reason became the primary arbiter of truth in the western world when interpreters turned to evolutionary models of historical development as the means to read biblical texts. The decipherment of ancient languages, such as Akkadian, Sumerian, Coptic, and others, together with archeological exploration of the ancient Near Eastern world, provided interpreters with a wealth of knowledge that often demonstrated parallels between ancient writings and biblical texts. Such advances prompted biblical interpreters, especially Protestant Christian interpreters, to imagine the possibility of recovering the most ancient—and therefore the most authentic—texts of the Bible in their efforts to understand the "true" meaning of biblical revelation.[1]

The most famous biblical scholar from this period was Julius Wellhausen (1844–1918), a German Lutheran Old Testament professor who built upon the works of earlier scholars in an attempt to reconstruct the original literary sources that were written and later combined to form the present text of the Pentateuch.[2] He identified four major sources in the Pentateuch.[3]

The first was the J source, based on its use of the divine name, YHWH (written as JHWH in German; Judaism does not pronounce the Holy Name of G-d, and so the name is not spelled out here). The J source is also characterized by its folkloristic-mythological world view, its human-like portrayal of G-d, its southern Judean setting, and its portrayal of face-to-face communication between humans and G-d. The narratives of Adam and Eve in the garden of Eden (Gen 2:4b–4:26); Abraham's covenant with YHWH (Gen 15); and major elements of the Balaam narrative (Num 22–24) are all considered J-source materials, which Wellhausen dated to the early Davidic monarchy in the ninth century BCE. Gerhard von Rad later pushed the date of J back to the tenth century BCE, when the House of David and a united kingdom of Israel emerged.[4]

The second was the Elohistic source (E), based on its use of the term *Elohim*, the generic term for G-d, until the time of Moses's encounter with YHWH at the burning bush (Exod 3). This source portrayed a more reserved understanding of the relationship between G-d and human beings, insofar as G-d would be represented by angels, burning bushes, dreams or visions, and other devices rather than portrayed in face-to-face communication with humans. E originated in the northern kingdom of Israel, and it had a more developed sense of moral concerns than J. Major E narratives include Abraham's binding of Isaac (Gen 22), Jacob's vision of G-d at Bethel (Gen 28), and Moses's encounter with G-d at the burning bush (Exod 3). Wellhausen dated the E source to the mid-eighth century BCE, at the apex of northern Israelite power.

The third source was the D source, named for the book of Deuteronomy. D was characterized by its exhortational, preaching style of speech, which appealed to the ears of its audience with characteristic phrases, such as "Hear, O Israel!" "you shall observe these commandments," "you shall love YHWH, your G-d," and so on. D employed the divine name, but it called for only one centralized place for worship where YHWH would cause the divine name to dwell, and it called for observance of the divine word of YHWH as the basis for the covenant and Israel's possession of the land of Canaan. Wellhausen identified the book of Torah discovered in the Jerusalem temple during King Josiah's reign (640–609 BCE; see 2 Kgs 22–23) as an early form of Deuteronomy that served as the basis for Josiah's seventh-century reforms.

The fourth and final source was P, the Priestly source, which appeared throughout Genesis, Exodus, Leviticus, and Numbers and in the concluding portions of Deuteronomy. P employed a formal literary style (e.g., "it was evening and it was morning, the first day," "be fruitful and multiply, and fill the earth," "these are the generations of . . . ," "this is the Torah of . . . ") as well as a focus on ritual and priestly concerns. P did not use the divine name until after Moses's encounter with YHWH in the burning bush, and so Exod 6 first presents the name of YHWH, explaining to Moses that YHWH was previously known as El Shaddai. P appears in the first creation narrative (Gen 1:1–2:4a), the covenant of circumcision with Abraham (Gen 17), the explanation of the divine name to Moses (Exod 6), and the ritual laws of Leviticus (Lev 1–26), among others. Wellhausen reasoned that the time of Ezra and Nehemiah, when the priesthood emerged as the rulers of Judah, formed the historical setting for P in the fifth and fourth centuries BCE.

Wellhausen's model emerged as the dominant model for reading the Pentateuch in the twentieth century. Nevertheless, there were many problems with Wellhausen's reconstruction. Wellhausen stated repeatedly that he was unable to distinguish between the J and E sources in many texts, and so he left them undefined. Scholars also note that he was unable to reconstruct a complete, freestanding narrative for any of his sources, even though this was one of the goals of his study. There was no clear ending to J and many gaps, neither E nor P had a fully coherent story line, and D was a block of material that stood apart from the rest of the Pentateuch.[5]

But the most fundamental problem with Wellhausen's work was that he allowed his own theological viewpoint to determine much of his historical model for the composition of the Pentateuch. His theological viewpoint was especially based in German theological idealism, which in turn is based on a Platonic model that posits that the earliest forms of religious expression are the most authentic or pure understandings of the living encounter between G-d and human beings, whereas later expressions become institutionalized, dead, and corrupt over time. Among his theological foundations were his commitment to the notions of messianism and prophecy and his disdain for ritual, law, and priesthood. These ideas are in keeping with his Lutheran faith, which valued prophecy and messianism as the most central expressions of true religion, whereas ritual, law, and priesthood were viewed as institutions of the Roman Catholic Church, deemed to be corrupt by the Protestant Reformers, and Judaism, understood to be superseded by Christianity.

Wellhausen's four sources gave expression to his theological views, especially by positing an initial ideal relationship between humans and G-d that declines over the course of time. J, the earliest source in Wellhausen's understanding, portrays direct, face-to-face encounters between G-d and human beings, much like the prophetic experience, and it is set in the period of the formation of the royal House of David, indicating messianic interests. E, the second source, written during the high point of northern Israelite power in the eighth century BCE, posits a somewhat more distant relationship between humans and G-d insofar as G-d appears only in visions, in dreams, in symbols, and through the agency of angels. D, the third source, set in the seventh century BCE, posits an even more distant relationship insofar as humans encounter G-d through the divine word as expressed in Deuteronomy. And finally, P portrays the greatest distance between G-d and human beings insofar as humans can relate to G-d only through the priesthood, law, ritual, and the temple.

Gerhard von Rad argued that J itself was the product of oral traditions found at the various sanctuaries of early Israel.[6] He pushed back Wellhausen's ninth-century BCE dating of J to the 10th century BCE, when the Davidic monarchy was founded, and argued that when Israel first united under the House of David, the J composer combined the oral traditions into a narrative that explained Israel's origins.

Martin Noth argued that Deuteronomy must be separated from the rest of the Pentateuch as a discrete work that served as a key foundation for Israelite historical writing in the Deuteronomistic History (DtrH), including Joshua, Judges, Samuel, and Kings.[7] The formation of Genesis, Exodus, Leviticus, and Numbers could be traced to a number of key motifs that served as the focal points for the collection of oral traditions to form narrative blocks that now constitute the Pentateuch, that is, the primeval history, the patriarchal history, the exodus, the wilderness journey, and the conquest of the land.[8]

Based on growing knowledge of ancient Near Eastern archeology, texts, history, and religious ideas, Thomas Thompson and John Van Seters raised questions concerning the early dating of J.[9] Many features of J, such as the account of the tower of Babel in Gen 11 or Abraham's traversing the land of Canaan in Gen 12, presupposed Babylonian or Assyrian imagery and practice. Van Seters observed that Israel did not come into contact with Assyria and Babylonia until the eighth through sixth centuries BCE, and therefore pushed the date of J's composition forward to the exilic period when Babylon conquered Judah.[10] Hans Heinrich Schmid pointed to J as a later interpreter of earlier tradition, and Christoph Levin likewise argued for a relatively late date for J.[11] Some therefore see J as a later redactional layer in a developing Pentateuch. Others argue that it is no longer possible to reconstruct an E source, insofar as E was always viewed as supplementary to J. Still others argue that our inability to separate J and E entails that we can no longer speak of a J source for the Pentateuch.

Frank Moore Cross Jr. observes that P does not simply stand as an independent source that has been combined with the others but that it appears to serve as a redactional composition that produces the final form of the Pentateuch.[12] He points especially to the *toledoth*, "generations," formulas ("these are the generations of . . . ")

that play such an important role in organizing the narrative presentation of Genesis and introducing its narrative components. He also points to the itinerary or travel formulas that appear throughout Exodus and Numbers as further evidence of P's attempts at editing the Pentateuchal narrative as a whole.

Although many scholars question the existence of J and E, most continue to hold that P constitutes the final layer of the Pentateuch.[13] David M. Carr probes the literary seams or fractures of Genesis in an attempt to distinguish the P stratum of the book from its underlying pre-P materials.[14] Joel Baden holds that D knows and presupposes E, but not J, and therefore calls for a new form of source criticism that upholds the literary integrity of the four discrete, self-standing sources.[15] David Wright demonstrates that the laws of the covenant code in Exod 21–24 were modeled on those of Hammurabi's Law Code.[16] Bernard M. Levinson demonstrates that the laws of Deuteronomy represent updated and revised versions of laws that had earlier appeared in the covenant code of Exod 21–24,[17] and Jeffrey Stackert demonstrates how the laws of the holiness code of Lev 17–26 read, interpret, and update earlier legal collections in the Pentateuch.[18] In a later study, Stackert demonstrates how Moses is characterized as a prophet at the earliest levels of E and J.[19]

Great progress has been made in rethinking the Wellhausenian paradigm, but more needs to be done. A number of issues remain to be considered:

(1) J is a much later source than Wellhausen and von Rad imagined. J presupposes the Assyrian and Babylonian periods in Israelite and Judean history ranging from the late eighth to the sixth centuries BCE.

(2) Wellhausen could not separate E and J, especially because he thought that E was a supplement for J. But with J as a later source, E then emerges as the foundational source for the Pentateuch and J becomes a later supplement. E would have been composed in northern Israel and brought south to be edited in southern Judah following the destruction of Israel by Assyria in 722–721 BCE.

(3) Mid-eighth-century northern Israelite prophets appear to know elements of the pentateuchal texts. Hosea cites Jacob, the exodus from Egypt, and the wilderness wanderings in Hos 12 and the Ten Commandments in Hos 4.[20] Amos, a Judean prophet at Bethel, cites the covenant code in Amos 2:6-16 and the exodus traditions at various points in his book.[21]

(4) Much of the pentateuchal narrative presupposes northern Israel.[22] Both Jacob and Joseph appear to be northern Israelite ancestral figures. Jacob is the eponymous ancestor after whom Israel is named, and he appears especially at northern Israelite sites. He founds the northern sanctuary at Bethel as a result of his visionary experience of G-d in Gen 28. His sons are the eponymous ancestors of the tribes of Israel. Some question why Judah is included as his fourth son, but we must remember that Judah was a vassal to northern Israel throughout the period of the divided monarchy.

(5) Jacob's conflicts with Laban reflect problems experienced by northern Israel during the ninth and eighth centuries BCE. During the ninth century BCE, Israel allied with Aram in an attempt to stop the Assyrians from pushing westward. The inscriptions of the Assyrian King Shalmaneser III relate his 853 BCE battle against

an Aramean-led coalition that included King Ahab of Israel and his two thousand chariots.[23] As Shalmaneser III repeatedly attempted to cross the Euphrates River to attack Aram, Israel apparently withdrew from the coalition and was then attacked by the Arameans, as related in the Elijah-Elisha narratives of 1 Kgs 17–2 Kgs 14.[24] King Ahab was killed in battle at Ramot Gilead, and his son, Jehoram, was killed in a coup launched by an Israelite general named Jehu. Jehu and his successors continued to suffer attacks from Aram. They turned to the Assyrians for support, as indicated in the pictorial portrayal of Jehu bowing at the feet of Shalmaneser III in the Black Obelisk of Shalmaneser III[25] and in the inclusion of Jehu's great-grandson, Joash, in the vassal list of Adad-Nirari III.[26] With the support of Assyria, Joash forced a settlement with Aram, enabling Jeroboam ben Joash (786–746 BCE) to rule over a united Israel in peace (2 Kgs 14).

(6) Jacob's conflicts with Esau, the eponymous ancestor of Edom, likewise reflect Israel's conflicts with its vassal, Edom. When Aram attacked Israel in the ninth century, Israel's Transjordanian vassals revolted and broke free from Israelite control (2 Kgs 8:16-22). The Tel Dan Stele relates the assassination of the kings of Israel and Judah.[27] The Deir Alla Inscription relates the words of the visionary, Balaam ben Beor, who apparently announces Israel's defeat.[28] The Moabite Stone relates how King Mesha of Moab overthrew Israelite rule and killed the men of Gad to set his kingdom free.[29]

(7) The Jacob narratives appear to have been edited by Judean (J source) editors. Genesis 26, an example of the wife-sister motif, appears to be a J composition that places Isaac in the southwestern border areas of Judah adjacent to Philistia.[30] At the close of the Jacob narrative in Gen 35:27-28, Jacob travels to Hebron in Judah to bury Isaac. Otherwise, Jacob spends his time in northern Israelite territory and in Aram in Gen 25–35. Other elements of Gen 35 appear to reflect Judean interests. Rachel dies at Bethel, the sanctuary of the northern kingdom of Israel, even though her tomb is located south of Jerusalem on the road to Bethlehem. Jacob's oldest son, Reuben, loses his position in the family as a result of an affair with Jacob's concubine, Bilhah. Jacob's second and third sons, Simeon and Levi, shame their father in Gen 34 when they attack the men of Shechem who had just circumcised themselves so that Shechem ben Hamor could marry their sister, Dinah. Shechem had raped Dinah, which raises questions about the city of Shechem, the central meeting point of the northern tribes where important decisions are made (see Deut 27; Josh 24; Judg 9; 1 Kgs 12).

(8) The Joseph narrative also appears to be a northern Israelite narrative that was edited by a Judean editor. The Joseph narrative portrays Joseph, the beloved son of Jacob and Rachel, as a young man who matures through great hardship to emerge as Israel's leader. Joseph fathers two sons, Manasseh and Ephraim, who ultimately become the leading tribes of northern Israel. But editorial inserts in the narrative indicate Judean or J interests. Genesis 38 portrays another instance of the endangered matriarch when Tamar, the daughter-in-law of Judah, disguises herself as a prostitute to ensure that Judah does not have Canaanite descendants. This episode thereby

contrasts Judah with Joseph, whose sons are born to an Egyptian mother. At two key points in the narrative, Joseph's older brothers associated with the northern kingdom act as heroes, but they are supplanted by Judah. When the brothers conspire to murder Joseph in Gen 37, Reuben stops the brothers from killing Joseph in vv. 21-22, but in vv. 26-28, it is Judah who proposes that they sell Joseph rather than murder him. When in Gen 42 Joseph demanded a hostage from the brothers to ensure Benjamin's return, Simeon was the hostage who remained with Joseph, but Judah later offered his own life to Jacob should any harm come to Benjamin. Jacob's blessing of his sons in Gen 49 condemns Reuben, Simeon, and Levi, but names Judah the royal tribe, indicating clear Judean interests at the end of the Joseph narrative.

(9) The Abraham narratives in Gen 12–25 appear to be more markedly Judean.[31] Although there are some E and P elements, the Abraham and Sarah narratives are largely a J composition that displays some characteristic Judean interests and serves as an editorial overlay over earlier E materials. For one, Abraham settles in Hebron, which was the capital of Judah; when Sarah dies, Abraham purchases the cave at Machpelah in Gen 23, indicating a contract for Abraham and thus Judah to own land in Hebron. Likewise, the account in Gen 14 of Abraham's deliverance of the hostages taken by Sodom highlights his piety by having him travel to Salem, which is identified with Jerusalem, where he pays the tithe to G-d Most High and meets King Melchizedek, who also serves as a priest. The narrative concerning Abraham's covenant with YHWH in Gen 15 highlights Abraham's need for a son, which interpreters note is a key concern of the royal House of David, and the land that Abraham is promised corresponds with the territory claimed by the Davidic dynasty. The identification of Abraham with Judean interests is a key consideration; it shows that the northern Israelite figures of Jacob and Joseph are ultimately descended from a Judean ancestor. Abraham appears as an ideal figure in Genesis, whereas Jacob and Joseph are flawed figures who ultimately lead Israel into Egyptian exile.

(10) The bulk of the primeval history in Gen 1–11 appears to be largely a combination of P and J elements. P would include the seven-day creation that culminates in the Shabbat in Gen 1:1–2:3 and elements of the flood narrative in Gen 6–9, as well as the genealogies that appear throughout the narrative. J would include the garden of Eden and Cain and Abel narratives in Gen 2:4b–4:26, portions of the flood narrative in Gen 6–8, and the tower of Babel episode in Gen 11. The J elements point to concerns with the Jerusalem temple insofar as various elements of the J creation narrative point to features of the Jerusalem temple, such as that the cherub that guards against entry to the garden represents the cherub embroidered on the veil that separates the holy of holies into which humans do not enter; that the tree of knowledge from which Eve ate is represented by the temple menorahs or lampstands, which are constructed on the pattern of a seven-branched tree and give light in the temple; that Adam himself is represented by the high priest, called ben Adam (or the son of Adam) in Ezekiel, who approaches YHWH in the holy of holies on behalf of the people; and that the engravings in the walls of the temple's interior replicate motifs from the garden, such as fruit, animals, and cherubim.[32] The flood narrative portrays Noah's

ark as a structure similar to the temple, and the tower of Babel (Heb. for Babylon) narrative is a polemic against the Babylonian ziggurat dedicated to the god Marduk. Such a concern is particularly important because Judah and Babylon were allied during the reigns of Judean kings such as Hezekiah and Josiah in the eighth and seventh centuries BCE.

(11) The exodus and wilderness narratives appear to be based in an E composition that was brought south and edited in Judah. Exodus 1–15 seems to display no overtly northern or southern motifs, but it is known to the northern prophet Hosea. It is a creation narrative that ties the creation of Israel as a nation to elements of the natural creation of the world such as the distinctive Sinai bush that appears afire when its red blossoms emerge in the spring; the first nine plagues, all of which explain the origins of various elements of creation in Egypt and Israel; and even the splitting of the Red Sea, which itself is a creation account insofar as it portrays dry land emerging from the waters. The narrative explains the origins of *Pesach* or Passover, the spring agricultural festival that celebrates the firstfruits of the harvest, flock, and herd. The firstfruits of grain are offered based on the account of the people baking unleavened bread because they had little time to prepare bread upon their departure from Egypt, and the firstfruits of the flock are offered based on the account of the lamb's blood smeared on Israelite doorposts to protect the people from the angel of death during the plague of the death of the firstborn.

(12) A focal point of the exodus narrative appears to be the redemption of the firstborn. Most interpreters correctly relate this motif to the Passover offerings of the firstborn of the flock and herd, but the human dimension of this motif is not fully understood. It also points to a feature of northern Israelite practice, the role of the firstborn sons as the priests of Israel. We are accustomed to thinking of the tribe of Levi as the priestly tribe, but Aaron and the Levites are not designated for this role until Num 17–18. Hidden within the often-overlooked narratives of YHWH's conversations with Moses in Num 1–10 are three instances in which YHWH indicates to Moses that the firstborn sons of Israel had served as priests in the past but in the future that role would be assigned to the Levites (Num 3:5-13, 40-51; 8:13-19). Elsewhere, Israelite law called for the redemption of the firstborn, who broke the wombs of their mothers (Exod 34:19-20), but the law does not state what the role of the redeemed firstborn should be. Here we should note the example of Samuel, who served as prophet, priest, and judge at the sanctuary at Shiloh in northern Israel. Although Samuel and his father, Elkanah, are identified as Levites in 1 Chron 6:12-15, 1 Sam 1:1 identifies Samuel's father, Elkanah, as an Ephraimite. Samuel himself is the firstborn son of his mother, Hannah, who bore Samuel after praying to YHWH at Shiloh. After she weaned Samuel, Hannah took him to the Shiloh sanctuary, where he had a visionary experience of YHWH while sleeping by the ark (chest) of the covenant and grew up to become a priest.[33] We must consider the possibility that northern Israel had a different understanding of priesthood than southern Judah. In northern Israel, non-Levites could serve as priests, but in southern Judah only Levites

could serve as priests (1 Kgs 12:31).[34] The redemption of the firstborn—to serve as priests in Israel—emerges as a fundamental concern of the E exodus narrative.

(13) But the E exodus and wilderness narratives have been edited by J to reflect Judean interests. A key episode in these narratives is the narrative of the gold calf at Mount Sinai in Exod 32–34. When Moses comes down from Sinai to find Israel worshipping the gold calf, he breaks the tablets of the covenant and calls for those zealous for YHWH to join him. The Levites respond, and slaughter those who worshipped the gold calf. This episode paves the way for the designation of the Levites as priests in place of the firstborn in Num 1–10 and 17–18. This narrative is clearly a polemic against northern Israelite worship. It has major parallels with the portrayal in 1 Kgs 12:25-33 of Jeroboam's practices, most notably his establishment of a gold calf for worship at Bethel and Dan. Exodus 32–34 draws upon the Jeroboam narrative in 1 Kgs 12:25-33 and others to portray Israel's wilderness rebellion in terms reminiscent of northern Israelite apostasy, and it employs this narrative to lay the foundations for the later choice of the tribe of Levi as the priestly tribe of Israel.

(14) Exodus 32–34 draws upon the Deuteronomistic Historian's narrative of Jeroboam's apostasy in 1 Kgs 12:25-33, but it also draws upon other Deuteronomistic and Deuteronomic texts.[35] The portrayal of Moses hidden in the cave on Mount Sinai, where he witnesses YHWH's revelation in Exod 34:1-9, is heavily indebted to the portrayal of Elijah's sojourn on Mount Horeb in 1 Kgs 19, where he received a revelation from YHWH in the form of a "still, silent voice." Likewise, the warning against making a covenant or intermarrying with the Canaanite nations in Exod 34:10-16 is dependent upon the prohibition of intermarriage with the Canaanite nations in Deut 7:1-11. The law code in Exod 34:17-28 is a revision of the earlier code presented in the so-called covenant code in Exod 21–24 as well as some elements in Deut 16:1-17. The J writer knew D and the DtrH and used them in formulating Exod 32–34.

(15) The Deuteronomic law code rewrites the older covenant code of Exod 20–24. D was written during the seventh century BCE and functioned as a support for King Josiah's reforms.[36] Although some scholars attempt to date the covenant code to the late monarchic period or the Babylonian Exile based on parallels to Hammurabi's Law Code,[37] the case law forms found in the covenant code and Hammurabi's Code were also in use during the Assyrian period when Shalmaneser III first made King Jehu of Israel a vassal in the late ninth century BCE. Furthermore, the problematic apodictic law forms present in the covenant code are dependent upon similar forms in use in Assyrian vassal treaties.[38] Israel knew these law forms and apparently used them in formulating its own covenant code.

(16) Questions concerning the leadership of Israel dominate the wilderness narratives of Num 10–25. Numbers 17–18 demonstrate a clear Judean interest in designating Aaron and the tribe of Levi as the priests in Israel to replace the firstborn sons who had previously functioned in this role (see Num 3; 8). But there are also signs of northern interests throughout the narrative. In Num 11 Moses designates Israel's seventy elders to share with him the burden of leadership, which looks quite similar

to the council of elders that appoints David as king of northern Israel in 2 Sam 5 and the seventy sons of the king who appear to function as a royal council in northern Israel (see Judg 9; 2 Kgs 10). In Num 12, Aaron and Miriam are rebuked for objecting to Moses's marriage to a Cushite (Egyptian or African) woman, which seems to predate the concern with intermarriage in Deut 7. In Num 13–14, Moses sends spies into southern Canaan, and only two prove to be faithful to YHWH's promises of the land, Hoshea ben Nun of the tribe of Ephraim (later identified as Joshua ben Nun) and Caleb ben Jephunneh of Judah. Insofar as Joshua is an Ephraimite who emerges as Moses's successor and leads Israel in the conquest of the land, this narrative appears to be an E narrative that was edited by the inclusion of Caleb, the leader of the tribe of Judah, who would have served J interests.

(17) A persistent problem in pentateuchal scholarship has been the question of the conclusion of the J narrative, but with our observations that the E narrative is foundational, it becomes a question of the culmination of the E narrative. The Balaam narrative in Num 22–24 comes to the forefront. Balaam's blessing of Israel provides an appropriate conclusion as Israel is encamped in Moab on the eve of its conquest of the land. Although often identified as a J narrative, the Balaam narrative's E elements need to be reconsidered, especially since Balaam blesses all Israel, or Jacob, which designates the northern kingdom of Israel and its Judean vassal. A key consideration is the narrative's intertextual relationship with the Deir Alla Inscription, mounted in a Transjordanian building across the Jordan River in Israel.[39] The Deir Alla Inscription presents the words of Balaam ben Beor, who cursed Aram's enemies and foresaw victory over them. The enemies, of course, would have been Israel at a time when the Arameans overran the Transjordan and subjugated Israel until the House of Jehu allied with Assyria and freed themselves from Aramean rule. Balaam's blessing of Israel in Num 22–24 appears to be a response to the Deir Alla Inscription, especially insofar as its vision of a mighty Israel dwelling peacefully in its own land included a notice of the defeat of Israel's enemies when a star rises from Jacob and a scepter from Israel, ensuring Israel's possession of Moab, Seth, Edom, Seir, and Ir. Such a portrayal would provide a resounding conclusion for an Israelite E narrative.

(18) The final P edition of the Pentateuch also demands attention. A number of narratives or narrative blocks appear very clearly to be P, such as the seven-day creation account in Gen 1:1–2:3; the genealogies in Gen 5, 10, and 11; the account of Abraham's covenant by circumcision in Gen 17; elements of the plague narratives and Passover regulations in Exod 7–12; instructions concerning the tabernacle (meeting tent) in Exod 25–30; the eternal covenant in Exod 31; the building of the tabernacle in Exod 35–40; the levitical laws in Lev 1–16; the holiness code in Lev 17–26; various laws in Num 5–6; 19; 28–30; 33–36; and elements of Deut 34. Although these narratives all appear to be self-standing accounts, their placement in relation to the earlier E, J, and D materials indicates their interpretative function, even if they were not explicitly written for such a purpose. Genesis 1:1–2:3 recounts the creation of the world at large, whereas Gen 2:4–4:26 focuses on human beings within that world. Genesis 17 presents an account of YHWH's covenant with Abraham, although Abra-

ham affirms the covenant by circumcision in Gen 17 whereas YHWH affirms it by symbolically passing between the pieces of the severed offering in Gen 15. Exodus 25–30, 31, and 35–40 relate the construction of the tabernacle and associated items that facilitate the transition from Sinai, conceived as a sanctuary in Exod 19, to a temple to be established in the land of Israel. Leviticus 1–16, 17–27, and the various laws of Numbers specify the holiness and conduct that Israel and Judah must observe to merit residence in the holy land of Israel, sometimes by rewriting earlier laws from D and E. Overall, the P materials edit the preceding materials.

(19) The *toledoth* ("generations") formulas demand special attention as part of the final P stratum of the Pentateuch. Cross observed that the *toledoth* formula, "these are the generations of PN," are strategically placed throughout the book of Genesis to provide a genealogical, structural overview for the entire Genesis narrative from the generations of Adam and Eve in Gen 2:4a through the generation of Jacob in Gen 37:2.[40] A study by Thomas extends Cross's observations to Num 3:1, "these are the generations of Aaron and Moses at the time that YHWH spoke with Moses on Mount Sinai," which points to the Pentateuch's interest in tracing the history of humanity in twelve stages from the time of Adam and Eve through the time of Moses's and Aaron's leadership of Israel in the Sinai and wilderness narratives.[41] Cross also observed that within the exodus and wilderness narratives, the itinerary formulas, "and the people of Israel travelled from Rameses to Succoth with six hundred thousand men on foot apart from the children" (Exod 12:37), trace the journey of Israel from Egypt to Sinai and on through the wilderness to the land of Moab from which they would then cross the Jordan River to take possession of the promised land of Israel. Thus, the narrative is especially interested in tracing the creation of Israel in relation to the creation of all the world and humanity at large. The synchronic literary structure of the final form of the Pentateuch appears as follows:[42]

Synchronic Literary Structure of the Pentateuch

History of Creation: Formation of People Israel

I. Creation of Heaven and Earth	Gen 1:1–2:3
II. Human Origins	Gen 2:4–4:26
III. Human Development/Problems	Gen 5:1–6:8
IV. Noah and the Flood	Gen 6:9–9:29
V. Spread of Humans over the Earth	Gen 10:1–11:9
VI. History of the Semites	Gen 11:10-26

VII. History of Abraham (Isaac)	Gen 11:27–25:11
VIII. History of Ishmael	Gen 25:12-18
IX. History of Jacob (Isaac)	Gen 25:19–35:29
X. History of Esau	Gen 36:1–37:1
XI. History of the Twelve Tribes of Israel	Gen 37:2–Num 2:34
A. Joseph and His Brothers in Egypt	Gen 37:2–50:26
B. Deliverance from Egyptian Bondage: Rameses	Exod 1:1–12:36
C. From Rameses to Succoth: Consecration of Firstborn	Exod 12:37–13:19
D. From Succoth to Etham: Pillar of Fire and Cloud	Exod 13:20-22
E. From Etham to the Sea (Pi-hahiroth/Baal-zephon): Deliverance at Sea	Exod 14:1–15:21
F. From Reed Sea to Wilderness of Shur/Elim: Water in Wilderness	Exod 15:22-27
G. From Elim to Wilderness of Sin: Quails and Manna	Exod 16:1-36
H. From Sin to Rephidim: Amalek and Jethro	Exod 17:1–18:27
I. From Rephidim to Sinai: Revelation of Torah	Exod 19:1–Num 2:34
1. Arrival at Sinai	Exod 19:1-2
2. Revelation from Mountain: Ten Commandments; Covenant Code; Building of the Tabernacle	Exod 19:3–40:38
3. Revelation from Tabernacle: Laws of Sacrifice and Holiness Code	Lev 1–27
4. Census and Organization of People around Tabernacle	Num 1:1–2:34
XII. History of Israel under the Guidance of the Levites	Num 3:1–Deut 34:12
A. Sanctification of the People Led by the Levites	Num 3:1–10:10

B. From Sinai to Wilderness of Paran/Kibroth-hattaavah: Rebellion in the Wilderness	Num 10:11–11:34
C. From Kibroth-hattaavah to Hazeroth	Num 11:35–12:15
D. From Hazeroth to the Wilderness of Paran	Num 12:16–19:22
E. From Paran to Wilderness of Zin/Kadesh: Water from Rock	Num 20:1-21
F. From Zin/Kadesh to Mount Hor: Death of Aaron	Num 20:22–21:3
G. From Mount Hor to Edom/Moab: Defeat of Sihon and Og	Num 21:4-35
H. Arrival at Moab: Balaam; Census and Organization of People	Num 22:1–36:13
I. Moses's Final Address to Israel: Repetition of the Torah	Deut 1:1–34:12

(20) By highlighting the leadership of Moses and Aaron and the journey from Egypt to the borders of the land of Israel, the Pentateuch points to Israel's establishment in the land of Israel as the culminating act of creation. Like many ancient Near Eastern creation myths, the Pentateuch points to the creation of a temple in honor of the creator god, in this case the wilderness tabernacle (meeting tent) dedicated to YHWH, as the holy center of creation that will represent and ensure the stability and sanctity of all creation. Thus, the wilderness tabernacle anticipates the establishment of YHWH's temple as the holy center of creation. But the Pentateuch does not tell us if that temple will be in Jerusalem, Shiloh, Bethel, Dan, Shechem, Gilgal, or any other location known in ancient Israel or Judah. From the standpoint of E, it might have been Gilgal, Shechem, Shiloh, Dan, or Bethel. But from the standpoint of J, D, and P, it could only be Jerusalem. Thus the Pentateuch, in both in its final P form and in its presumed earlier compositional stages in E, D, and J, provides the foundations for Israel's and Judah's identity in the context of YHWH's creation of the world at large.

Genesis

I

Genesis introduces the formation of the nation Israel. The formal, synchronic literary structure of Genesis leads the reader from creation to a focus on Israel by a succession of formulaic statements that include "these are the generations of PN."[1] The first appears in Gen 2:4a, immediately following the account of creation in Gen 1:1–2:3, and reads, "These are the generations of the heavens and the earth when they were created." Some have read this statement as the conclusion of the initial creation narrative in Gen 1:1–2:3, but several factors point to its introductory role for the following material. First, there is no conjunction that joins Gen 2:4a to the preceding narratives. Second, the term generations, *toledoth* in Hebrew, is based on the Hebrew verb root *yld*, which means "to give birth," and thereby points to the human beings generated or given birth by creation whose narratives then follow. Third, the other examples of the formula throughout Genesis focus on a figure who is the ancestor of those whose narratives follow the formula. The *toledoth* formulas shift the focus of the reader from all humanity to the tribes of Israel. They tie Genesis into the larger narrative structure of the Pentateuch as a whole. As the final example of the formula in Num 3:1—"and these are the generations of Aaron and Moses on the day that YHWH spoke with Moses on Mount Sinai"—identifies Aaron and the tribe of Levi as the priesthood of Israel that would guide the nation in observance of YHWH's teachings throughout its history.

The following *toledoth* formulas in Genesis demonstrate their function. Following the initial account of creation in Gen 1:1–2:3, the first *toledoth* formula, in Gen 2:4a, "these are the generations of the heavens and the earth when they were created," introduces the account of the first humans in Gen 2:4–4:26, which focuses on the origins of human beings and their characteristics. The second *toledoth* formula, in Gen 5:1, "this is the account of the generations of Adam," introduces the development of humans and the problems that arise among them in Gen 5:1–6:8. The third *toledoth* formula, in Gen 6:9, "these are the generations of Noah," introduces Noah and the flood in Gen 6:9–9:29. The fourth *toledoth* formula, in Gen 10:1, "these are the generations of the sons of Noah:

Shem, Ham, and Japheth," introduces the spread of human beings over the earth in Gen 10:1–11:9. The fifth *toledoth* formula, in Gen 11:10, "these are the generations of Shem," shifts the focus to the Semites, the ancestors of Israel, in Gen 11:10-26. The sixth *toledoth* formula, in Gen 11:27, "and these are the generations of Terah," shifts the focus to the family of Terah among the Semites in Gen 11:27–25:11. Insofar as Terah is the father of Abraham, Gen 11:27–25:11 focuses on the history of Abraham (and Isaac). The seventh *toledoth* formula, in Gen 25:12, "and these are the generations of Ishmael, son of Abraham," introduces the history of Ishmael in Gen 25:12-18. The eighth *toledoth* formula, in Gen 25:19, "and these are the generations of Isaac, son of Abraham," introduces Isaac's son, Jacob, in Gen 25:19–35:29. The ninth *toledoth* formula, in Gen 36:1, "and these are the generations of Esau, who is Edom," introduces Esau, Jacob's brother, in Gen 36:1–37:1, in an effort to prepare the reader for the following account of Jacob's sons. The tenth *toledoth* formula, in Gen 37:2, "these are the generations of Jacob," introduces Jacob's twelve sons, who go on to become the ancestors of the twelve tribes of Israel. Although the initial narrative appears in Gen 37:2–50:26, this narrative block also includes the exodus from Egypt and a major portion of the revelation at Sinai in Exod 1:1–Num 2:34. The *toledoth* formula in Num 3:1, "and these are the generations of Aaron and Moses on the day that YHWH spoke with Moses on Mount Sinai," introduces Aaron's and Moses's leadership of Israel from Sinai to the Jordan River in Num 3:1–Deut 34:12.

The synchronic literary form of the Pentateuch appears as follows:[2]

Synchronic Literary Structure of the Pentateuch:

History of Creation/Formation of People Israel

I. Creation of Heaven and Earth	Gen 1:1–2:3
II. Human Origins	Gen 2:4–4:26
III. Human Development/Problems	Gen 5:1–6:8
IV. Noah and the Flood	Gen 6:9–9:29
V. Spread of Humans over the Earth	Gen 10:1–11:9
VI. History of the Semites	Gen 11:10-26
VII. History of Abraham (Isaac)	Gen 11:27–25:11
VIII. History of Ishmael	Gen 25:12-18
IX. History of Jacob (Isaac)	Gen 25:19–35:29

X. History of Esau	Gen 36:1–37:1
XI. History of the Twelve Tribes of Israel	Gen 37:2–Num 2:34
XII. History of Israel under the Guidance of the Levites	Num 3:1–Deut 34:12

Altogether, the pentateuchal narrative recounts the origins of Israel from the time of creation to the eve of their possession of the promised land of Israel. Insofar as the Pentateuch begins with creation to explain the origins of a nation, it is typical of many ancient Near Eastern creation accounts, such as the Babylonian Enuma Elish or the Ugaritic Baal Cycle, which employ the motif of creation to explain the origins of nations and their gods. The Enuma Elish explains the origins of the Babylonian empire and its leading god, Marduk, who created the world following a revolt against the earliest gods, Apsu and Tiamat.[3] The Baal Cycle explains the origins of the kingdom of Ugarit and its leading god, Baal, who assumed power following the decline of the creator god, El.[4] In each case, a temple is erected at the center of the principal city to commemorate the god and point to the leading role of the city in the nation or the world. The Pentateuch points to the construction of the tabernacle at Mount Sinai (Exod 25–30; 35–40), a portable sanctuary carried by Israel through the wilderness, which would serve as the pattern for the construction of YHWH's temple in the land of Israel.[5]

II

Genesis 1:1–2:3 presents G-d's seven-day creation of the world that serves as the foundation for the final synchronic form of the pentateuchal narrative.[6] Genesis 1:1–2:3 is a P-stratum text as indicated by its formulaic literary style; its initial use of *Elohim*, the generic term for G-d; and its focus on the institution of the Shabbat. Insofar as the process of creation presented in Gen 1:1–2:3 culminates in the holy Shabbat, the Shabbat both completes and sanctifies creation and thereby provides the epistemological basis that defines the character of creation and the means by which life, including human life, functions ideally within it.[7]

In order to understand how Gen 1:1–2:3 presents the Shabbat as the foundation of creation, readers must consider a number of issues.

The first issue is the initial statement of creation in Gen 1:1-2. Non-Jewish interpreters have understood these verses to describe a process of creation out of nothing or *creatio ex nihilo*.[8] Such an understanding holds that G-d is the supreme creative power in the universe and the beginning point or alpha of creation, which entails an omega, or a point at which creation will come to an end. But such a conception is not supported by the text of Gen 1:1-2. The conception of G-d as absolute creator presupposes a finite understanding of Gen 1:1, "in the beginning, G-d created the heavens and the earth," followed by a second set of finite statements in Gen 1:2, "and the earth was formless and void, and darkness was over the deep and the spirit of G-d was hovering over the face of the waters." Genesis presents a sequence of statements in which the earth is first created out of nothing in v. 1 and then v. 2 describes the state of the earth following its initial creation.

Such a reading is grammatically impossible based on the Hebrew Masoretic Text (MT).[9] As the medieval Jewish Bible interpreter R. Solomon ben Isaac (Rashi, 1040–1105 CE) demonstrated nearly a millennium ago, the Hebrew term, *bere'shit,* often translated "in the beginning," cannot stand as an independent clause. The Hebrew term, *reishit,* is a construct form that must be read in relation to the following term in the sentence so that *bere'shit* can only read, "in the beginning of . . . " Thus the sentence, *bere'shit bara' 'Elohim et hashamayim ve'et ha'arets* must read, in awkward English, "in the beginning of the creating of (by) G-d of the heavens and the earth," in better English, "when G-d began to create the heavens and the earth" (cf. the Common English Bible). In such a reading, Gen 1:1 can only be read as a subordinate clause that requires a following clause to serve as the primary assertion of the sentence, that is, "when G-d began to create the heavens and the earth, the earth was formless and void and darkness was upon the face of the deep and the wind of G-d was hovering over the waters." In such a statement, the earth is an unformed, preexisting entity at the outset of G-d's creation. G-d's act of creation is not *creatio ex nihilo* or "creation out of nothing"; rather it is the shaping and definition of the unformed chaos that existed before G-d commenced creation.

The reading that presents the notion of *creatio ex nihilo* is derived from the Greek Septuagint (LXX) text, *En archē epoiēsin ho theos ton ouranon kai tēn gēn,* "in the beginning, G-d created the heavens and the earth," an interpretative reading of the Hebrew influenced by hellenistic notions of creation circulating during the third through second centuries BCE.

Such a difference in interpretative perspective points to a divine model for human action in the world. Whereas the LXX Greek reading of the text presents a model of divine action that humans are unable to emulate, the MT Hebrew reading of the text presents a model of divine action that humans are able—and even expected—to emulate. Just as G-d takes a situation of unformed chaos and creates order and definition out of the chaos, so human beings, who are given "dominion," are expected to create order out of chaos in the world in which we live.

The seven-day process of creation in Gen 1:1–2:3 entails that holiness is inherent in creation. Creation in Gen 1:1–2:3 proceeds on the basis of six days of divine action and one day of divine rest. The six days of creation are highly ordered to provide the basic structure of creation in two parallel three-day sequences.[10] The first sequence in days one through three calls for the creation of the basic structures of creation, beginning with the differentiation between light and darkness on day one; the differentiation between the waters of the earth and the waters of the heavens on day two; and the differentiation between the dry land, which produces plant life, and the waters of the sea on day three. The second sequence on days four through six fills in details for the basic structures. The second sequence therefore includes the lights of the heaven, which reckon time, and the sun and the moon, which distinguish day and night on the fourth day; the creation of sea creatures and the birds of the heavens on day five; and the creation of living creatures culminating in human beings on day six.

Creation remains incomplete without the sanctification of the seventh day, Shabbat. Genesis 2:2 makes it clear that G-d completes the work on the seventh day, not on the sixth, "and G-d completed his work which he had done on the seventh day, and G-d ceased on the seventh day from all the work which he had done." The full creative process of creation requires both the six days of divine labor and the seventh holy day of divine rest.

This raises the question of the role of the human being, who was created on the sixth day. The human, created as male and female in the image of G-d, is endowed with the responsibility to master the earth and to rule it. The usual English interpretations of the Hebrew words used for mastery (Heb. *vekivshuha*, "and master it") and dominion (Heb. *uredu*, "and rule it") envision total domination. The Hebrew root *kbs* means "to subjugate" in reference to nations and slaves and as "to violate" in reference to women.[11] The Hebrew root *rdh* means "to tread" in reference to a wine press or "to rule" (as in to oppress) in reference to the earth, nations, peoples, and so on.[12] Such understandings suggest that human beings are given virtually unlimited autocratic and oppressive rule over the earth and its creatures.

A basic principle of power in politics holds that such autocratic rule is impossible without the consent of those governed. Such consent might be gained through use of force, but in the long run, such models prove to be unviable. Effective dominion is best gained by demonstrating to those ruled that they will benefit from the actions of their rulers.

But what does this mean? For one, Shabbat calls for a day of rest for all creation so that creation might rejuvenate itself and thereby better ensure its viability or sustainability. Such a principle of rejuvenation applies to land, animals, and human beings. But it is not limited to simple rest and rejuvenation. As Lev 17–26 indicates, holiness also entails a combination of moral and ritual principles, such as the proper treatment of blood, appropriate marriage and sexual relations, appropriate ownership and care for land, proper observance of sacred times and offerings, proper treatment of the elderly, and more. The use of Shabbat as an epistemological principle in creation signals an entire code of conduct that is incumbent upon human beings to ensure their proper, holy, just, and sustainable life in the land that G-d grants to them.

The placement of the P account of creation in Gen 1:1–2:3 immediately prior to the J account of creation in Gen 2:4–4:26 is key. Under the influence of source criticism, readers are accustomed to reading these narratives diachronically and independently of each other. But the more recent recognition of intertextual reading strategies demands consideration of the synchronic literary context in which a narrative appears. Genesis 1:1–2:3 sets the basic holy structure of creation and the place, role, and responsibility of human beings within it. Genesis 2:4–4:26 then examines the character of human beings within that creation.

III

The next four units of Genesis recount aspects of the origins and development of human beings and their spread throughout the earth. Genesis 2:4–4:26 recounts human origins. It includes three basic episodes, that is, the creation of human beings within creation as a whole in Gen 2:4-25; Eve's encounter with the snake and the expulsion from the garden of Eden in Gen 3:1-24; and Cain's murder of Abel in Gen 4:1-26. Because of the use of the divine name, YHWH, the anthropomorphic portrayal of YHWH in relation to the human beings, and the overall fairytale-like character of the narratives, interpreters consider this unit to be J.

The first episode, in Gen 2:4-25, presents an alternative account of creation from that of Gen 1:1–2:3. YHWH plants a garden in Eden that will become the scene of the creation of the first human and the creatures that will provide him with companionship. The garden of Eden provides a model of the world insofar as it is watered by a river with four branches which represent the major watercourses of the world. The first, the Pishon, remains unidentified, although the name of the land through which it winds, Havilah, means "sandy" in Hebrew and may refer either to Egypt or to Arabia. The Tigris and the Euphrates are the two major rivers that define Mesopotamia. The Gihon is a small stream that provides water for Jerusalem in the biblical period. Archeologists have now uncovered evidence that a rich and vast garden full of plants and trees was located in the Kidron Valley just outside the eastern main gate of ancient Jerusalem. Its purpose was likely to emulate the gardens planted in major capital cities of the world, such as the famed Hanging Gardens of Babylon, that were intended to represent the ideal beauty of creation and perhaps to provide fruits and vegetables for the royal kitchens. The portrayal of the garden of Eden is likely based on this Jerusalem garden.

The first human placed in the garden to till it is often understood as Adam, but the Hebrew term, *ha'adam*, means "the *adam*" or "the human being."[13] YHWH permits the human to eat of all the trees of the garden except for the tree of the knowledge of good and evil. YHWH notes that the first human is alone, and YHWH creates animals to keep the human company. When this proves to be inadequate, YHWH casts a deep sleep on the human and divides it in two to create a man and a woman. Although many translations depict taking a rib from Adam's side, the Hebrew term, *tsela'*, often translated "rib," actually means "side."[14] Thus the original human is divided into two gendered figures, the male who will henceforth be known as Adam and the female, whom Adam will call "woman" and later "Eve" (*khavvah*), which means "living" or "mother of all living" (Gen 3:20). Both the man and the woman are naked (*'arummim*), but they are not ashamed. Although some have attempted to portray Eve as subordinate to Adam, her designation as "a helper corresponding to him" (*'ezer kenegdo*) in Gen 2:18 indicates that Eve is a partner with Adam.[15]

The second episode, in Gen 3:1-24, presents the woman's encounter with the snake and the resulting expulsion from the garden. The snake is described as "clever" (*'arum*), a deliberate play of words on the Hebrew word for "naked" (*'arummim*) in Gen 2:25. The snake challenges the woman to eat the fruit of the tree by arguing that she will not die if she eats. The snake's argument turns on the question of *when* the humans would die if they eat the fruit, immediately or at some later time. With two conflicting claims, the woman must use her own reason to decide what to do. After examining the fruit and finding it desirable, she eats the fruit and gives some to the man beside her. The narrative neglects to mention why the man does not take part in the conversation with the snake even though he was there. As a result of eating, the man and the woman recognize that they are naked and make clothing to cover themselves. When YHWH searches for them and finds that they are hiding because they know that they are naked, YHWH asks who was responsible. After each character dodges responsibility, YHWH passes judgment, that is, the man will work for his food and eventually die; the woman will desire the man, suffer labor pains at childbirth, and forever be in conflict with the snake; and the snake will crawl on its belly in the dirt. Although many charge Eve with sin, she introduces the knowledge of good and evil to humanity.

The ancient Near Eastern background for the Adam and Eve narrative lies in the Canaanite and Egyptian worship of the goddess Hathor or Kadeshah.[16] She is a goddess of fertility and wisdom who typically appears naked to represent sexuality. She holds fruit tree branches in one hand to represent fertility and a snake in the other hand to represent immortality, and she is mounted on a lion to represent royalty or dominion.[17] Snakes were a symbol of immortality in the ancient world because they shed their skin, which suggests that they live forever. She is flanked by Resheph, the Canaanite/Egyptian god of plagues, to represent death and the ithyphallic Min, the Egyptian god of fertility, to represent life. As a J text, Gen 3:1-24 is a polemic against the Egyptian and Canaanite gods to encourage worship of YHWH instead.

The final episode, in Gen 4:1-26, portrays Cain's murder of Abel. Interpreters maintain that the narrative portrays the conflict between the settled agricultural population of Canaan/Israel and the seminomads of the desert who so frequently raided farming settlements. The agriculturalist setting of the narrative appears in Cain's punishment: he loses his right to land and is forced to wander in the wilderness as an outcast. Israel traces its origins to the wilderness wandering and frequently idealizes desert dwellers, such as Jethro, the priest of Midian, who becomes the father-in-law and key advisor of Moses (Exod 3; 18), or the Rechabites, to whom Jeremiah points as ideal adherents of YHWH (Jer 35). The key element of the narrative is the shedding of blood, which defiles the sacred soil of creation. This motif continues when Lamech, a descendant of Cain, kills a young boy who wounded him, thereby pointing to increased bloodshed which leads to the flood. The narrative ends with a notice that humans began to call on the name of YHWH at that time.

Genesis 5:1–6:8 presents a combined P and J account of the line of Adam through Noah and his sons, Japheth, Ham, and Shem. It also notes that the sons of G-d mated with the daughters of Adam, transgressing the boundaries between heaven and earth and between the divine and the human. The shedding of blood and the mixing of the human and divine points to a return to chaos and human evil, which prompts YHWH to destroy the earth.

Genesis 6:9–9:29 recounts Noah and the flood. This narrative explains YHWH's decision to establish an eternal covenant to maintain creation. It is a combination of the J and P strata of the Pentateuch. The J narrative focuses on Noah's efforts to save one pair each of all the living creatures on earth from a flood, which lasts for forty days. The P narrative focuses on Noah's efforts to save seven pairs each of all the clean living creatures on earth and one pair each of the unclean creatures during a flood that lasts for one hundred fifty days. P thereby shifts the narrative from functioning simply as an account of YHWH's attempt to punish humanity to an account that establishes the means to ensure the holy boundaries of the world and to channel human violence by allowing them to eat meat.

The biblical flood story responds to the well-known Mesopotamian flood narratives, including the Sumerian account of the flood hero, Ziusudra; the Babylonian Atrahasis narrative; and the Babylonian Gilgamesh epic, which includes a flood story based on the hero, Utnapishtim.[18] The three narratives are actually variants of the same basic account that develops through time and across cultures. All are focused on the question of human mortality. The Atrahasis narrative posits that the flood is an attempt by the gods to destroy human beings because their noise prevents the gods from sleeping. The humans are aided by Enki or Ea, the god of fresh water, who advises Atrahasis to build a vessel to save his family and animals from the flood. During the flood, the gods discover that they need humans to feed them or they will starve. When they find humans alive after the flood, they impose labor, death, disease, and stillbirth to control their numbers and to reduce the noise. Zuisudra, Atrahasis, or Utnapishtim, however, are granted eternal life.

Genesis 10:1–11:9 presents a combined P and J text that discusses the development of the lines of Noah's sons, Shem, Ham, and Japheth. Japheth's descendants populate Asia Minor and Europe. Ham's sons dwell throughout Canaan, Africa, and Mesopotamia. The sons of Shem (the Semites) live throughout Western Asia and the Arabian Desert and ultimately move into Mesopotamia. The tower of Babel narrative in Gen 11:1-9 recounts how YHWH divided the various peoples of the world into different cultures, nations, and language groups in order to prevent them from uniting to reach heaven and disrupt the order of creation and its division between heaven and earth. Thus, the narrative is a polemic against Babylon, which was built on the plain of Shinar and featured a temple in the form of a ziggurat or stepped pyramid at its center dedicated to Marduk, the creator and city-god of Babylon. Babylon saw itself as the ruler of all the nations of the world. By destroying the tower of Babel, YHWH confuses all the languages of the world and ensures that no such union of human beings would ever overturn creation.

IV

Genesis 11:10-26 presents a history of the Semites from Shem to Terah and his sons, Abram, Nahor, and Haran. This brief P genealogy prepares for the history of Terah.

Genesis 11:27–25:11 presents the history of Terah, which focuses on Abram/Abraham as the ancestor of Israel, including the birth of his sons, Ishmael to the Egyptian concubine, Hagar, and Isaac to Abraham's wife, Sarah. Genesis 11:27–25:11 is the product of P composition and the editing of an underlying EJ stratum. P material appears especially in the genealogical account in Gen 11:27, 31, and 32; brief notices in Gen 12:4b, 5; 16:1a, 3, 15, 16; and 19:29; the account of Abraham's covenant by circumcision in Gen 17:1-27; the birth of Isaac in Gen 21:1b-5; and Abraham's purchase of the cave at Machpelah for the burial of Sarah in Gen 25:7-11a. Genesis 20:1b-17, 18; 21:6, 8-20, 21, 22-27, 28-31, 32, 33, 34; and 22:1-14, 15-18, 19 are commonly identified as E, but with the later dating of J, the underlying narrative is fundamentally an E narrative from northern Israel that has been edited and expanded by J following the collapse of northern Israel.

Scholars engaged in considerable debate during the twentieth century concerning the historical background of Abraham and Sarah.[19] Two potential periods were identified, but neither proved entirely satisfactory. The earliest was the Amorite period, ranging from 2300 BCE when the Amorite invasions of the ancient Near East commenced through 1800 BCE when King Hammurabi of Babylon (1792–1750 BCE), the founder of the first Amorite dynasty, commenced his rule. The term Amorite is derived from Akkadian *amurru*, "westerners," which refers to the seminomadic, Semitic-speaking peoples who began to move into Babylonia and the rest of the Fertile Crescent from the Arabian Desert (west of Babylonia) 2300–1800 BCE. Although the portrayal of the Amorites corresponds to the portrayal of Abraham and Sarah, the Amorites have a very questionable reputation in the Hebrew Bible (Gen 15:16-19; Deut 1:7), especially because they are identified with the kingdoms of Sihon of Heshbon and Og of Bashan, who attempted to block Israel from passing through their land while the Israelites were journeying through the wilderness (Num 21:21-35; Deut 1:4; 2:24-37; 3:1-13; Judg 11:19-24).

The second period is the so-called Amarna period from the mid-thirteenth century BCE. This period is named after the discovery in the Egyptian town of Amarna of a cuneiform archive containing letters sent by the governors of the city-states of Canaan to their Egyptian overlords, especially Pharaoh Amenhotep IV, also known as Akhenaton, who ruled Egypt and Canaan ca. 1353–1336 BCE.[20] The Canaanite governors requested troops from Egypt to suppress King Labayu of Shechem and his sons, who were harassing the territories of Jerusalem, Megiddo, and other Canaanite city-states with the aid of *habiru*, seminomadic tribespeople who were moving into Canaan and settling in areas around the major Canaanite cities. The Akkadian term *habiru* (Egyptian pronunciation *apiru*) means "barbarian" or "people outside the law." It is sometimes identified as a cognate for the Hebrew term, *'ivri*, "Hebrew," which is used to describe Abram and the Israelite slaves in Egypt (Gen

14:13; 43:22; Exod 1:15; 2:11, 13), but this identification is disputed. Even as late as 1216 BCE, the Merneptah Stele portrays Israel as a seminomadic people among the settled peoples of Canaan. Overall, the portrayal of the *habiru* in the Amarna letters appears to resemble that of the Hebrews in the Pentateuch, although critics point out that the chronology of the Pentateuch would call for the ancestors to have lived in a much earlier period. Nevertheless, the *habiru* hypothesis has some possibilities, especially since Shechem, named as the city of Labayu, was situated on the border between Ephraim and Manasseh (Josh 17:2, 7; 20:7), and it was never destroyed prior to Israel's emergence in the land. Shechem functioned as northern Israel's central gathering point (Deut 27; Josh 24; Judg 9) and the place where the northern kingdom of Israel chose Jeroboam ben Nebat as its first king (1 Kgs 12).

There is no clear evidence concerning the historical existence or setting of Abraham and Sarah. The narratives about them in Gen 11:27–25:11 are the product of later reflection by the E, J, and P writers who produced the final form of Genesis.

The Abraham and Sarah narratives in Gen 11:27–25:11 are an idealized account of Israel's first ancestors. Abraham—or Abram—is portrayed as a righteous figure placed in difficult positions by YHWH, the G-d to whom he swears allegiance as the foundation of the covenant with Israel. The narrative is designed to raise questions about YHWH's integrity and fidelity to the covenant made with Abraham.[21] The question of YHWH's integrity is based on the further question as to whether or not Sarah—or Sarai—will bear a son to Abraham and thereby enable the covenant with YHWH to pass on to future generations. The Abraham and Sarah narratives introduce considerable tension concerning YHWH's integrity and intentions. Will Sarah bear children to the Egyptian Pharaoh when she is taken in to his harem in Gen 12:10-19? Will Abraham's line continue through Ishmael, born to his Egyptian concubine, Hagar, in Gen 16? Will Abraham offer his son Isaac, born to Sarah in Gen 21, as a sacrifice demanded by YHWH in Gen 22? In the end, YHWH emerges as a G-d who shows fidelity.

The Abraham and Sarah narrative begins in Gen 11:27-32 with the genealogy of Terah, initially placed in the city of Ur of the Chaldeans. This designation is a clue concerning the dating of the text. Although Ur is known from Sumerian times in the third millennium BCE, the reference to the Chaldeans indicates the Neo-Babylonian empire, founded by King Nebopolassar, the father of Nebuchadnezzar, in 627 BCE. Terah takes his family to Haran in Aram, from which Abram and his family journey to Canaan. A key notation in Gen 11:30, "and Sarai was barren; she had no child," serves as the *Leitmotif* of the narrative, thereby raising the question as to whether YHWH's promises to make a great nation of Abram mean anything at all.

The narrative proceeds in episodes. The first, in Gen 12:1-9, presents YHWH's commands to Abram to journey from Haran to the land of Canaan, together with YHWH's initial promise to make Abram into a great nation. The episode begins with YHWH's instruction to Abraham to leave his native land and his father's house to go to an unnamed land that YHWH will show him. YHWH's promise to make Abram into a great nation that will bless all the families of the earth then follows. Without having much of an idea of who YHWH is or where YHWH expects him to go, Abram proves himself to be an obedient servant of YHWH who does not argue with his G-d or demand clarification concerning what YHWH has just asked him—at the age of seventy-five—to do. The identification of the cities to which Abram travels points to northern interests, Shechem in v. 6, Bethel and Ai in v. 8, and on into the Negev in v. 9. Shechem and Bethel are two key cities of northern Israel. Shechem is King Jeroboam ben Nebat's first capital (1 Kgs 12:25) and Bethel is one of northern Israel's major temple sites (1 Kgs 12:29; 13:1-34; cf. Gen 28), which suggests that Gen 12:1-9 is originally an E narrative concerning Abram's connections with two major sites in northern Israel. Abram is portrayed as ruler of the land analogous to the Assyrian kings from the late ninth through the seventh centuries BCE. Following the spring plantings and harvests, the Assyrian kings would gather their armies for a *palu* campaign, an expedition throughout the territory ruled by the Assyrian king to show force to his subjects, intimidate them into submission, and collect the annual tribute.[22] The Assyrian kings thereby ensured the loyalty of their subjects and kept control of their lands. Abram demonstrates his own "sovereignty" over the land as granted to him by YHWH.

Having moved to the land of Canaan on YHWH's instructions, Abram and Sarai are placed in jeopardy in Gen 12:10-20 due to a famine in the land. Some interpreters claim that Abram's willingness to abandon Canaan demonstrates his lack of faith in YHWH, but such a contention ignores the fact that YHWH is the G-d of fertility who brings rain and therefore food to the land, without which Abram and Sarah cannot survive. YHWH's credibility is in question here, not Abram's. The family is forced to migrate to Egypt looking for food, not unlike migrant workers coming into the United States and other developed countries looking for work. As aliens, they are vulnerable in Egypt. Their vulnerability comes to the forefront when the narrative introduces the first of the "endangered matriarch" narratives in which a mother of Israel is put at risk of bearing children to a foreign man rather than to her Israelite/Judean husband. The "endangered matriarch" narratives in Gen 12; 20; 26; 34; and 38 play a key role in tying the Genesis narratives together by raising tension as to whether the ancestors of Israel will maintain their distinctive identities or assimilate into a more powerful Gentile culture, whether Egyptian, Philistine, or Canaanite.[23] In all cases but one (Dinah in Gen 34), the women are delivered and go on to bear children who will become the leaders of Israel and Judah. In the present narrative, the Egyptians note Sarai's beauty, and Abram rightly fears that she will be taken and he will be killed, an experience common to many homeless people in the world even today. He tells her to claim that she is his sister to save their lives, which is an indication of just how desperate their circumstances are. If Abram dies, neither of them leaves Egypt and the covenant is void. Sarai is indeed noticed by Pharaoh, the most powerful man in Egypt, and he takes her into his harem. It is only when YHWH sends plagues against Pharaoh that Pharaoh realizes Sarai's identity and releases her back to Abram. Abram takes his wife and leaves Egypt.

The following narratives in Gen 13 and 14 aid in building up Abram's righteous character and indicate J authorship insofar as they are set in Judah. Genesis 13 presents an account of Abram's interaction with his nephew, Lot, over grazing rights in the Negev. Abram's and Lot's shepherds were in conflict over territorial rights for their flocks, but Abram settles the matter by offering Lot whichever lands he might choose. Such an act demonstrates Abram's magnanimity. As the senior male in a patriarchal society, Abram had the right to choose. The Jordan plain, including Sodom and Gomorrah, was well watered, and Lot chose that territory. The narrator, however, signals coming trouble for the region by noting the wickedness of Sodom and Gomorrah. Abram retains Canaan and makes his home by the oaks of Mamre near Hebron in what would become the land of Judah.

Genesis 14 likewise demonstrates Abram's righteousness. A Mesopotamian coalition attacked Sodom, Gomorrah, and their allies and carried off Lot as well as other hostages and a great deal of wealth. Abram assembled men from his own household to rescue Lot and recover the spoils. When Abram returned Lot and the others, he declined a reward from the king of Sodom, which ensured that he would not be beholden to the king of a city that has already been identified as wicked in Gen 13:13. Melchizedek, the king of Salem, identified with Jerusalem and the future site of the temple, and priest of El Elyon, "G-d on High" (Ps 110), also met him and gave him El Elyon's blessing. Abram demonstrates his piety by giving to Melchizedek a tithe, or one-tenth, of everything he had gained, in keeping with the later requirement to pay the tithe to support the temple and the Levites (Lev 27:30-33; Num 18:21-32; Deut 14:22-29).[24] Such an act demonstrates Abram's piety and righteousness and identifies him with YHWH, identified with El Elyon in Gen 14:21, and the future Jerusalem temple.

Genesis 15–17 presents the account of YHWH's covenant with Abraham. When read synchronically, it presents a coherent account in which YHWH affirms the covenant in Gen 15 by passing through the pieces of sacrificial animals, the birth of Ishmael in Gen 16 introduces an element of tension concerning the identity of Abraham's heir, and Gen 17 presents Abraham's affirmation of the covenant through circumcision. When read diachronically, these narratives present a combination of EJ material in Gen 15–16 and P material in Gen 17.

Genesis 15 begins with YHWH's promise of great wealth to Abram in a vision, but Abram responds by noting that he has no son to whom to pass on such wealth.[25] Abram's responses raise the level of tension in the narrative concerning YHWH's fidelity. Whereas Abram has been loyal to YHWH, YHWH has made many promises but has still not granted Abram and Sarai a son. When YHWH reiterates the promise of land and descendants, Abram asks for a sign to demonstrate the validity of YHWH's promise. Although many read Gen 15:6 as a statement of YHWH's reckoning of Abram as righteous, the Hebrew states that Abram believed in YHWH and reckoned YHWH as righteous, "And he (Abram) believed in YHWH, and he (Abram) reckoned it to him (YHWH) as righteous." YHWH's sign calls for the presentation of a number of sacrificial animals that have been cut in half. A deep sleep falls upon Abram, and YHWH tells him that YHWH will deliver his offspring from slavery in a foreign nation. YHWH then makes a covenant with Abram, symbolized by a blazing torch and smoking firepot that passes between the pieces of the sacrificial animals, and promises Abram the land extending from the river Euphrates in Mesopotamia to the river of Egypt, sometimes identified with the Nile, but best identified with the Wadi el-Arish, which formed the boundary of the land of Canaan and the Sinai wilderness. The ceremony of passing through the pieces was common to Assyrian treaty texts in the ninth through seventh centuries BCE. When a party to the treaty would pass between the pieces of the animals, he would declare that the same thing should happen to him if he does not abide by the treaty.[26] The smoking firepot and flaming torch are common divine symbols in the ancient world, indicating that YHWH passed between the pieces and therefore affirmed the treaty. Altogether, Gen 15 appears to be an E text edited by J that envisions the full extent of the Davidic-Solomonic kingdom.

Genesis 16 presents the birth of Ishmael to Abram though Sarah's Egyptian maidservant, Hagar. Genesis 16 introduces an element of narrative tension insofar as it suggests that Abram's heir might be Egyptian (see Gen 12:10-20). Although such an act might seem bizarre, Sarah is within her rights to offer Hagar to her husband. Women could be divorced in the ancient world if they did not produce offspring, in which case they would return to their father's family or be forced to fend for themselves. Hammurabi's law code sections 144–147 allow a woman to give a maidservant to her husband so that she might provide him with children and thereby avoid a divorce.[27] Should the maidservant attempt to supplant the wife, the wife may sell her.

Genesis 17 then presents the covenant by circumcision in which Abram affirms the covenant with YHWH. The practice of circumcision is known from as early as the twenty-third century BCE Naga ed-Dêr Stele, which presents the account of a young man who is circumcised with one hundred twenty others for priestly service.[28] Circumcision may have originated as a puberty ceremony that prepared a young man for marriage (Ishmael is 13 when circumcised, and Moses's son is circumcised as a "bridegroom of blood" by Zipporah in Exod 4:24-26). But ancient Israel and Judah understood circumcision, which is performed on the eighth day following the boy's birth, as a holy obligation of service to YHWH. The practice may indicate a symbolic offering of the boy to YHWH analogous to the firstborn of flock and herd (Exod 22:28-29).

Genesis 18–22 returns to the presentation of Abraham as a righteous servant of YHWH. The first episode is the Sodom-Gomorrah narrative in Gen 18–19 in which YHWH destroys the two cities for their wickedness. Sodom and Gomorrah were known cities of the ancient world, having been cited as trading partners with the third-millennium city of Ebla. They were located along the southern region of the Dead Sea, perhaps in the area of the southern shallower portion of the Dead Sea, which flooded as a result of earthquakes in antiquity. The narrative features YHWH's reiteration of the promise that Sarah will have a son, which prompts her to laugh (*vatitzkhaq*, "and she laughed"; Gen 18:12; cf. Gen 21:6), which in turn stands as the basis for Isaac's name *yitzkhaq*, "he laughs." A key element in the narrative is when YHWH discloses to Abraham plans to destroy Sodom and Gomorrah, which prompts Abraham to ask the moral question of YHWH, "Will you indeed destroy the righteous with the wicked?" in Gen 18:23. The question places the onus on YHWH to demonstrate righteousness. The attempted rape of the two angels who visit the city points to its immorality and indicates a potential E origin with J editing (see Judg 19–21).

Genesis 20 presents another instance of the endangered matriarch motif in which the Philistine king Abimelech desires Sarah. The passage demonstrates that Sarah is indeed Abraham's half-sister. The episode aids in tying the ancestral narratives together by introducing a threat to their Israelite identities. Genesis 21, widely viewed as an E narrative, then follows with the birth of Isaac to Sarah and the expulsion of Hagar and Ishmael.

Although the birth of Isaac would seemingly resolve the issue of Sarah's barrenness, Gen 22, known as the binding of Isaac, raises the tension once again by presenting YHWH's demand that Abraham sacrifice his son as a test of his faithfulness. Ironically, readers have seen a fully obedient Abraham, even when he raises questions to YHWH, and Abraham here obeys without protest. When Abraham's knife is about to strike, an angel of G-d intervenes and puts a stop to the sacrifice, indicating that Abraham has passed the test. Readers might rightly ask who actually is tested here: Abraham, who has been obedient all along, or YHWH, whose promises of a son to Abraham have come into question throughout the narrative? In the end, YHWH proves to be a reliable deity, but the narrative forces the reader to consider this dimension of YHWH for some eleven chapters before finally demonstrating the point. The background to this narrative is the Israelite practice of redeeming the firstborn (to the mother's) sons of Israel (Exod 34:19-20). Ancient Israel initially dedicated firstborn sons as priests (Samuel is the firstborn of Hannah, 1 Sam 1–3) until the tribe of Levi was appointed to serve as a dynastic priesthood (Num 17–18).

Genesis 23:1–25:11, considered a J text, closes out the Abraham-Sarah narratives. Genesis 23 reports Sarah's death and burial in Kiriath-arba or Hebron. Abraham's purchase of the cave at Machpelah establishes ownership of the land, and it serves as the burial site for the entire ancestral family except for Rachel. Genesis 24 recounts Abraham's efforts to secure a bride for Isaac by sending his servant Eliezer to Haran. Rebekah, the daughter of Bethuel and granddaughter of Abraham's brother, Nahor, agrees to the offer to marry Isaac and accompanies Eliezer to Hebron for the marriage. Genesis 25:1-11 recounts Abraham's marriage to Keturah and the births of his other children together with his burial at Machpelah with Sarah.

Genesis 25:12-18 then recounts the descendants of Ishmael. The P account portrays the Ishmaelites as a great nation that encamps alongside their kinsmen from Egypt to Assyria.

V

Genesis 25:19–35:29 presents the account of the descendants of Isaac, which focuses on his fraternal twin sons, Jacob and Esau. The Jacob narratives are set largely in the territory that would eventually become the northern kingdom of Israel and its problematic ally Aram. Such a setting, which highlights key northern Israelite locations, such as Bethel, Penuel, Succoth, Mahanaim, and others, suggests that the Jacob narratives are fundamentally an E, or Ephraimite, narrative that has been brought south following the destruction of the northern kingdom of Israel in 722–721 BCE to be edited by J, or Judean, redactors.

The narrative makes it clear that major characters are the eponymous ancestors of Israel and its neighbors Edom and Aram.[29] Thus Jacob is renamed as Israel in Gen 32:29 when he wrestles with the man at Penuel and again in Gen 35:10 when G-d blesses him at Bethel. Esau is the eponymous ancestor of Edom as indicated in Gen 25:30 (see Gen 36:1), and Laban is the eponymous ancestor of Aram as indicated by his residence in Haran and the association of his name with the Lebanese Mountain Range, which separates Aram from Phoenicia to the west. Laban's name means "white," and the Lebanese mountains are so named because of their white, snow-capped peaks. Jacob's twelve sons become the ancestors of the twelve tribes of Israel.

Through the use of the eponymous ancestors, the narrative focuses on relations between Israel and its neighbors Edom and Aram, particularly in the late ninth to early eighth centuries BCE when Israel and Aram, formerly allies against the Assyrian monarch Shalmaneser III, went to war, resulting initially in major Israelite setbacks from the reigns of the Omride monarchs through the rule of the Jehu dynasty (1 Kgs 16–2 Kgs 14). Israel's loss of the Transjordan to Aram during this period is documented in several inscriptions, including the Tel Dan Inscription, which notes the deaths of the kings of Israel and Judah; the Deir Alla Inscription, in which the Aramean prophet Balaam speaks of Aram's victory over its enemies; and the Moabite Stone, in which the Moabite king Mesha celebrates his victory over Israel.[30]

Israel recovered and reestablished its boundaries with Aram, although it lost control of Edom (2 Kgs 8:22). Israel's recovery is due to the alliance between the Jehu dynasty and the Assyrian empire, which would threaten Aram's northern borders. Evidence of Israel's alliance with Assyria includes the Black Obelisk of Shalmaneser III (859–824 BCE), in which King Jehu of Israel (842–815 BCE) is pictured bowing at his feet, and the inclusion of King Jehoash of Israel (801–786 BCE) in the tribute list of the Assyrian monarch Adad Nirari III (811–783 BCE).[31] Israel's alliance with Assyria would eventually cause its destruction in 722–721 BCE when it revolted against Assyria to reestablish its alliance with Aram.

The Jacob narrative portrays this period from the perspective of Israel's ancestor Jacob.[32] The narrative begins in Gen 25:19-24 with accounts of the birth of Jacob and Esau and their interactions as boys. The overall orientation of the Jacob narratives to the north suggests that these episodes are due to J editing of the E account. Edom is located to the east of Judah, southeast of the Dead Sea, but throughout the late ninth through the early eighth centuries BCE, Judah was Israel's vassal. Insofar as Edom was Judah's vassal, it was also Israel's vassal.

Genesis 25:19-26 recounts the birth of the two boys and indicates the national significance of the entire Jacob cycle. Rebekah has a difficult pregnancy due to the struggle of the two boys in her womb. When she inquires of YHWH about her condition, the oracular response is that "two nations are in your belly, and two peoples shall separate from your body; one people shall be stronger than the other people, and the greater one shall serve the younger." The birth of the two boys indicates their characteristics and their characters. The first to be born is covered with red hair, and so he is called Esau. The statement actually constitutes a pair of puns that point to Esau's role as the ancestor of Edom. First, he is described as "red" or *'admoni* in Hebrew, which recalls the name, Edom, *'edom*. Second, he is described as hairy, employing the Hebrew term *se'ar*, "hair," which recalls the alternate name for the region of Edom, Seir, *se'ir*. The second boy emerged holding on to his older brother's heel, *'aqeb* in Hebrew, and so he is named Jacob, *ya'aqob*, which is a pun on Hebrew *'aqeb*. By holding on to his older brother's heel, Jacob attempts to pull Esau back into their mother's womb so that he might be born first and have all the rights that pertain to firstborn sons (see Deut 15:18-21).

The following episode in Gen 25:27-34 provides some perspective concerning the characters of the two boys, especially concerning their attitudes toward their birthrights. Esau is a hunter who roams in the wild, whereas Jacob is a "mild" or "perfect" (Heb., *tam*) man who remains by the tents. The boys are further distinguished by the fact that Isaac loves Esau, whereas Rebekah loves Jacob, thereby setting up the motif of sibling rivalry that will dominate the Jacob/Esau relationship. The characterization deepens when Esau returns from a day of hunting without having caught anything, only to find Jacob cooking some "red" stuff, *ha'adom*, which provides the occasion once again to remind the reader of Esau's Edomite association. The red stuff is likely lentils. When Esau demands some to eat, Jacob demands in return that Esau sell him his birthright. Esau does not hesitate to give Jacob his birthright for some lentils, which shows how he regards such a serious issue.

Genesis 26 presents another instance of the endangered matriarch in which Isaac and Rebekah are dwelling in southwestern Judah close to the Philistine border. When Isaac crosses the border to go to Abimelech (the king of the Philistines in Gerar), he seeks the same Abimelech who wanted Sarah in Gen 20. Two results follow. First, YHWH reaffirms the covenant of Abraham with Isaac, so that Isaac will possess the land. Second, the Philistines notice Rebekah's beauty, prompting Isaac to declare that she is his sister for fear that the Philistines might kill him to take her. The matter is quickly resolved, however, when Abimelech spots Isaac fondling Rebekah and figures out that she is his wife. Once again, the motif signals concern with the identity of the people of Israel. Will they be assimilated into the Philistine or Canaanite population? After all, Esau marries Canaanite and Hittite women, prompting Isaac to alleviate Rebekah's concerns by sending Jacob to Haran to find a bride from the family in Gen 27:46–28:2 (Gen 26:34-35). Otherwise, Gen 26 explains how Isaac founds the city of Beer-sheba, Hebrew for "well of seven" or "well of oath," which again places the narrative in southwestern Judah along the Philistine border. The Judean settings point to Gen 26 as a J-stratum text, like the other examples of the endangered matriarch texts. It therefore serves as a means to frame an E-stratum text with a Judean narrative. The fixing of Judah's and Philistia's borders would have been an ongoing concern throughout the monarchic period.

Genesis 27 brings the motif of sibling rivalry to a head. Isaac is old, his eyes are dim, and he is ready to give his blessing to his favored son, Esau. When he asks Esau to prepare a dish of hunted game, Rebekah overhears and makes arrangements for her favored son, Jacob, to receive his father's blessing instead of Esau. She prepares food for Jacob to take to his father. When Jacob protests that he is smooth-skinned unlike his hairy brother, Rebekah covers him with wooly lambskins and Esau's clothing so his father might not notice. Jacob's reference to his smooth skin, *khalaq*, "smooth," is another opportunity for a pun that signals national identity insofar as the town of Halak guarded the border between Israel/Judah and Edom according to Josh 11:17. Isaac's blessing includes clauses that peoples and nations, Esau's brothers' and his mother's sons, will serve him, and it curses anyone who curses him and blesses anyone who blesses him. When Esau later returns to find that his father had already blessed Jacob, he is outraged. Isaac gives him a qualified blessing indicating that he will indeed serve his brother, but ultimately he will break free, thereby anticipating Edom's revolt from Judah mentioned in 2 Kgs 8:22. Jacob's ruse incenses Esau, who vows to kill Jacob in revenge. It is at this point that Rebekah ensures that her husband will send Jacob to her brother's family in Paddan-aram to find a wife for her favored Jacob and ensure that Esau won't be able to kill him.

Jacob's vision of YHWH at Bethel in Gen 28:10-22 is a key element in the narrative, both concerning the transmission of the covenant of Abraham and Isaac to Jacob and the northern Israelite setting of the Jacob narratives. Bethel is the site of the later northern Israelite sanctuary established by King Jeroboam ben Nebat, the first king of northern Israel, in 1 Kgs 12:25-33. Bethel is vilified in the book of Kings for the worship of the gold calf, but here it is lauded as the site where Jacob, the ancestor of Israel, had a vision of YHWH and received the covenant that granted him the land of Israel. The narrative employs the motif of a vision through which YHWH speaks to Jacob, identifying it with the E, Ephraimite stratum of the Pentateuch.

Some interpreters note the association of Bethel with Babylon.[33] The stairway ascending to heaven is called a *sullam*, and it replicates a key feature of the Babylonian ziggurat dedicated to Marduk, which was also equipped with such a stairway to ascend the structure. Jacob declares that the site is "the gate of the heavens" in v. 17, which calls to mind the name Babylon, or *bab-ilu*, "gate of the gods," in Akkadian. Upon awakening from his dream, Jacob anoints the stone on which he had been sleeping, sets it up as *matzebah*, or pillar that would signify a cultic site, and renames the site from Luz to Bethel, Hebrew for "house of G-d." Some see the association with Babylon as an indication that Gen 28 is a J narrative that must be set in the time of the late monarchy or the exilic period, when Babylon was a major concern to

Judah. But Babylon was a cultural icon even in the Assyrian empire and would have sparked the imaginations of northern Israelites in the ninth century BCE when King Jehu of Israel first submitted to Shalmaneser III of Assyria, thereby paving the way for Assyrian influence in Israel.

Genesis 29–30 presents the account of Jacob's marriages to Leah and Rachel, the daughters of Laban, and the birth of his twelve sons and one daughter. These chapters introduce the motifs of role reversal for Jacob. Whereas he was easily able to best his twin brother, Esau, in securing the birthright of the firstborn and the blessing of his father, he meets his match in Laban, who compels him to marry both of his daughters and to work for him for a total of twenty years to pay the bride price for each sister and to secure the flocks necessary to support his family. His sibling rivalry with Esau comes back to plague him when he marries the two sisters, Leah and Rachel, who make his life miserable by competing with each other incessantly for his attention. Compare Lev 18:18, which prohibits a man from marrying two sisters within their lifetimes. The present narrative illustrates a fundamental reason for such a prohibition.

Most interpreters regard Gen 29–30 largely as a J-stratum narrative, but this view must be reconsidered. The birth order of Jacob's sons indicates the political standing of each tribe within the twelve tribes of Israel as a whole. Overall, that standing appears to represent the northern kingdom of Israel. Joseph and Benjamin are the two most important tribes among the twelve insofar as they are born to Jacob's favored wife, Rachel. Joseph becomes the father of Ephraim and Manasseh, the two key tribes of the northern kingdom of Israel located in the highlands of Israel. Benjamin, also located in the highlands of Israel, becomes the first royal tribe of Israel, insofar as Saul ben Kish of Benjamin is selected as the first king of Israel in 1 Sam 8–12. The sons born to Leah—Reuben, Simeon, Levi, Judah, Issachar, and Zebulun—are marginal tribes when considered in relation to those that inhabit the central highlands of Israel. Reuben is located in the Transjordan, just north of Moab, and eventually disappears. Simeon is located to the southwest of Judah by the Philistine border, and it too disappears. Levi becomes the priestly tribe, and it inhabits no land. Judah lives in the highlands and Negev desert south of Israel. Judah was a vassal of northern Israel during the reigns of the Omride and Jehu monarchs during much of the ninth and eighth centuries BCE until northern Israel was destroyed by Assyria in 722–721 BCE. Issachar and Zebulun live in the Galilee hills, separated from the Israelite highlands by the Jezreel Valley. Because she is a woman, Dinah does not become the ancestor of a tribe, and her rape in Gen 34 further marginalizes her. The handmaiden tribes are also marginalized in relation to those of the central Israelite highlands. Gad and Asher, the sons of Leah's handmaiden, Zilpah, live in the Transjordan to the north of Reuben in the case of Gad and along the borders of Phoenicia in the case of Asher. Dan and Naphtali, the sons of Rachel's handmaiden, Bilhah, live to the east and north of the Galilee hills, even farther away from the central Israelite highlands. Overall, the birth identities of the twelve sons and one daughter of Jacob indicate their standing in the northern kingdom of Israel.

The role reversal begins almost immediately with Jacob's arrival in Paddan-aram where he first lays eyes on his beloved Rachel. He comes to a well, which is a common motif associated with an upcoming marriage (see Exod 2:16-22). He sees three flocks of sheep waiting for all the shepherds to gather so that they might lift the stone covering the well together, thereby ensuring that everyone gets a fair share of the water. Upon seeing Rachel approach, a love-smitten Jacob rolls the stone off the well himself in an adolescent show of muscle power intended to impress the young woman. Jacob introduces himself as a kinsman and goes to his Uncle Laban's house to be welcomed. Jacob, of course, volunteers to work for seven years to marry Laban's daughter Rachel. The background for such a proposal appears in the debt slave laws of Exod 21:2-11, which call for a Hebrew man to work for six years to pay a debt.

Laban readily agrees, but the narrator notes that Laban has two daughters. Leah, the older daughter, has soft, beautiful eyes, whereas Rachel, the younger daughter, has a nice, beautiful shape. The wedding is held, the marriage is consummated, but in the morning, the not-very-observant Jacob awakens to find that he had married Leah, not Rachel. When he demands an explanation, Laban tells him that it is the custom to marry older daughters first. But if Jacob wants to marry Rachel, he is welcome to do in return for an additional seven years of service.

The sibling rivalry between the Leah and Rachel is well underway. The narrative states that Jacob loves Rachel, but not Leah. And the narrative tension increases as Leah bears son after son while Rachel remains barren. Readers have seen this motif before when the barren Sarah gives Hagar to Abraham in Gen 16. The motif also appears in 1 Sam 1 when Elkanah, ultimately the father of Samuel, loves the barren Hannah, but Peninnah bears all the children.

Rachel demands that Jacob give her sons or she will die, but Jacob can only respond that he is not G-d to do such a thing. So Rachel follows Sarah's example and gives her handmaiden, Bilhah, to Jacob so that he might have children with her. Dan and Naphtali are born. Leah immediately gives her handmaiden, Zilpah, to Jacob for the same purpose. Gad and Asher are born to counter Rachel's move. A desperate Rachel is forced to make a deal with Leah. If Leah will give her some mandrakes that Reuben had found, apparently understood to be an ancient aphrodisiac and fertility drug, Rachel will give Leah even more nights with Jacob. Leah immediately bears Issachar, Zebulun, and Dinah. Finally, Rachel bears Joseph.

It is at this point that Jacob wants to return home, but he finds that he lacks the means to support his huge family. Laban agrees to provide Jacob with a share of his flocks, but he requires that Jacob work for him for another six years, raising the total to twenty. Again, Laban has outwitted Jacob. But Laban doesn't stop there. The two men agreed that Jacob would get the striped and spotted sheep of the flock, but Laban made arrangements to remove those sheep so that Jacob would be left with nothing. When Jacob discovers the ruse, he waters the sheep by fresh poplar, almond, and plane shoots that had been peeled to appear striped so that when the sheep mated by the shoots, their lambs would be born striped and spotted.

Jacob had finally found a way to outwit his father-in-law, but Jacob is also a tragic figure. When it came time for Jacob to return his family to the land of Israel after twenty years of service to Laban in Aram, Jacob's beloved Rachel took her father's *teraphim* or family gods and hid them in her baggage. When he discovered the theft, Laban pursued Jacob to recover his property. Jacob, unaware of the theft, told Laban that he could search the baggage, and declared that if anyone had stolen Laban's property, that person should die. Jacob's solemn pledge would later be realized when his dearly loved Rachel died while giving birth to Benjamin (Gen 35:16-21). Laban is unable to find his gods because Rachel sat on her baggage and declared that she was having her menstrual period. Her declaration constitutes a way to defame the gods, and it prompted Laban not to search her baggage. Laban and Jacob reconcile and set up boundary markers, called "a heap of witness" in both Hebrew and Aramaic, to define their territories. The settlement of boundaries corresponds to the settlement between Israel and Aram in the early eighth century BCE.

Genesis 32–33 recounts Jacob's return to the land of Israel and his reconciliation with Esau. The focus on locations in the Transjordan, which was part of the northern kingdom of Israel, indicates that this material is E with some J editing. The demonstration of Jacob's connection to this land is a northern Israelite effort to assert its claims to the Transjordan.

Upon returning to Israel, Jacob learns that his brother, Esau, is coming to meet him with four hundred men, a clear sign of Esau's intent kill him after a twenty-year grudge. To protect his family, Jacob divides them into groups or camps, Hebrew *makhanot*, reasoning that if Esau finds and destroys one group, others might survive. The name Mahanaim becomes the name of an important Israelite city in the north Transjordan. When Jacob crosses the Wadi Jabbok in the north Transjordan, he spends the night alone by the banks of the wadi, where he is attacked by a man during the night. The man is obviously a divine being according to v. 31; Hos 12:5 identifies him as messenger. When Jacob overpowers the man, the man injures Jacob's groin, leaving him with a limp. The man then changes Jacob's name to Israel, claiming that the meaning of the term is that "you have striven with G-d and with men and have prevailed," although the philological meaning of the name *yisra'el* is "G-d rules." The narrative serves as an etiology for the city Penuel, one of Jeroboam's fortified cities in the Transjordan according to 1 Kgs 12:25. The name is understood to mean "face of G-d," due to Jacob's encounter with the divine being. Other etiologies include the name of the Wadi Jabbok, which is based on the Hebrew verb for wrestling; the practice of not pronouncing G-d's name indicated by the man's refusal to give his name; and the prohibition against eating the hind quarters of an animal which are given only to G-d based on Jacob's injured thigh. Indeed, the limping suggests that the once arrogant Jacob was humbled by his encounter with G-d. When Jacob finally does encounter Esau, he humbles himself before his brother. He declines Esau's offer to escort him back to their father's home, and the two brothers separate as indicated in Isaac's blessings in Gen 27.

Genesis 34, which relates Jacob's return to Shechem, constitutes another example of the endangered matriarch motif. Shechem was the most important gathering place for the northern kingdom of Israel in its earliest times. It is situated on the border between Ephraim and Manasseh. Deuteronomy 27 and Josh 24 portray it as the place where the tribes of Israel gathered to affirm their covenant. Judges 9 portrays it as the place where Abimelech ben Gideon sought to press his claims to rule as king of Israel, and 1 Kgs 12 portrays it as the place where the northern tribes rejected Rehoboam and instead selected Jeroboam as the first king of northern Israel.

But Gen 34 presents Shechem as a city of sordid reputation where Jacob's daughter, Dinah, was raped by Shechem ben Hamor. It is therefore not likely an E narrative, but a J narrative that polemicizes against Shechem. When Dinah goes out on her own to meet the daughters of the land, she meets Shechem, who rapes her but then later decides he wants to marry her. Jacob, who appears as a negligent father for allowing his daughter to go out alone, agrees to the marriage despite the rape and the issues that such an assault would raise (Deut 22:28-29). Dinah's brothers, Simeon and Levi, are outraged at the treatment of their sister and conspire to kill the men of Shechem while they are recovering from their circumcisions. In the end, Jacob only worries about his reputation among the Canaanites, whereas Simeon and Levi are outraged that their sister had been treated like a whore. The narrative clearly defames both Shechem and Jacob, thereby indicating its J, or Judean, perspective.

Finally, Gen 35 presents Jacob's return to Bethel where YHWH reiterates the covenant made with Jacob and his ancestors granting them the land of Israel. G-d once again changes Jacob's name to Israel, indicating the E, or Ephraimite, interest in the narrative, although P elements, such as the command to be fruitful and multiply, also appear in G-d's blessing. But there is a tragic dimension to this narrative as well. On the road to Ephrath near Bethlehem, Jacob's beloved Rachel dies while giving birth to Benjamin. The location of Rachel's death indicates later J or P editing, insofar as 1 Sam 10:2 indicates that Rachel's tomb was located in the tribal territory of Benjamin (Jer 31:15), not that of Judah, as depicted here. The concluding episodes of the chapter likewise point to J editing. Verse 27 notes Reuben's adultery with his father's concubine, Bilhah, which undermines his role as firstborn son. When considered in relation to Simeon's and Levi's roles in defaming Jacob in Gen 34, this clears the way for Judah, the fourth-born son, to emerge as the leader of the tribes. Finally, vv. 27-29 report Isaac's death and burial in Kiriath-arba/Hebron, which reunites Jacob and Esau in Judah.

Genesis 36, recognized as a P text, provides a lengthy genealogy for Esau, who then disappears from the narrative. The final notice in Gen 37:1 indicates resolution insofar as it recounts Jacob's settlement in the land of Canaan where his father had lived.

VI

Genesis 37:2–Numbers 2:34 constitutes the history of the twelve tribes of Israel. This is an extraordinarily large unit that includes accounts of Joseph, the exodus from

Egypt, and the wilderness and Sinai narratives. Discussion here focuses on the Joseph narratives in Gen 37:1–50:26 as the first major subunit of the history of the twelve tribes of Israel.

Interpreters view the Joseph narrative as a relatively unified work known as the Joseph novella because of its well-developed plot structure and use of characterization throughout the whole.[34] The focus of the novella is Joseph ben Jacob, a spoiled and arrogant young man, who suffers for his arrogance at the hands of his brothers, matures through adversity, and ultimately becomes the leader of his people to save them from trouble. Interpreters view the Joseph novella as a J document with some E supplements and light P editing, but such a view is difficult to defend when Joseph emerges as the father of Ephraim and Manasseh, the two central tribes of the northern kingdom of Israel. Readers since antiquity have noted the strong parallels between Joseph in Gen 37–50 and Jeroboam ben Nebat, the first king of northern Israel, in 1 Kgs 11–14.[35] Both Joseph and Jeroboam serve a pharaoh; Joseph is self-explanatory, but Jeroboam's master, Solomon, is known for marrying the daughter of the pharaoh of Egypt (1 Kgs 3:1) and for imposing state slavery on the northern tribes of Israel (1 Kgs 5; 9).[36] Both Joseph and Jeroboam take refuge in Egypt when their lives are threatened. Both overcome obstacles to rise to high office while serving their masters. Both ultimately save their people when they are threatened by famine or oppressive rule. Both become leaders of their people.

It seems appropriate to recognize that the Joseph novella is fundamentally an E composition that has been edited by J following the collapse of Israel in 722–721 BCE. Such an understanding also explains why pro-Judean narratives bracket the basic Joseph story in Gen 38, an endangered matriarch episode in which Tamar ensures the Judean identity of the descendants of Judah, and in Gen 49, the blessing of Jacob in which Judah emerges as the royal tribe of Israel. The Tamar narrative provides an interesting contrast between the descendants of Judah, who will not be Canaanite thanks to Tamar, and the descendants of Joseph, who were born to his Egyptian wife, Asenath bat Potiphera, the priest of On (Heliopolis), who bore him Manasseh and Ephraim. Unlike Sarah and Abraham's descendants, Joseph's descendants are Egyptian. The introduction of Gen 38 indicates an attempt to defame Joseph by contrast with Judah, and the introduction of Gen 49 indicates an attempt to assert Judah as the leading tribe of Israel. Other indications of Judean editing appear in Gen 37:25-28, when Judah emerges as the brother who would save Joseph's life following Reuben's attempt to do so in Gen 37:18-24, and in Gen 43:8-10, when Judah offers his own life to his father as surety for the protection of Benjamin whereas Simeon had been Joseph's hostage for the return of Benjamin in Gen 42:18-26.

The novella begins in Gen 37 with the portrayal of Joseph as an arrogant adolescent who sees himself as superior to his brothers and even his parents. Although the literary style of the Joseph narratives differs markedly with its well-developed, consistent plot and characterization from the far choppier presentation of the Jacob narratives, the Joseph narrative depends heavily on Joseph's identity as the son of Jacob's favored wife, the late Rachel. It appears that Jacob has overindulged his favored son to the neglect of the others. The narrative says as much, and it reinforces this perception by noting Jacob's special treatment of Joseph in the form of a sleeved cloak, like that worn by King David's daughter Tamar (2 Sam 13:18-19), to indicate his favored status among his brothers. Joseph's capacity for relating his dreams, which again indicate his dominance over his brothers and even his parents, only builds the resentment of his brothers until a disaster occurs. The opportunity to seek revenge comes when Joseph follows his brothers to Shechem, where they conspire to kill him, strip him of his cloak, and throw him in a pit to consider how to go about the deed. First Reuben and then Judah insist that Joseph should not be killed. While the brothers consider Judah's proposal to sell Joseph to the Ishmaelites, Midianite traders pull Joseph from the pit and sell him to the Ishmaelites instead. The brothers tell their father that Joseph was killed by a wild animal and show Jacob the cloak, which they had smeared with the blood of a lamb. In the meantime, the Ishmaelites take Joseph to Egypt and sell him to Potiphar, an official in the court of Pharaoh.

Genesis 38 presents the final example of an endangered matriarch episode in Genesis in which an Israelite woman is placed in a position that might compromise her descendants. The narrative focuses on Judah, who marries a Canaanite woman and fathers three sons, Er, Onan, and Shelah. Judah marries Tamar, presumably an Israelite woman, to his firstborn son, Er, but Er dies. Following levirate law, in which a childless widow is married to her dead husband's brother to provide a son who will serve as the dead man's heir, Tamar is married to Onan (see Deut 25:5-10; Ruth). But Onan spills his seed on the ground to avoid the birth of a son whom he would have to raise but who would not be his own heir. When Onan dies for displeasing YHWH, Judah tells Tamar to wait until the youngest son, Shelah, grows up, and so she returns to her own father's house. But Judah fails to marry Tamar to the half-Canaanite Shelah even when he does grow up. When Judah goes to Timnah for sheep shearing, Tamar disguises herself as a prostitute, finds Judah on his way to Timnah, and sleeps with him in return for his pledge of payment with his seal, cord, and staff. When Tamar later turns up pregnant, she is threatened with death for acting as a whore, but she saves herself when she displays Judah's seal, cord, and staff, stating that they belong to the man who fathered her yet-unborn child. Judah recognizes his belongings, and realizes that Tamar has acted to preserve the integrity and the Judean identity of Judah's family line. Judah's fully Israelite/Judean descendants stand in marked contrast to Joseph's half-Egyptian sons, Manasseh and Ephraim. Genesis 38 serves Judean interests and therefore must be recognized as a J-stratum text.

Joseph's process of maturation gets underway in Gen 39 when he is purchased by Potiphar, an officer in Pharaoh's court, and placed in charge of Potiphar's house. Although Joseph is a slave, he is given the responsibility for overseeing the administration of Potiphar's home and business interests, and demonstrates his capabilities as a future leader. The problem arises when Potiphar's wife notices how handsome and well-built he is and consequently demands that he sleep with her. Joseph refuses, the wife persists, and she is able to grab Joseph's garment as he flees from her. Potiphar's wife then denounces Joseph by claiming that he attempted to rape her. Joseph is arrested and imprisoned for his alleged offense.

This episode represents a retelling of a well-known thirteenth century BCE Egyptian narrative concerning two brothers, Anubis and Bata.[37] Anubis was the older brother; he was married and had a fine house. Bata, the younger brother, was a handsome and strong young man who did a great deal of the work in his older brother's household and slept in the stable. One day during plowing season, Bata came to the house to ask Anubis's wife to provide him with seed for the planting. As she was busy combing her hair, she told him to get it himself. When she saw Bata lifting the heavy sacks of grain, she was impressed with his strength and demanded that he sleep with her. Bata refused and upbraided his sister-in-law for her demand, but she was incensed at his rejection of her charms and informed her husband that Bata had tried to rape her. When Anubis tried to kill him, Bata confronted his older brother by telling him what really happened. To underscore his honesty, Bata cut off his penis. Finally convinced, Anubis went home, mourning for what had happened to his younger brother, and killed his wife.

Genesis 40 portrays Joseph in prison where he is joined by the cupbearer and chief baker of the king. Joseph displays his wisdom and leadership potential by interpreting their dreams. When Joseph interprets the cupbearer's dream as a sign that he would be released in three days, Joseph asks the cupbearer to remember him and help to secure his release. As for the chief baker, Joseph interprets his dream as a sign that he would be executed in three days.

Although Joseph remains in prison, the episode prepares for Joseph's release in Gen 41. Pharaoh dreams that seven beautiful and fat cows emerged from the Nile to graze on the bank followed by seven thin cows of poor appearance, who ate the seven beautiful and fat cows. Pharaoh's second dream featured seven fat and good ears of grain growing on one stalk followed by seven thin ears that swallowed up the fat ones. When the cupbearer tells Pharaoh about Joseph's ability with dreams, Pharaoh summons him, and Joseph proceeds to interpret the dreams. Egypt would enjoy seven years of plenty followed by seven years of famine. On the basis of his interpretation of the dreams, he advises Pharaoh to appoint a man to oversee the gathering and storage of grain during the seven prosperous years so that Egypt might prepare for the seven lean years. Pharaoh recognizes Joseph's talents and appoints him as an Egyptian official to undertake the task, granting Joseph powers second only to his own. Pharaoh renames Joseph with an Egyptian name, Zaphenath-paneah, and grants him Asenath bat Potiphera, daughter of the priest of On, as a wife. She bears him two half-Egyptian sons, Manasseh and Ephraim. Under Joseph's administration, Egypt prospers, and Joseph buys grain at cheap prices. When the famine comes, Joseph sells grain back to the people at a huge profit for Egypt.

Genesis 42–45 relates Joseph's reconciliation with his brothers. The plot of this segment is set against the backdrop of the famine that had seized Canaan and Joseph's preparations for the famine by storing grain. Jacob continues to display his self-destructive and debilitating favoritism by sending his remaining sons down to Egypt to buy grain but insisting that Benjamin, the son of his favorite wife, Rachel, and brother of his lost Joseph, remain behind for his own protection. They appear before their brother, Joseph, when they arrive in Egypt to buy grain, but they don't recognize him although he recognizes them. This provides Joseph with the opportunity to exact some measure of love and revenge. Joseph accuses the brothers of spying against Egypt, throws them in prison, and threatens to keep them there until their youngest brother, Benjamin, appears before him to verify their story of who they are and why they are there. Joseph proposes that they return to Canaan to retrieve Benjamin, but he will keep one of them as a hostage to ensure their return. And so he binds Simeon to remain with him, but he gives them their grain, returns their money, and gives them provisions for their journey home.

When the famine persists, the brothers must return to Egypt to obtain more food. Although Jacob has refused Reuben's offer to ensure Benjamin's safety, Jacob must relent, but he does so only after Judah offers to guarantee Benjamin's safe return. Judah's supplanting of Reuben as protector indicates J editing of an earlier E narrative. When they appear before Joseph, he still does not disclose his identity but frequently leaves the room to weep upon sight of his brother Benjamin. Joseph treats the brothers to a banquet, gives them their grain, and returns their money, but he also gives instructions to place his silver cup in Benjamin's bag to provide a pretext for arresting them and returning them to his presence. When the brothers are arrested upon leaving the city and brought back to appear before Joseph, Judah again acts as spokesman and offers himself in place of Benjamin. At this point in the narrative (Gen 45), Joseph clears the room and, in one of the most dramatic and emotionally charged scenes in the Bible, reveals his true identity to his brothers, "I am Joseph. Is my father still living?" (Gen 45:3). With that, the family is reunited, the brothers reconciled, and Joseph makes arrangements with the Pharaoh to bring his father and the rest of the family to Egypt.

Genesis 46, which interpreters consider to be largely P, presents a census of the family of Jacob that came down to Egypt, and Gen 47 relates how Joseph was able to enrich Pharaoh by selling grain to the Egyptians as the famine continued, effectively reducing the Egyptian population to slavery. Joseph's actions toward the Egyptians provides background for the Egyptian decision to enslave the Israelites in Exod 1, but his treatment of Israel provides a model for understanding Jeroboam as a far more generous ruler of Israel than Solomon, who is portrayed in 1 Kgs 3–11 as a pharaoh-like ruler who imposed state slavery on Israel, or his son Rehoboam, who promised to be even harder than his father in 1 Kgs 12.

Genesis 48–50 then brings the Joseph novella to a close with accounts of Jacob's death and his testament or legacy for his sons, his burial, and finally Joseph's death. The first major episode in Gen 48 focuses on Jacob's adoption of Joseph's sons Manasseh and Ephraim, apparently to overcome any questions about their Israelite identity and thus their share in the inheritance of their father and place among the tribes of Israel. Interpreters consider this narrative to be largely E and reflective of early Israelite history. Although Manasseh is the older of Joseph's sons, Jacob designates Ephraim as the firstborn. Many believe that Manasseh was indeed the older tribe due in part to its place in the Transjordan, along the Jezreel Valley, and the northern portion of the Israelite highlands, but that Ephraim supplanted Manasseh as the predominant tribe of the Israelite federation. Ephraim threatened war with Gideon of Manasseh in Judg 8; Ephraim actually went to war with Jephthah of Gilead, which would have included the Transjordanian territory of Manasseh, in Judg 12; and Josh 22 relates how the Ephraimite leader, Joshua ben Nun, took measures to ensure that the Transjordanian tribes of Manasseh, Gad, and Reuben remained loyal to all Israel during the conquest of Canaan.

Genesis 49 presents the testament of Jacob in which he announces the legacy of each of his sons. Interpreters frequently consider this to be a non-source text, but its portrayal of the tribe of Judah demonstrates its Judean, or J, inclinations. Indeed, Gen 49 is aware of the preceding Jacob and Joseph narratives and incorporates elements from each in its portrayal of the future for Jacob's sons. Reuben is firstborn but disgraces himself when he has relations with his father's concubine Bilhah (Gen 35:22). Simeon and Levi are to be scattered due to their attack on the people of Shechem for raping Dinah (Gen 34); Simeon disappears, but Levi later uses its proclivity for violence to kill those who worshipped the gold calf (Exod 32–34) and to be selected to offer the sacrifices of Israel (Num 17–18). Judah will hold the scepter over the other tribes, which indicates Judah's assumed role as spokesman for the sons of Jacob in the Joseph narrative and the future role of Judah as the royal tribe of David. Zebulun's boundaries would abut Sidon in Phoenicia and yet have some access to the sea. Issachar would raise sheep in the Galilean hills, which were subject to rule by the Israelite highlands. Dan would be a serpent that bites the heels of its foes, which would be especially important once it moved north to form the northernmost boundary of Israel, first to be invaded. Gad would be raided due to its exposed boundaries in the Transjordan where it would be eventually seized by Aram and Moab. Asher would become rich due to its location along the sea with access to seaborne trade. Joseph would become a warrior, which likely explains the preeminent role of Ephraim and Manasseh as the tribes that controlled the northern Israelite coalition. The notice that Joseph's blessing might surpass those of Jacob's ancestors in v. 26 suggests that Gen 49 might originally have been an Ephraimite text that was revised to account for Judah as the ruling tribe. Benjamin is a wolf who divides the spoil, which might explain its role as the first royal tribe.

Genesis 50 relates Jacob's death and Joseph's journey to Hebron to bury his father in the cave at Machpelah in Judah, which Abraham bought to bury Sarah. Jacob's burial at Machpelah in Judah very clearly serves J's interests. The account of Joseph's death ends with his embalmment and entombment in Egypt, later to be transported to Shechem for burial by Israel as it departed from Egypt (Exod 13:19; Josh 24:32). The account of Joseph's death clearly serves Ephraimite, or E, interests, especially because it portrays him as a beneficent leader who will secure the future of his people. Joshua 24:32 notes that Joseph was ultimately buried in Shechem on the land purchased by Jacob for his dwelling and an altar (Gen 34:18-22), although the passage makes no mention of any intent to use it for burial. Once again, Gen 50 appears to be an E, or Ephraimite, text revised to serve J, or Judean, interests.

Exodus

I

Exodus marks a distinct transition in the pentateuchal narrative from the ancestral narratives in Genesis to the accounts of Israel's exodus from Egyptian bondage, the revelation of the Torah at Mount Sinai, and the journey through the wilderness to the promised land of Israel. Exodus 1 facilitates the transition by naming the sons of Jacob who would constitute the tribes of Israel and by recounting the rise of a new pharaoh in Egypt who imposed state slavery. Some argue that the combination of the ancestral narratives in Genesis and the exodus/wilderness narratives in Exodus–Numbers must have occurred at a relatively late stage in the history of the Pentateuch's composition.[1] But several features indicate an early association of these narratives, including the shared interest in northern Israelite figures, such as Jacob and Joseph; the interest in northern Israelite institutions, such as the Bethel sanctuary; the role of the firstborn sons of Israel, in the E strata of both Genesis and Exodus–Numbers; and the citation of both the Jacob narratives and the exodus/wilderness narratives by the late eighth-century prophet, Hosea ben Beeri, in Hosea 12. These features point to the combination of these narratives at the time of the mid-eighth-century BCE composition of the E stratum.[2]

Exodus is integrated into the *toledoth* literary structure of the Pentateuch as part of the account of the "history of the twelve tribes of Israel" in Gen 37:2–Num 2:34. Exodus continues the focus on the twelve tribes of Israel by shifting to the narratives concerning the exodus from Egypt, the revelation at Sinai, and most of the journey through the wilderness until the final example of a *toledoth* formula appears in Num 3:1 to introduce the history of Israel under the guidance of the Levites in Num 3:1–Deut 34:12.

But Exodus also introduces a new and very different structural principle from the *toledoth* formula in the presentation of its narratives, that is, the itinerary report, which recounts Israel's journey from one location to another.[3] The first example appears in Exod 12:37, "and the Israelites journeyed from Rameses to Succoth as six hundred thousand men on foot apart from the children." The itinerary formula generally includes a form of the verb *nsʿ*, "to journey," and a statement of both the starting and the concluding location for the segment of Israel's journey through the wilderness. Insofar as the itinerary formula structure holds the entire exodus/Sinai/wilderness narrative together, it must constitute the earliest literary form of the narrative, that is, the E stratum of Exodus–Numbers.

Indeed, the itinerary formula defines the foundational literary structure of the account of the "history of the twelve tribes of Israel" in Gen 37:2–50:26 from the time of their arrival in Egypt in the time of Joseph through their exodus from Egypt and their arrival at Mount Sinai for YHWH's revelation of Torah. Genesis 37:2–50:26 recounts Israel's arrival in Egypt during the time of Joseph. Exodus 1:1–12:36 recounts Pharaoh's enslavement of Israel at the Egyptian cities of Pithom and Rameses and YHWH's efforts to free Israel from Egyptian bondage through the agency of Moses. Exodus 12:37–13:19 recounts the journey from Rameses to Succoth and the consecration of the firstborn of Israel. Exodus 13:20-22 briefly recounts the journey from Succoth to Etam and the role of the pillar of fire (lightning) and cloud to symbolize YHWH's guidance of Israel out from Egypt. Exodus 14:1–15:21 relates Israel's journey from Etam to the Reed Sea as well as YHWH's deliverance of Israel from the pursuing Egyptian army. Exodus 15:22-27 recounts the journey from the Reed Sea to the Wilderness of Shur, or Elim, where YHWH provides water in the wilderness. Exodus 16:1-36 recounts the journey from Elim to the Wilderness of Sin where YHWH provides the people with manna and quail for food. Exodus 17:1–18:27 recounts the journey from Sin to Rephidim where Moses and Israel defeat the treacherous attack of the Amalekites and where Moses's father-in-law, Jethro, visits the camp and advises Moses on the institution of judges for the people. Exodus 19:1–Numbers 2:34 recounts the journey from Rephidim to Sinai where YHWH reveals the Torah to Israel. This lengthy unit is further subdivided into accounts of Israel's arrival at Sinai in Exod 19:1-2; revelation from the mountain in Exod 19:3–40:38; revelation from the tabernacle in Lev 1–27; and the census and organization of Israel around the tabernacle in Num 1:1–2:34. Numbers 3:1 employs the final example of the *toledoth* formula to introduce the account of the history of Israel under the guidance of the Levites in Num 3:1–Deut 34:12. Although Israel remains at Sinai in Num 3:1–10:10, the itinerary-based structure of the wilderness continues beginning in Num 10:11 through the end of the pentateuchal narrative.

The literary structure of Exodus–Deuteronomy within the history of the twelve tribes of Israel appears as follows:

Synchronic Literary Structure of the Pentateuch:

History of the Twelve Tribes of Israel

XI. History of the Twelve Tribes of Israel	Gen 37:2–Num 2:34
A. Joseph and His Brothers in Egypt	Gen 37:2–50:26

B. Deliverance from Egyptian Bondage: Rameses	Exod 1:1–12:36
C. From Rameses to Succoth: Consecration of Firstborn	Exod 12:37–13:19
D. From Succoth to Etam: Pillar of Fire and Cloud	Exod 13:20-22
E. From Etam to the Sea (Pi-hahiroth/Baal-zephon): Deliverance at Sea	Exod 14:1–15:21
F. From Reed Sea to Wilderness of Shur/Elim: Water in Wilderness	Exod 15:22-27
G. From Elim to Wilderness of Sin: Quails and Manna	Exod 16:1-36
H. From Sin to Rephidim: Amalek and Jethro	Exod 17:1–18:27
I. From Rephidim to Sinai: Revelation of Torah	Exod 19:1–Num 2:34
1. Arrival at Sinai	Exod 19:1-2
2. Revelation from Mountain: 10 Commandments; Covenant Code; Building of the Tabernacle	Exod 19:3–40:38
3. Revelation from Tabernacle: Laws of Sacrifice and Holiness Code	Lev 1–27
4. Census and Organization of People around Tabernacle	Num 1:1–2:34
XII. History of Israel under the Guidance of the Levites	Num 3:1–Deut 34:12
A. Sanctification of the People Led by the Levites	Num 3:1–10:10
B. From Sinai to Wilderness of Paran/Kibroth-hattaavah: Rebellion in the Wilderness	Num 10:11–11:35a
C. From Kibroth-hattaavah to Hazeroth	Num 11:35b–12:15
D. From Hazeroth to the Wilderness of Paran	Num 12:16–19:22
E. From Paran to Wilderness of Zin/Kadesh: Water from Rock	Num 20:1-21
F. From Zin/Kadesh to Mount Hor: Death of Aaron	Num 20:22–21:3

G. From Mount Hor to Edom/Moab: Defeat of Sihon and Og	Num 21:4-35
H. Arrival at Moab: Balaam; Census and Organization of People	Num 22:1–36:13
I. Moses's Final Address to Israel: Repetition of the Torah	Deut 1:1–34:12

Exodus is more than just an account of Israel's itinerary. The Song of the Sea in Exod 15 makes it clear that YHWH will guide Israel to YHWH's "holy abode" (v. 13) and to the mountain of YHWH's "sanctuary" (vv. 17-18). Although the initial reference would be to Mount Sinai, the narrative looks beyond Mount Sinai to the temple that would be established for YHWH once the people return to the promised land of Israel. Israel's journey appears as a pilgrimage.[4] Just as the people of Israel and Judah would embark upon a pilgrimage from their homes throughout the land to come to YHWH's temple for the major holidays, so Israel's journey through the wilderness is formulated as a pilgrimage to YHWH's sanctuary, first at Sinai, which provides the model or paradigm for YHWH's temple as the place of divine revelation, and later at YHWH's sanctuary established in the land of Israel.

Exodus–Numbers is also a creation account that both differs from and continues the creation accounts of Genesis. Temples in the ancient world are generally conceived to stand as the holy center of creation.[5] Just as the Entemenanki in Babylon commemorates Marduk's creation of the world and the temple at Ugarit commemorates Baal's defeat of Yamm, thereby ensuring order in the world of creation, so YHWH's temples in Jerusalem, Bethel, Shiloh, and elsewhere commemorate YHWH's creation of the universe and of Israel. The exodus narrative highlights the role that creation in nature plays in the creation of Israel. The burning bush where Moses first encounters YHWH in Exod 3 represents a type of red-flowered bush that grows in the Sinai wilderness. The first nine plagues in Exod 7–10 each represent a known feature of the natural world in Egypt and Canaan. The parting of the Reed Sea employs the creation motif of dry land emerging from the waters as the means to save Israel from Egypt. The provision of water, quail, and manna in the wilderness all represent natural features of Sinai. The portrayal of Mount Sinai, from which YHWH reveals divine Torah, represents one of the most conspicuous features of the Sinai wilderness. Exodus correlates the creation of Israel with creation at large.

But the creation motif points to one of the most prominent literary goals of Exodus, that is, the creation of the wilderness tabernacle, which will ultimately provide the model for the establishment of YHWH's temple in the land of Israel. Michael Fishbane notes the parallels between the account of creation in Gen 1:1–2:3 and the construction of the tabernacle in Exod 39–40.[6] Specifically, Gen 1:31; 2:1, 2, 3 are cited in Exod 39:43, 32; 40:33; 39:43 respectively, indicating the close linkage between the two accounts. The texts in Genesis point to the role that the tabernacle and the later Jerusalem temple will play as the holy center of creation that ensures and symbolizes order and stability in the world of creation. The construction of the tabernacle now signals that YHWH's revelation will proceed from the tabernacle as Israel makes its way to the promised land where YHWH's temple will ultimately be established.

One more feature requires consideration: the motif of the firstborn sons. The slaying of the firstborn is the tenth of YHWH's plagues to be visited upon Egypt. It does not represent an element of creation like the other nine plagues; its significance lies elsewhere. The firstborn sons of Israel are delivered from death by the smearing of lamb's blood on the doorposts of Israelite households. The lamb's blood signifies the Passover offering, that is, a lamb that will be offered to YHWH on the temple altar, much as the unleavened bread or *matzah* eaten by the Israelites as they fled Egypt is represented by the *minkhah*, or grain offering, that accompanies the Passover offering. But what of the firstborn sons who are redeemed from death? Interpreters generally consider their deliverance from death to be the major concern of the narrative, but closer attention to Israelite law and other features of the Exodus–Numbers narrative indicates that the firstborn were originally intended to serve as Israel's priests. Interpreters assume that the tribe of Levi will fulfill this role, but the Levites only demonstrate their zeal for YHWH in the gold calf episode of Exod 32–34, and they are only selected to serve as priests in Num 17–18.

The editors of the Pentateuch are well aware that the Levites are relative latecomers to priestly service. On three separate occasions, in Num 3:11-14, 40-51; 8:13-19, YHWH instructs Moses that the Levites will replace the firstborn sons of Israel to be consecrated for service to YHWH. "And I, behold, I have taken the Levites from the midst of the sons of Israel in place of every firstborn who breaks the womb, and the Levites shall be mine. Because all the firstborn were mine on the day that I smote all the firstborn in the land of Egypt. I consecrated for myself all the firstborn in Israel, including human and animal. They shall be mine. I am YHWH" (Num 3:12-13). The firstborn of the animals, herd and flock, are presented as Passover offerings at the altar, but the firstborn sons play a different role. According to Exod 34:19-20, the firstborn human being is to be redeemed, apparently for divine service to YHWH as the above-cited passages in Num 3:11-13, 40-51; 8:13-19 indicate. The firstborn is one who breaks the womb, that is, the firstborn of the mother, not the father. A telling example of such a birth is Samuel, who was the firstborn to his mother, Hannah, who was married to his father, Elkanah, identified as an Ephraimite in 1 Sam 1:1.[7] When little Samuel was weaned, Hannah took him to the sanctuary at Shiloh where he was raised to become a priest. While sleeping by the ark of the covenant in the holy of holies of the sanctuary, Samuel had a visionary experience in which YHWH called him to become a prophet as well. Access to the holy of holies and the ark was reserved only for the priests, which would suggest that Samuel's visionary experience was part of his ordination as a priest of YHWH (see Exod 29; Lev 8; Num 8). Insofar as Shiloh was a northern sanctuary located in Ephraim, Samuel's priestly status suggests that the consecration of the firstborn as priests was a northern practice. Indeed, Jeroboam ben Nebat, the first king of northern Israel, is condemned by the Judean narrator in 1 Kgs 12:31 for appointing non-levitical priests.

These considerations indicate that the exodus account is fundamentally concerned with the firstborn sons of Israel. A major agenda of the narrative is to explain the origins of Israel's priesthood together with the origins of Passover, the revelation of Torah at Sinai, and the construction of the wilderness tabernacle as elements in the creation of Israel. Such an agenda suggests that the exodus account was originally written as a northern Israelite, or E-stratum, narrative, but the interest in replacing the firstborn with the Levites in Exod 32–34 and YHWH's instruction of Moses in Num 3 and 8 points to Judean redaction, including both J and P elements, interested in establishing the tribe of Levi as a dynastic priesthood for Israel.

II

Exodus 1:1–12:36 focuses on the twelve tribes in Egypt following the lifetime of Joseph. Exodus 1:1–12:36 is defined by its setting in the Egyptian cities of Pithom and Rameses where the Israelites are enslaved and put to work in building these two store or garrison cities for Pharaoh.[8] Most interpreters consider this text to be a combination of J, E, and P strata texts with good reason. Insofar as E appears to be the foundational text, the present form of the narrative would be the product of successive J and P redactions. Exodus 1:1–12:36 is fundamentally concerned with the conflict between YHWH and Pharaoh, who was considered to be a god in Egypt, to demonstrate who was the true G-d of creation, Israel, and all the other nations of the earth. It proceeds episode by episode with a special focus on the plagues visited by YHWH on Egypt in an effort to compel the Egyptian Pharaoh to let the people of Israel go.

Exodus 1:1–2:25 forms the first major subunit of Exod 1:1–12:36. It functions as a prologue for the Exodus narrative insofar as it makes the transition between the ancestral narratives of Genesis and the focus on Israel as a nation. Exodus 1:1-7 begins this subunit with a summation of the names of the sons of Jacob who came with their families and their father to Egypt and a notice of Joseph's death as well as the deaths of that generation. But the passage employs formulaic P language to emphasize that the people of Israel were "fruitful" and "multiplied" in keeping with G-d's commands to the first humans in Gen 1:28.

The EJ narrative follows in Exod 1:8–2:25 with a focus on the rise of a new pharaoh who did not know Joseph. The unnamed pharaoh's concerns play upon fears of the ever-growing numbers of Israelites and thereby signal the beginning of the conflict between Pharaoh and YHWH. Part of YHWH's role is to ensure the continuing life of the people of Israel, which means that YHWH ensures the fertility and well-being of Israel as promised to the ancestors in Genesis. These promises were not yet fulfilled, and the narrative introduces tension by presenting Pharaoh, a god in Egypt, as the foil to YHWH. Such opposition provides the opportunity to demonstrate who the true G-d of the universe, Israel, and the nations really is.

Pharaoh's efforts begin with the enslavement of the Israelites and their assignment to build the store cities of Pithom and Rameses. This notice has historical ramifications because Egypt did in fact hold thousands of Habiru/Apiru slaves, especially following the overthrow of the Hyksos dynasty in the mid-sixteenth century BCE.[9] The Hyksos were foreign rulers, originally from Canaan, who took control of Egypt from the mid-nineteenth through the mid-sixteenth century BCE when they were expelled by the rise of a new native Egyptian dynasty.[10] Although some see Joseph as an example of Hyksos rule, there is no indication that Joseph was the ruler of Egypt—he was always second to Pharaoh—nor that the pharaoh himself was not native to Egypt. Nevertheless, the Hyksos capital was located in the city of Tanis, also known as Zoan, which was later renamed Rameses during the reign of Pharaoh Rameses II (1290–1224 BCE). The identification of Rameses in the narrative has prompted many to identify Rameses II as YHWH's opponent throughout the narrative and his father, Seti I (1310–1290 BCE), founder of the Nineteenth Egyptian Dynasty, as the Pharaoh who initially enslaved the Israelites. The identification is supported by the appearance of the Merneptah Stele, dated to ca. 1220 BCE, which refers to Israel as a seminomadic people among Pharaoh Merneptah's enemies in Canaan.[11] But there is no historical evidence of a mass exodus of slaves from Egypt either during the reign of the Nineteenth Dynasty or any other time. Merneptah (1224–1216 BCE) erected his stele to claim victory over a Canaanite coalition, including Israel, but archeological evidence indicates the decline of Egyptian influence in Canaan following his reign.

Pharaoh's efforts continue with his orders to the Hebrew midwives, Shiphrah and Puah, to kill any male children born to the Israelites. When the midwives refused to kill the infant males, they explained their action by claiming that Israelite women were more vigorous than Egyptian women so that the babies were born before the midwives arrived.

Pharaoh's order is ironically thwarted by his own daughter in the birth of Moses. The narrative very carefully identifies Moses as a member of the tribe of Levi, although it is only in Exod 6:16-19, 20 and Num 26:59 that his parents are named as Amran ben Kohat and Jochebed bat Levi. Moses's mother saved her son by placing him in a basket sealed with bitumen and pitch and setting him adrift on the Nile while his sister, later named as Miriam in Num 26:59 (Exod 15:20-21; Num 12:1), watched over him. The daughter of Pharaoh retrieved Moses when she went to the Nile to bathe and subsequently raised him as her own son with a Hebrew wet nurse, identified in Rabbinic tradition as Jochebed, in the house of Pharaoh. The daughter of Pharaoh named him Moses because "I drew [*meshiti*, a pun on *mosheh*, "Moses"] him from the water," although the Hebrew name *mosheh* is actually derived from the Egyptian term, *mesis*, "mose," which means, "son of" (Rameses, "son of Ra"; Thutmose, "son of Thut").

Moses's birth story has strong parallels with the birth account of Sargon I, the king of Agade (2334–2279 BCE), who founded the Akkadian dynasty that ruled

Pharaoh

Moses, birth's story

much of Mesopotamia prior to the rise of the Amorite rulers of Babylonia.[12] Sargon was born illegitimately to a mother who placed him in a basket and floated him down the river until he was rescued by Akki the Drawer of Water. Sargon won the favor of the goddess Ishtar and went on to become king of the black-headed people (a term employed by the Sumerians of Mesopotamian to describe themselves) and the founder of a great empire. Such accounts of infants saved from early death appear throughout the ancient world to explain the origins of great leaders or heroes, such as Cyrus of Persia, Hercules of Greece, and Romulus and Remus, the founders of Rome.

Moses's Israelite identity comes to the forefront in the account of his killing of an Egyptian taskmaster who was beating a Hebrew slave. Moses is compelled to flee to the land of Midian in the Sinai wilderness after he learned that he had been observed and that Pharaoh sought to kill him. Moses's arrival in Midian brought him to a well where the seven daughters of the priest of Midian were drawing water. Such a scene typically portends marriage as the example of Jacob in Gen 29:1-30 indicates. When Moses defends the women from the shepherds at the well, they take him home to meet their father, Reuel, who is elsewhere identified as Jethro (Exod 3:1) and Hobab ben Reuel (Num 10:29; Judg 4:11).

Exodus 2:23-25 closes the first subunit in Exod 1:1–2:25 with the death of the pharaoh; a reminder of YHWH's covenant with Abraham, Isaac, and Jacob; and the auspicious notice that G-d saw what had happened to Israel.

Exodus 3:1–4:31 constitutes the second major subunit of Exod 1:1–12:36. The interplay between the names YHWH and G-d indicates that this passage is a combination of E and J materials that present YHWH's commission of Moses as a prophet who will return to Egypt to redeem Israel. Exodus 3:1–4:31 begins with Moses's prophetic commissioning narrative in Exod 3:1–4:17. It portrays Moses shepherding the sheep of his father-in-law, Jethro, at Mount Horeb, an alternative name for Mount Sinai typically used by the E and D strata. The narrative is formulated as a visionary account in which an angel addresses Moses from the midst of a burning bush that is not consumed by the flames. The bush has been identified as the *Rubus sanctus*, a red-flowering bush native to the Sinai wilderness that appears to burn when viewed from a distance.[13] Its appearance in the narrative signals YHWH's role as creator, insofar as creation plays a key role in YHWH's efforts to free the Israelite slaves. The narrative likewise invokes the imagery and role of the temple, which functions as the holy center of creation in ancient Israelite and Judean thought, insofar as YHWH tells Moses to remove his shoes because he is standing on holy ground. The encounter then follows the typical pattern of a prophetic commissioning or call narrative, which includes (1) an encounter between YHWH and the prospective prophet (vv. 1-6); (2) a word of commissioning (vv. 7-10); (3) an objection by the prospective prophet (vv. 11, 13); (4) an answer to the objection (vv. 12, 14-15); and (5) a sign of the commissioning or an ordination procedure (v. 12).[14]

When Moses asks YHWH's name, YHWH states, "I am who I am [*'ehyeh asher 'ehyeh*]." YHWH's response is a rhetorical device known as the *idem per idem* in which a thing is defined in relation to itself. It provides no explicit information concerning the identity of YHWH or YHWH's name and instead functions as a device to deflect Moses's question. The reason for YHWH's response is that the divine name is holy and not to be pronounced by human beings. In Egyptian culture, priests were able to invoke the power of Egyptian deities by invoking their names as part of a blessing or cursing ritual, which entailed that the priests were able to gain power over the gods by pronouncing their names.[15] Pronunciation of the divine name is forbidden in Judaism, except on the day of Yom Kippur when the high priest enters the holy of holies of the temple to atone for the nation Israel before YHWH. Indeed, YHWH's response to Moses presents an early interpretation of the divine name. The Hebrew verb *'ehyeh*, "I am," is a first-person future/imperfect tense conjugation of the verb *hyh*, "to be." If it was conjugated in third person masculine form, it would appear as *yihyeh*, "he is," a variation of the consonantal form of the divine name *yhwh*, suggesting that "YHWH is" the true G-d.

Exodus 3:16-22 presents YHWH's further commissioning statement to Moses, and Exod 4:1-17 presents Moses's further objections and YHWH's signs that are meant to answer Moses. When Moses objects that the Egyptians will not believe him, YHWH instructs Moses in the sign of the rod turned into a snake, which presupposes the Egyptian practice of snake charming. Other signs include YHWH's ability to inflict leprosy and to turn the water of the Nile into blood. When Moses objects that he is unable to speak effectively, YHWH responds that Moses's older brother, Aaron, will accompany him to Egypt to act as spokesman. Such a role suggests a priestly identity for Aaron as an interpreter of YHWH's words given through Moses. Aaron's status as the firstborn son qualifies him for this task in the E-stratum narrative.

Moses, Zipporah, and Gershom are attacked by YHWH in Exod 4:24-26; this episode plays a strategic role in the narrative insofar as it depicts Moses's and Gershom's circumcision. Circumcision sanctified Egyptian priests, but it sanctifies all men in Israel.

Exodus 5:1–6:13 constitutes the next subunit of Exod 1:1–12:36 with an account of Moses's and Aaron's confrontation with Pharaoh. Pharaoh's question in Exod 5:2—"Who is YHWH that I should listen to his voice in order to release Israel?"—constitutes the *Leitmotif* of the entire Exodus narrative, which is designed to demonstrate to Pharaoh, Egypt, Israel, and the reader just who YHWH is. The encounter is a complete failure, insofar as Pharaoh refuses Moses's demand to allow the people to go on a three-day journey to the wilderness to present offerings to YHWH. The three-day journey signals ancient Israelite pilgrimage patterns in which they would journey for as much as three days to present offerings at the temple during the major holidays of the year when all Israelite males are to appear before YHWH with offerings (Exod 23:14-17). The encounter builds upon YHWH's prior promise in Exod 4:21 to stiffen Pharaoh's heart, which raises theological questions concerning YHWH's willingness to punish those who cannot exercise free will. Pharaoh's refusal and his imposition of a greater workload build dramatic tension in the confrontation between YHWH and Pharaoh. The encounter also provides an opportunity for the P writer to introduce the divine name in Exod 6:1-13 to reassure Moses. YHWH states in Exod 6:2, "I am YHWH," so there is no ambiguity concerning the identity of the divine name left over from Exod 3:1–4:17. It also enables P to explain the name El Shaddai and YHWH's earlier promises to Abraham, Isaac, and Jacob. El is the name applied to the creator G-d in Canaanite mythology, which signals the historical reality that ancient Israel and ancient Israelite religion actually developed from Canaanite religious practice.

Exodus 6:18–12:36 presents the account of YHWH's confrontation with Pharaoh in the form of the ten plagues to be visited by YHWH upon the Egyptians. The text combines J and P elements to demonstrate YHWH's role as the true creator G-d of the universe as well as the true master of human events. The J text may well be a redacted version of an underlying E narrative. The text begins with a P genealogy in Exod 6:18-30, which focuses on the descendants of Jacob's sons Reuben, Simeon, and Levi. The genealogy explains the levitical origins of Moses and Aaron as the key figures in YHWH's confrontation with Pharaoh.

The confrontation with Pharaoh begins in the P narrative of Exod 7:1-13 with YHWH's instructions to Moses to prepare for what is to come. YHWH makes several key points. First, YHWH appoints Moses in the role of G-d to Pharaoh with Aaron as his prophet. Moses will speak and act on YHWH's behalf to carry out the plagues with an outstretched arm and rod that symbolizes YHWH's outstretched arm. Aaron will address Pharaoh to demand the release of the people. Second, YHWH will harden Pharaoh's heart so that he and Egypt will suffer the full punishment of YHWH and thereby answer the question that Pharaoh posed in Exod 5:2. When Egypt suffers the plagues, the Egyptians will know that YHWH is the true G-d. YHWH's statements raise theological questions as to why Egypt is not given the chance to exercise free will and come to understand YHWH on its own, but the demonstration of YHWH's divine power as the true creator and master of human events is key to the narrative. Third, YHWH further instructs Moses and Aaron to confront Pharaoh with their rods that turn into snakes. Although the Egyptian magicians performed similar feats, Aaron's rod/snake swallowed those of the Egyptians thereby providing an initial indication of YHWH's divine power.

The account of the ten plagues follows in Exod 7:14–12:36. The plague narrative includes all ten plagues, that is, the Nile turns to blood (Exod 7:14-25), frogs (Exod 8:1-15), gnats (Exod 8:16-19), flies (Exod 8:20-32), cattle disease (Exod 9:1-7), boils (Exod 9:8-12), hail and thunder (Exod 9:13-35), locusts (Exod 10:1-20), darkness (Exod 10:21-29), and the death of the firstborn (Exod 11:1–12:36).[16] Another version of the plague account, in Ps 78:43-51, includes only seven plagues (Nile, frogs, flies, cattle disease, hail and thunder, locusts, firstborn), and there are only eight plagues in Ps 105:27-36 (Nile, frogs, gnats, flies, hail and thunder, locusts, darkness, and firstborn). The J account of the plagues also includes only eight plagues, that is, Nile, frogs, flies, cattle disease, hail, locusts, darkness, and firstborn. The J narratives are identified by a narrative pattern in which YHWH commands Moses to demand that Pharaoh release the slaves and to threaten plagues if he does not; the plagues then strike; Pharaoh summons Moses for dialog; Moses intercedes with YHWH, and the plague ends; Pharaoh's heart remains hardened; the pattern resumes (Exod 7:14-24, 25-29 [Eng. 7:25–8:4]; 8:4-11 [Eng. 8:8-15], 16-28 [Eng 8:20-32]; 9:1-7, 13-35; 10:1-20, 21-29; 11:1-8; 12:21-36). The P plague account follows a pattern in which YHWH instructs Moses and Aaron to perform actions involving the staff; Moses and Aaron comply and the plague ensues; the Egyptians unsuccessfully attempt to match the plague; and Pharaoh's heart remains hardened (Exod 7:8-22; 8:1-3 [Eng. 8:5-7], 11-15 [Eng. 8:16-19]; 9:8-12; 11:9-10; 12:1-20, 28).

The final form of the plague narratives presents the first nine plagues in a well-crafted literary pattern of three groups of three plagues with the tenth plague, the slaying of the firstborn, as the climactic event that finally prompts Pharaoh to set the people of Israel free. It is no accident that the first nine plagues represent natural features of the world of creation, particularly as found in ancient Egypt and Canaan. The first plague, the Nile turning to blood, possibly represents a natural feature of the Nile River. Every year at springtime, the headwaters of the Nile fill the river with an overabundance of water from melting snow and rain that carries with it the red sediment from the Ethiopian highlands, thereby flooding the Nile River Valley with red-colored water that looks like blood. The river deposits rich, fertile silt throughout the valley, which provides the foundation for Egypt's agricultural production. But this leads to the second plague, insofar as the waters carry living creatures, such as frogs, that inundate the land. The third and fourth plagues, gnats and flies, then appear as the flood waters recede and the frogs and other creatures begin to die, attracting winged insects that feast on their corpses. The fifth and sixth plagues, cattle disease and boils, then result when the gnats and flies bite animals and humans, thereby transferring various ailments to their victims. The seventh plague, hail and thunder, is a familiar feature in the land of Egypt in antiquity and in the present. The eighth plague, locusts, is likewise a recurrent feature in both Egypt and the land of Israel. The ninth plague, darkness, is sometimes explained as an eclipse of the moon, but it more likely presupposes the dry desert sirocco wind, known in Hebrew as the *sharav* and in Arabic as the *ḥamsin*, which blows tremendous quantities of dust and dirt into North Africa, Western Asia, and Southern Europe. This wind is analogous to the Santa Ana winds of southern California that appear at times of seasonal transition, reversing the normal airflow from west to east to a flow from east to west, thereby bringing the heat and dryness of the desert to the more temperate areas located by the Pacific. This wind is known as the "east wind" in the Bible, and it is credited with splitting the Red Sea in Exod 14–15. When the sirocco is at its height, the quantities of dust and dirt blown in by the winds block out the sun during the day and make the moon appear red at night. The account of the first nine plagues reinforces the portrayal of YHWH as the creator.

Exodus 11:1–12:36 presents the account of the tenth plague unleashed by YHWH against Egypt, that is, the slaying of the oldest male child. The plague of the firstborn differs from the previous nine plagues in that it does not represent an element from the natural world of creation. Rather, the slaying of the firstborn provides the means to explain the celebration of the Passover holiday in ancient Israel and

Judah insofar as Passover functions as an ancient equivalent of Independence Day. In presenting the slaying of the firstborn, the narrative presents various elements that are part of the Passover celebration in Exod 12:1-20. The festival is celebrated at the beginning of the first month of the year (Nisan, March–April) for seven days beginning on the fourteenth day of the month. Each family group is to present a yearling lamb for sacrifice. Its blood is to be smeared on the lintel and doorposts of the house to protect the family against the angel of death that will kill the firstborn in Egypt. The people will roast the lamb on the first night and eat it before morning while dressed for travel out of Egypt. They will also eat unleavened bread for seven days until the twenty-first day of the first month as they depart from Egypt. The instructions to the Israelites concerning the plague of the firstborn sets the pattern for later temple worship for the Passover holiday in Israel, that is, a seven-day holiday that begins with the offering of a lamb, which is roasted and eaten by the people on the first night followed by the celebration of the Festival of Matzot, Unleavened Bread, for seven days to symbolize the hurried departure from Egypt, which allowed the people time only to bake unleavened bread on their backs.

III

Exodus 12:37 begins the presentation of Israel's itinerary as they depart from the city of Rameses to commence their wilderness journey, first to Sinai and afterwards to the promised land of Israel. Six major stages mark their progress to Sinai. The first appears in the journey from Rameses to Succoth in Exod 12:37–13:19, which discusses the significance of the firstborn. The second appears in the journey from Succoth to Etam in Exod 13:20-22, which discusses the pillar of fire and cloud that leads Israel through the wilderness. The third appears in the journey from Etam to the sea (Pi-hahiroth/Baal-zephon) in Exod 14:1–15:21, which presents YHWH's deliverance of Israel at the sea. The fourth appears in the journey from the Red Sea to the Wilderness of Shur/Elim in Exod 15:22-27, which discusses water in the wilderness. The fifth appears in the journey from Elim to the Wilderness of Sin in Exod 16:1-36, which discusses quails and manna. The seventh appears in the journey from Sin to Rephidim in Exod 17:1–18:27, which discusses Amalek and Jethro. Exodus 19:1 marks Israel's arrival at Sinai.

The presentation of the plague of the slaying of the firstborn in Exod 11:1–12:36 left open one important dimension of the celebration of Passover, that is, the redemption of the firstborn. Exodus 12:37–13:19 turns to that question as it portrays the journey from Rameses to Succoth. Although this text contains some J and P elements, Exod 13:1-16 is considered a non-source text that was composed on the basis of Deuteronomic patterns. But this is a legal text set in narrative form that explains the Israelite understanding of the redemption of the firstborn. It draws heavily on the language of the law code in Exod 34:10-28 that represents a J revision of the covenant code in Exod 21–24, which served as the basic law code of the northern kingdom of Israel. Such a relationship suggests that Exod 13:1-16 is in fact a J revision of underlying E laws. The passage begins with the command to consecrate the oldest male offspring of Israel, including humans and animals, to YHWH. Firstborn is here defined as the firstborn to the mother. The practice is explained as a means to recall what YHWH did for Israel at Egypt. It reiterates instruction to observe the Passover festival for seven days and to teach one's children the significance of the holiday. Once Israel is in the land, the firstborn of the herd and flock are to be presented as offerings to YHWH. The oldest male human child is to be redeemed. But for what purpose is the firstborn redeemed? In the present form of the text, the redemption of the firstborn is meant as a reminder of the tenth plague and the observance of Passover at large.

Although Exod 12:37–13:19 provides no explanation concerning the purpose for which the firstborn are redeemed other than the opportunity to teach the significance of the holiday, later elements in the pentateuchal narrative indicate that the firstborn sons of the mother had special sacred duties within the family so that they functioned as the priests in ancient Israel. Num 3:11-13, 40-51; and 8:13-19 are three instances in which YHWH informs Moses that YHWH will take the Levites in place of the firstborn of Israel to serve as priests. Indeed, Num 17–18 marks the point where Aaron and the Levites are consecrated as priests to YHWH in the pentateuchal narrative. Other texts in the Hebrew Bible point to a northern Israelite practice of consecrating firstborn sons as priests. First Samuel 1–3 relates the birth of Samuel to his mother Hannah and his Ephraimite father, Elkanah.[17] After weaning her firstborn son, Hannah takes little Samuel to the sanctuary at Shiloh and places him under the care of the high priest Eli, who raises Samuel as a priest even though he is of Ephraimite descent. Samuel apparently points to a northern practice of consecrating firstborn sons as priests. This would explain why Jeroboam ben Nebat, the first king of the northern kingdom of Israel, is charged with allowing non-Levites to serve as priests in 1 Kgs 12:31 and why non-priestly figures, such as Elijah and Elisha, can engage in priestly activity, such as building the altar at Mount Carmel in 1 Kgs 18 or playing liturgical music in 2 Kgs 3.[18] It would appear that our narrative was originally intended to explain that the firstborn sons of Israel were to be consecrated to serve as priests and that their function was to teach the people the significance of the holiday and to present the offerings of the people at the temple altar. But J and P presupposed that the Judean practice of exclusively employing the Levites as Israel's priesthood was correct.

Exodus 13:20-22 presents the journey from Succoth to Etam. It is a J text that describes YHWH going before the people in a pillar of cloud by day and a pillar of fire by night. The imagery is that of the altar of the later temple, which would be recognized by the pillar of smoke and fire that would rise from the altar as offerings were burned. Such an image represents divine presence and anticipates the construction of the tabernacle and altar in Exod 25–30 and 35–40.

Exodus 14:1–15:21 present the journey from Etam to Pi-hahiroth, before Baal-zephon and between Migdol and the sea together with YHWH's deliverance of Israel at the sea. The Hebrew text generally refers to the sea in Exod 14:1–15:21, but Exod

15:4, 22 identifies the sea as *yam-suph*. Many Christian translations identify the sea as the Red Sea, based on the LXX text which reads in Greek, *thalasses erythras*, "Red Sea." The Hebrew term *yam-suph*, however, does not refer to the Red Sea; instead it refers to "the sea of Reeds," based on the fact that *suph* is a loan word from Egypt, *tjouf*, which means "reeds."[19] The *yam-suph* is therefore identified with the marshy area around Lake Manzaleh in the vicinity of the present-day Suez Canal. Such a setting would better explain Israel's departure from Egypt into the wilderness, insofar as a journey to the Red Sea would require a sharp turn to the south and a great distance to travel. It also explains why the wheels of the Egyptian chariots were stopped in Exod 15:25, apparently because they could not negotiate the mud of the marshes.

Overall, Exod 14:1–15:21 presents a dramatic confrontation at the sea in which Pharaoh, his heart hardened by YHWH, pursues Israel to the sea with his army and chariots, while YHWH or the angel of YHWH, represented by the pillar of smoke and fire, moved between the Egyptians and Israelites to ensure Israel's safe passage through the sea. The confrontation prompts the Israelites to rebel and complain that YHWH brought them into the wilderness to die, a motif that will appear repeatedly throughout the wilderness narratives. YHWH commands Moses to lift up his rod to represent the outstretched arm of YHWH before the eyes of all Israel and Egypt to see YHWH's power. YHWH employs the east wind to drive back the sea, thereby revealing dry land in the midst of the waters for Israel to cross. The parting of the sea thereby represents another act of creation by YHWH analogous to the initial creation in Gen 1:1–2:3 when dry land emerged from the midst of the waters. But this time, the redemption of Israel is included as a major element of YHWH's act of creation, demonstrating YHWH's power as creator and as the true G-d who redeems Israel.

The Song of the Sea in Exod 15:1-19 is an expanded example of the psalm of praise that extols YHWH for delivering Israel from the Egyptians.[20] It is considered by many scholars to be one of the oldest compositions in the Hebrew Bible. Although the song is identified as a non-source text, it appears to derive from northern Israel. Exodus 15:20-21 portrays Miriam the prophet, the sister of Aaron and Moses, leading the women in song and dance. The women sing the same psalm, but they worship separately from the men under the leadership of a woman, a feature that seems to be known in northern Israel.[21]

Exodus 15:22-27 presents the account of the journey from the sea to the Wilderness of Shur. This is basically a J narrative with a P framework that ties into the creation and wilderness rebellion motifs once again. When the people complain that they have no water to drink because the water in the wilderness is bitter, Moses throws a piece of wood into the water to make it fit to drink. The passage appears to be related to 2 Kgs 2:19-22 in which the northern prophet, Elisha, purifies water with salt. The rebellion is easily settled, and a characteristic natural feature of the wilderness is explained.

Exodus 16:1-36 recounts the journey from Elim to the Wilderness of Sin. The narrative has a J foundation and P editing. Again, it presents the wilderness rebellion motif coupled with elements of creation. The people complain because they are hungry, and the narrative deliberately highlights the tension of the rebellion motif by portraying the people as longing for the sumptuous food of Egypt, neglecting the fact that they had been slaves and would have eaten only the worst food possible. But such a portrayal serves a J agenda which portrays the rebellious people as northern Israelites who were punished by the fall of their kingdom to Assyria in 722–721 BCE. When the people demand bread, YHWH and Moses give them manna, a Hebrew term that plays upon the exclamation of the people, *mah-hu'?* "what is it?" (v. 15), when they are asked to eat it. Manna is a characteristic feature of the natural environment of the Sinai akin to honey. It is a sweet substance formed when insects feed on the sap of tamarisk trees and secrete the manna, which coagulates into a form that may be eaten by humans. When the people demand meat, YHWH provides them with quail that they can easily catch. The provision of quail presupposes the migratory travel patterns of quail and other birds who fly through the Sinai on a regular seasonal basis like that observed at San Juan Capistrano in Southern California. The interests of the P stratum appear when the narrative links the provision of quail and manna to the Shabbat, the foundation of creation according to P in Gen 1:1–2:3.

Exodus 17:1–18:27 presents the combined E, J, and P account of the journey from the Wilderness of Sin to Rephidim as the background for the encounter with Amalek and Jethro's visit to see Moses. The motifs of Israel's rebellion and the natural features of the Sinai wilderness appear as the people complain about lack of water in the J narrative of Exod 17:1-7. When Moses strikes the rock at Horeb, water gushes forth, apparently presupposing places in the Sinai wilderness where water can be found by breaking into the brittle surface of limestone rocks which cover underground water sources. Horeb is the alternative name for Sinai. Insofar as Sinai is configured like a temple in Exod 19, it is noteworthy that temples in ancient Israel were understood as the holy centers of creation from which water flowed.

The encounter with the Amalekites is key because it presents Israel's right to defend itself against enemies who seek to destroy it in the J narrative of Exod 17:8-16. The Amalekites were a seminomadic tribal group that lived in the Sinai and Negev regions, frequently raiding Israel and Judah with deadly attacks in an attempt to steal animals, produce, and other items of value. They are known as the implacable enemies of Israel who must be destroyed before they destroy Israel (see Judg 3:13; 6:3-5; 1 Sam 15).

Finally, Exod 18:1-27 presents the account of Jethro's visit to the camp of Israel. The narrative is largely an E composition, and it is important for several reasons. First, it suggests that Jethro comes because of some problem between Moses and Zipporah insofar as Moses has sent her away. Some interpreters maintain that Moses had divorced her because the Cushite woman of Num 12 might be a different woman from his Midianite wife, Zipporah.[22] Indeed, Num 25 indicates that Midianite women might be a source of apostasy. A second issue is Jethro's alleged conversion to Judaism. As priest of Midian, Jethro would represent a tradition different from that of Israel, although many interpreters speculate that Israelite religion originated among seminomadic desert-dwelling tribes. Jethro's blessing of YHWH in v. 10 is frequently read as a statement of his adherence to YHWH and therefore of his conversion to Israelite religion or Judaism.[23] Finally, the narrative allows Jethro to advise Moses on how to organize his court system. Jethro advises him to teach the people what they should know and to establish lower courts to hear most cases; only the most difficult cases would then come to Moses as chief magistrate of the nation (Deut 16:18–17:13 which calls for the high priest to serve as the chief magistrate). The narrative signals the origins of the Israelite judicial system.

IV

Exodus 19:1–Numbers 2:34 presents the journey from Rephidim to Sinai where the revelation of Torah to Israel takes place. This chapter concentrates only on the initial account of the arrival at Sinai in Exod 19:1-2, and the account of YHWH's revelation from the mountain in Exod 19:3–40:38. Subsequent accounts of revelation from the tabernacle in Lev 1–27 and the census and organization of the people around the tabernacle in Num 1:1–2:34 are treated below.

The revelation at Sinai is the centerpiece of the pentateuchal narrative, insofar as it establishes the relation between YHWH and Israel and provides the covenantal and legal foundations for a just and holy society. The text is largely a P composition, although elements of E and J are apparent at various points. The Sinai pericope actually extends all the way to Num 10:10, but the P *toledoth* formula in Num 3:1 indicates that the narrative has been edited by P for its present place in the final structure of the Pentateuch.

Exodus 19:1-2 is a P text that works the Sinai pericope into the travel itinerary structure of the narrative. It signals Israel's arrival and encampment at Sinai from Rephidim on the third month following the exodus from Egypt. The beginning of the third month is the traditional time for the observance of Shavuot, which celebrates the revelation of Torah at Sinai. Numbers 2:11 marks the twentieth day of the second month of the second year as the date for Israel's departure.

Exodus 19:3–40:38 focuses on YHWH's revelation from the mountain as part of the larger Sinai pericope in Exod 19:3–Num 2:34/10:10. It commences with the focus on Mount Sinai as the location from which G-d reveals Torah to Israel. The completion of the tabernacle and the movement of the divine pillar of fire and smoke into the tabernacle structure in Exod 40 concludes this subunit. Revelation from the tabernacle then follows beginning in Lev 1.

The narrative proceeds with a sequence of episodes. First is the theophanic revelation of YHWH at Sinai in Exod 19:3-25. Second is the presentation of YHWH's laws, including the Ten Commandments and covenant code in Exod 20:1–23:33. Third is the account of YHWH's conference with Moses on the mountain, including instructions to build the tabernacle, in Exod 24:1–31:18. Fourth is the account of the gold calf in Exod 32:1–34:35. Fifth is the account of Israel's compliance with YHWH's instructions to build the tabernacle (Exod 35:1–40:38).

The account of the theophanic revelation of YHWH on Mount Sinai in Exod 19:3-25 presents the mountain as a holy site in the midst of creation that serves as a pattern for the structure and function of the temple. YHWH announces that the people of Israel are to observe YHWH's instructions and keep the covenant so that they will be recognized as YHWH's treasure (*segullah*), a term normally employed for a personal treasure, from among all the nations as well as a kingdom of priests and a holy people. YHWH's statements in vv. 5-6 are a development of the covenant formula which establishes the relationship between YHWH and Israel. The language is similar to that employed in Assyrian vassal treaties in which the Assyrian king establishes a treaty relationship with a weaker client state that swears loyalty to him.[24] The theophany, or appearance of G-d, employs the imagery of thick cloud of smoke, lightning, and thunder, which emulates the imagery of the temple in operation with its incense burners producing thick smoke, the *menorot* or candelabrae flashing light, the shofars blowing, and the temple choir singing loudly (1 Kgs 7; Isa 6). Moses instructs the people to self-sanctify by washing themselves and their clothing as they would before going to the temple; by not moving beyond the bounds at the base of the temple, which is construed as a model for the holy of holies in the temple where the ark of the covenant will reside and only the priests may enter; and by not going near a woman. The last condition presumes sexual contact, forbidden for those who have consecrated themselves. Sexual relations require purification; seminal emission desecrates a man because it is a living substance that dies following release from the body.

When Moses and Aaron ascend the mountain to hear YHWH, YHWH begins, in Exod 20:1-23, by announcing the Ten Commandments and the altar law. This version of the Ten Commandments is an E-stratum text, although its rationale for observance of the Shabbat is creation. The Ten Commandments are already known to the eighth-century northern prophet Hosea ben Beeri, who cites them in Hos 4:2, and to the seventh- to sixth-century priestly prophet Jeremiah ben Hilkiah, who cites them in Jer 7:9. They are not laws per se, because it would be impossible to adjudicate them in a court of law. Rather they are statements of principle for both civil and religious issues that are to be addressed in the law codes. An alternative version appears in Deut 5, with somewhat different wording. They employ the apodictic or command form of statement common in ancient Assyrian treaty texts and once again indicate that YHWH is portrayed in relation to the imagery of an Assyrian monarch who makes a vassal treaty with a client nation.[25] Verses 2-3 present the first commandment in which YHWH self-identifies, much as an Assyrian king would do in a treaty text, and then issues a command that the people shall have no other gods. Idolatry is prohibited. Proper use of the divine name ensures YHWH's sanctity, and remembrance of the Shabbat as the foundational command of Judaism (Gen 1:1–2:3; Exod 31:12-17; Isa 56:1-8). Honoring one's parents preserves family integrity. Prohibitions against murder, adultery, theft, false oaths in court, and coveting a neighbor's house, wife, slaves, animals, and so on, protect social order. The subsequent altar law in vv. 19-23 provides instruction on how to build the structure that serves as the focal point for Israel's relationship with YHWH in the later temple compounds. Unlike Deuteronomy, which allows only one altar (Deut 12), Exod 20:21 allows for altars wherever G-d is worshipped. The command to use unhewn stones is an attempt to symbolize the integrity of the created world.

Exodus 21:1–23:33 presents the so-called covenant code, which constitutes the foundational law code of the northern kingdom of Israel, cited by the mid-eighth-century Judean prophet Amos of Tekoa in Amos 2:6-16 in his indictment of northern Israel. Although some argue that this is a non-source text, more now agree that this is an E-source composition due to its northern Israelite roots. David Wright correctly argues that it was composed on the basis of Hammurabi's law code, but he is mistaken in arguing that it is exilic.[26] The Jehu dynasty of Israel submitted to the Assyrian monarch, Shalmaneser III, in the late ninth century BCE. Jehu's submission to Assyria would have provided the opportunity for Mesopotamian legal texts, such as Hammurabi's law code and Assyrian vassal treaty texts, to be introduced into Israel. The covenant code portrays YHWH and not the Assyrians as the true source of Israelite law. But the code is not entirely indebted to Hammurabi's code. The case law forms, which state a case or a condition, "if a man does such and such," and its resolution, "then he shall be such and such," certainly presuppose the forms employed in Hammurabi's code, but the apodictic forms, "thou shalt/thou shalt not," are derived from Assyrian vassal treaty texts.

The covenant code addresses a variety of civil and religious issues. The slave law in Exod 21:2-11 defines the treatment of a Hebrew man or woman who must submit to debt slavery. The term of service is limited to six years (Jacob in Gen 29). Laws here are statements of precedent from which legal principles are derived and applied to other situations, much like contemporary American law. There are a number of goring-ox laws in the covenant code like those of Hammurabi's code. Oxen did not pose a particular problem; rather they functioned as templates for adjudicating issues of liability in the case of death, personal injury, and property damage.[27] Religious laws appear as well, such as those concerning the major holidays. The laws concerning the harvesting of fields combine civil and religious concerns by requiring that fields lie fallow during the seventh year of the Shabbat cycle so that the poor may find food. The conclusion to the covenant code in Exod 23:20-23 functions like the blessings and curses of Assyrian treaties insofar as G-d's angel will protect the people if they abide by the covenant.

Exodus 24:1–31:18 presents the account of Moses's ascent to Mount Sinai to receive YHWH's instructions for building the tabernacle. This text begins in Exod 24:1-18 with an account of the vision of YHWH and the covenant ceremony that will seal the relationship between Israel and YHWH. It continues in Exod 25:1–30:38 with YHWH's instructions to build the tabernacle and ordain the priests. It concludes with accounts of YHWH's appointment of Bezalel ben Uri ben Hur as the master craftsman for the tabernacle in Exod 31:1-11 and YHWH's reiteration of the observance of the Shabbat in Exod 31:12-18.

The account of the vision of YHWH and the covenant ceremony in Exod 24:1-18 is a combination of E, J, and P elements. It points to the leadership of Israel in the wilderness, Aaron, his sons Nadab and Abihu, and the seventy elders of Israel as the representatives of the people, as those who will encounter YHWH in a visionary experience. The seventy elders of Israel are a northern institution of tribal leaders who play the key role in selecting the kings of northern Israel. Aaron appears to act as a priest although he is not designated as such until Num 17–18; he is, however, the firstborn son of his mother, Jochebed. His sons, Nadab and Abihu, share the names of the sons of King Jeroboam ben Nebat of Israel, Nadab and Abijah, which suggests an attempt to portray Aaron as a corollary to the king. Some argue that vv. 3-8 are non-source texts because Moses erects an altar at the foot of the mountain whereas the covenant is made on the mountain itself, but these verses portray only one part of the process of covenant making in which the people swear to observe all that Moses has written. The leadership of the people must still engage in a festival meal with YHWH, apparently representing the consumption of the offerings on the altar. The portrayal of YHWH takes place in a visionary context, typical of E, which attempts to avoid portrayal of YHWH in anthropomorphic terms. The reference to YHWH's feet appears only to describe the placement of the likeness of a work of sapphire, apparently a representation of the blue skies of the heavens to indicate that YHWH resides in the heavens above. There is no depiction of YHWH per se. The work of sapphire is described only in terms of a simile to avoid describing the boundary between heaven and earth in finite terms.

The J and P version of the encounter then follows in Exod 24:12-18 where Moses, accompanied by his future successor, Joshua, ascends the mountain to meet YHWH. P's interests are clear with the depiction of YHWH's presence as "the glory of YHWH" (Heb., *kevod-yhwh*) ensconced in cloud for six days. Moses enters the cloud, like the priest entering the holy of holies of the temple, while the incense burners fill the structure with smoke, to ascend the mountain alone and receive YHWH's instruction for forty days.

Exodus 25:1–30:38 is a P composition that presents YHWH's instructions to Moses concerning the building of the tabernacle and the ordination of the priesthood. The tabernacle (*mishkan*) is a portable sanctuary that functions as YHWH's symbolic dwelling amongst the people until such time as the temple in the land of Israel is built. The tabernacle functions as a model for the future temple, which is built according to the same pattern. YHWH's first instruction to Moses in Exod 25:1-9 is to tell the people to bring the various building materials that will be necessary for the construction of the tabernacle, its furnishings, and the ordination of its priesthood.

YHWH then turns to instructions concerning the building of the various fixtures and furnishings connected to the tabernacle. The first is the ark of the covenant in Exod 25:10-22, which will house the tablets of the covenant between YHWH and Israel. The ark is a portable chest made of acacia wood, overlaid with gold, and carried by poles inserted through rings constructed on its sides (cf. 2 Sam 6, where the ark is conveyed by cart). Its function is to house the tablets of the covenant in the tabernacle much as ancient Assyrian treaty texts were housed in temples. The *kapporeth*, or cover, for the ark functions as YHWH's footstool on earth (cf. Isa 66:1). It is protected by two cherubim, composite animal figures who typically guard the thrones of kings and the gates of cities in ancient Near Eastern iconography. They contribute to the imagery of the ark of the covenant as throne of YHWH who sits invisibly above it, indicated by the phrase, "YHWH who sits above the cherubim" (1 Sam 4:4; 2 Sam 6:2; cf. Isa 66:1).

Instructions for the building of the table for "the bread of the presence" and its utensils for the offering of libations appear in Exod 25:23-30. The table with the bread of the presence stands before the holy of holies in the temple as an ongoing offering to YHWH. Twelve loaves of bread are placed on it each week, after which they are eaten by the priests (Lev 24:5-9). Exodus 25:31-40 provides instruction for the building of the tabernacle menorah, or lampstand. The menorah is designed with six branches to represent the six days of creation together with a central branch to represent the Shabbat. Its treelike structure indicates fertility in creation. Each branch is built with cups to hold the oil and the wicks. The menorah provides light for the interior of the tabernacle (later, the temple in Jerusalem), which symbolizes YHWH's Torah. The image of the menorah apparently stands behind the tree of the knowledge of good and evil in Gen 3.

Exodus 26:1–27:21 presents YHWH's instructions for building the tabernacle, its courts, and its interior features, which in turn serve as the pattern for the construction of the temple. Because the tabernacle structure is portable, it is constructed as a tent structure, whereas the temple will later be built from stone and wood. The structure of the holy of holies is formed by constructing ten cloth panels made of linen with cherub designs clasped together to form the interior of the tabernacle tent. The exterior covering of the tent is formed by eleven cloth panels made of goat's hair (Exod 26:7-14). The reason for the eleventh panel is that it functions as the covering for the entrance which faces east. The goat's hair covering is overlaid with coverings of tanned ram skins and another of dolphin skins so that the tent actually comprises four layers. The planks or vertical support beams are made from acacia wood overlaid with gold, each 10 cubits (15 feet) long and 1 ½ cubits (27 inches) wide (Exod 26:15-25). Each beam is supported by two silver posts on either end. The result is a tent structure that measures 30 cubits (45 feet) on the north and south by 10 cubits (15 feet) on the east and west with a 10-cubit (15 foot) entrance on the east. Fifteen bars of acacia wood overlaid with gold are constructed and fitted to form the interior of the holy of holies from the north, south, and west, leaving the east open (Exod 26:26-30). A curtain woven from colored threads provides a cover for the holy of holies where the ark is to be placed in the tent (Exod 26:31-35). The table and the menorah are placed before the curtain, and the screen is constructed to shield the eastern entrance of the tent (Exod 26:36-37).

Exodus 27:1-8 presents the instructions for constructing the altar and its utensils. It is to be 5 by 5 cubits (7.5 feet) square and 3 cubits (46 inches) high with four horns to represent the four winds or directions of the world of creation. The altar is constructed of acacia wood overlaid with copper, apparently because copper is best suited for the fires of the offerings. It includes poles for transporting the structure through the wilderness.

Exodus 27:9-19 presents instructions for constructing the meeting tent (tabernacle) that covers the holy of holies. The cloth for the structure is made from goat's hair supported by posts with sockets of copper. It measures 100 cubits (150 feet) along the north and south sides, and 50 cubits (75 feet) along the west and east sides. Exodus 27:20-21 instructs the people to bring olive oil for the lamps.

Exodus 28:1–29:46 provides instruction concerning the priestly vestments and the ordination of the priests. The instructions concerning the vestments in Exod 28:1-43 presume that Aaron and his sons, Nadab, Abihu, Eleazar, and Ithamar, will become the priests of Israel, although Nadab and Abihu will die in Lev 10, and Aaron and his remaining sons will be named as priests in Num 17–18. The vestments are holy and are to be worn when the priests perform the service of the sanctuary. The ephod and the breast piece include precious stones engraved with the names of the twelve tribes of Israel and the Urim and Thummim, indicating that it was meant to function as an oracular device with which priests would divine the will of YHWH. The robe of the ephod is pure blue with a hem woven with pomegranate features and golden bells. The diadem is formed from gold and engraved with the phrase, *qodesh layhwh*, "holy for YHWH." The tunic, turban, and breeches are all made from linen.

The ordination of the priests in Exod 29:1-37 is a rite of passage that calls for six actions: washing, robing, anointing, and the presentations of three offerings, including the sin or purification offering (*khatta't*), the entirely burnt offering (*'olah*), and the ordination offering derived from the peace offering (*zebakh shelamim*). The ordination offering is the breast of the ram, which functions as the breast of ordination (*khazeh hammillu'im*) or as an elevation offering (*tenuphah*) and the thigh of the animal functions as a gift offering (*terumah*). These portions of the animal are given to the priests for their own support as part of the Israelite peace offering, *zebakh shelamim*. The ordination process then lasts for seven days as the priests purify the altar for service to YHWH. Additional instruction concerning the priests includes the daily *tamid*, or entirely burnt offering, (Exod 29:28-42) and YHWH's instruction that the meeting tent (tabernacle) is the place that YHWH will meet with Israel through the agency of the consecrated priests.

Further instruction concerning the tabernacle include the incense altar (Exod 30:1-10), a census for the half-shekel temple tax (Exod 30:11-16), the laver for washing (Exod 30:17-21), the anointing oil (Exod 30:22-33), and the sacred incense (Exod 30:34-38).

Finally Exod 31:1-11 presents Bezalel ben Uri ben Hur of Judah as YHWH's master craftsman and Oholiab ben Ahisamach of Dan as his assistant in building the tabernacle and making the priestly vestments and other sacred items. The instruction concludes in Exod 31:12-17 with a reminder to observe the Shabbat as the foundation of the covenant.

Exodus 32:1–34:35 relates the infamous gold calf episode, which indicates problems among the people while Moses was up on the mountain with YHWH. This text combines E, J, and P elements and points to the need to purge Israel of those who would stray from YHWH as well as the need to provide appropriate leadership for the people. It ties into the wilderness rebellion motif in that the people become anxious while Moses is away for forty days, and they demand that Aaron, functioning in his priestly role as a firstborn son, build them a gold calf to worship in place of YHWH. Aaron agrees readily and calls upon the people to give their gold, much as they were to do for the construction of the tabernacle, to produce a gold calf. When Moses comes down from the mountain and sees the people worshipping the calf, he breaks the covenant tablets, and demands an explanation from Aaron, who fails to take full responsibility for what he has done by stating that he cast the people's gold into the fire and a calf came out. Moses then calls for those who are zealous for YHWH. The Levites answer Moses's call and proceed to kill those who were engaged in the illicit worship. Moses returns to the mountain to seek YHWH's forgiveness and returns with a second set of tablets for the covenant.

This brief summary hardly does justice to the narrative, and so discussion must turn to its key features. It will become obvious that this text is heavily dependent on other texts from Deuteronomy and the Deuteronomistic History which it employs to cast the sin of the gold calves in relation to the worship practices of the northern kingdom of Israel.[28] It explains the destruction of northern Israel and points to Judean patterns of worship as legitimate. The text defends YHWH's holiness and righteousness and instead holds Israel responsible for its own suffering. Its purpose is to promote fidelity to YHWH as the true course for the future of Israel. Such an agenda indicates that the text is a J composition that has been edited by P.

The first issue is the portrayal of the gold calf. The gold calf and Aaron's statements about it relate intertextually to the portrayal in 1 Kgs 12:25-33; 13:1-34 of King Jeroboam ben Nebat, the first king of northern Israel, and his construction of the gold calves at the sanctuaries at Bethel and Dan for the worship of the people. Aaron's statement to the people in Exod 32:4, "Behold your G-d, O Israel, who brought you out from the land of Egypt," is nearly identical to Jeroboam's statement to Israel in 1 Kgs 12:28. Aaron's two older sons, Nadab and Abihu, who will ultimately die in Lev 10, correspond to Jeroboam's sons, Nadab and Abijah. There seems to be a deliberate attempt to correlate Aaron and the gold calf of the wilderness with Jeroboam and the gold calves of northern Israel.

But there is polemical intent to such a portrayal. In 1 Kgs 12:25-33, Jeroboam is portrayed as an apostate king who leads his people into sin. He becomes the model for the northern Israelite kings, each of whom is condemned for following the lead of Jeroboam in leading the people astray.[29] Jeroboam's apostasy becomes the basis for explaining the destruction of northern Israel in the Deuteronomistic History, apparently as a basis for calling for the people of Judah to repent and adhere to YHWH alone. But we must ask whether the gold calves of Jeroboam were indeed sinful as portrayed in the Judean-authored text in 1 Kgs 12:25-33. Animals such as bulls, lions, and so on, were commonly portrayed as mounts for gods and goddesses in the ancient Near Eastern world. The mounts were not worshipped as gods; rather the gods and goddesses who sat astride or stood upon the animals were the objects of worship. YHWH was understood to be a divine presence who could not be portrayed in finite terms. In Judah, YHWH was understood to be enthroned above the cherubim of the ark of the covenant as indicated in 1 Sam 4:4; 2 Sam 6:2. The covenant chest was a throne for YHWH in Judah, just as the gold calf was a mount for YHWH in northern Israel. The issue was not one of apostasy but a different iconography. But the Judean authors of Kings did not want to charge YHWH with wrongdoing in the fall of northern Israel; instead, they portrayed the fall of Israel as a case of human wrongdoing, and pointed to Jeroboam's gold calves as idolatry that justified Israel's destruction. It would appear that the authors of Exod 32–34 made the same choice.

The narrative recognizes the theological problems inherent in YHWH's anger against Israel. Before Moses descends from the mountain, YHWH asks him to see what the people are doing in Exod 32:7-14. YHWH proposed to destroy the people of Israel and to create a new nation from Moses. But Moses must serve as the moral voice of the narrative. Moses reminds YHWH that such destruction would result in charges that YHWH was evil in bringing the people out from Egypt; that YHWH made a covenant with Abraham, Isaac, and Jacob; and that YHWH promised to make Israel a great nation that would possess the land of Israel. Upon hearing these reasons, YHWH decided against destroying Israel, but nevertheless permitted a purge. The zeal of the Levites demonstrates their suitability to serve YHWH. The levitical priesthood was the only legitimate priesthood in Judah, and it supplanted the practice of using the firstborn sons as priests in the pentateuchal narrative. Aaron is a firstborn son whose inadequacy as a priest is apparent, but his descendants will serve as a dynastic priesthood in Num 17–18.

YHWH's actions prompt Moses to ask that he might know YHWH's presence. Moses is portrayed throughout the narrative as a visionary prophet who meets with YHWH, first in the burning bush and later in the meeting tent. Consequently, YHWH agrees to present Moses with a revelation of YHWH's divine presence. YHWH instructs Moses to go to a cave on Sinai and YHWH passes before Moses stating YHWH's divine characteristics of mercy and judgment, "YHWH, YHWH, a G-d merciful and gracious, slow to anger and great in fidelity and truth, extending fidelity to the thousandth generation, forgiving iniquity and rebellion and sin, but who does not remit punishment, bringing punishment for the iniquity of the fathers upon sons and the sons of sons and upon the third and fourth generations" (Exod 34:6-7). This remarkable statement of YHWH's essential nature appears at many points throughout the Bible as a means to understand YHWH's character. It is noteworthy, however, that Moses's encounter with YHWH is similar to Elijah's encounter with YHWH in 1 Kgs 19. Elijah flees King Ahab and Queen Jezebel and hides in a cave on Mount Horeb, the alternative name of Sinai in Deuteronomic and Deuteronomistic literature. Here he sees three visions of power—wind, earthquake, and fire—but realizes that none of them is YHWH, until he hears a voice of absolute silence (Heb., *qol demmamah daqqah*), which is the voice of YHWH. It would appear that our Judean authors in Exodus once again drew upon the Deuteronomistic History and its portrayal of Elijah's struggle against idolatry in northern Israel to fashion the present exodus narrative.

Finally, readers must consider the new covenant tablets that YHWH gives to Moses. The new law code in Exod 34:10-26 is essentially a revision of the covenant code in Exod 21–23, although it, too, has been influenced by Deuteronomic texts.[30] It begins with YHWH's promise to drive out the various foreign nations, but it also draws upon Deut 7:1-7 in prohibiting Israel from marrying their sons and daughters to these nations and thereby exposing themselves to the influence of their foreign gods. Deuteronomy, or D, is a Judean text, written during the reign of King Josiah of Judah, and the law code in Exod 34:10-26 provides a brief sample of Deuteronomic law and thinking.[31] The first command to follow the prohibition on intermarriage is a prohibition on making molten gods, like the gold calf, which indicates the influence of the literary context. Laws concerning the observance of the Festival of Matzot and the redemption of the oldest male child then follow together with laws concerning the observance of the other festivals, modeled on texts from Exod 23 and Deut 16.

Moses is changed. YHWH's holy presence requires him to wear a veil when he leaves the meeting tent to speak with the people. His exposure to YHWH renders his face radiant as he now functions like Elijah as a man of G-d. Because the Hebrew term (*qeren*) meaning "rays" also means "horn," medieval art depicted Moses with horns upon his forehead.

The book of Exodus closes in Exod 35–40 with a compliance report in which the people carry out the instructions for building the tabernacle and ordaining the priests as stated in Exod 25–30. Interpreters recognize these chapters as a P-stratum text that, like Exod 25–30, focuses on the details of the construction of the tabernacle as a model for the future temple.

It begins in Exod 35:2-3 with instruction to observe the Shabbat, emphasizing once again the fundamental character of Shabbat observance in Judaism (see Gen 1:1–2:3). A number of intertextual references in Exod 39–40 correlate with statements from the creation account in Gen 1:1–2:3, pointing to the construction of the tabernacle as a culminating act that advances the completion of creation. These references appear in Gen 1:31 and Exod 39:43; Gen 2:1 and Exod 39:32; Gen 2:2 and Exod 40:33; and Gen 2:3 and Exod 39:43, all of which signal the correlation between the completion of creation on the Shabbat and the completion of the tabernacle. Genesis 1:1–Exodus 40:38 thereby emulates many ancient Near Eastern creation narratives by portraying the building of a temple to the creator god as the culmination of creation.

The narrative concludes in Exod 40:33-39 with the account of the glory or presence of YHWH entering the tabernacle. From this point on, the account of the revelation of Torah (instruction) from the mountain in Exod 19:3–40:38 concludes, and the account of revelation from the tabernacle in Lev 1–27 begins.

Leviticus

I

Leviticus begins the segment of the Pentateuch concerned with revelation from the tabernacle in Lev 1:1–Num 2:34. Exodus 19:3–40:38 constitutes revelation from the mountain, but with the construction of the wilderness tabernacle in Exod 35–40, the divine presence or "glory of YHWH" transfers to the tabernacle so that revelation may continue from the sacred structure that serves as the model for the holy temple to be built in the land of Israel.[1] The content of the revelation shifts as well. Exodus 19:3–40:38 focuses on instruction concerning the laws necessary for a just and holy Israelite society as well as instructions for the building of the tabernacle, which will serve as the holy center of Israel and creation at large. Leviticus 1:1–27:34 focuses on the laws of holiness that Israel must observe to ensure the sanctity of the tabernacle/temple so that it might serve as the holy center of Israel and creation.

Leviticus includes two major compositions, the priestly laws of sacrifice and priestly practice in Lev 1–16 and the laws of holiness or the so-called holiness code in Lev 17–26.[2] These sections are distinguished by their very different contents and literary styles. Leviticus 1–16 focuses especially on instruction concerning the roles and obligations of the priesthood in performing the sacred rituals of the tabernacle and temple, whereas Lev 17–26 focuses on the laws of holiness that pertain to the people and priesthood. The repeated emphasis on the formula, "you shall be holy because I, YHWH, am holy," indicates that Lev 17–26 is a discrete composition that scholars have labeled the holiness code. Leviticus 27 then resumes the priestly instruction of Lev 1–16 with laws concerning vows made by the people for the support of the temple and priesthood. Leviticus 1–16 actually includes two types of composition, the laws in Lev 1–7 and 11–26 and the narratives in Lev 8–10 concerning the priesthood.[3]

Most twentieth-century interpreters associate Leviticus with the P source, or stratum, set in the postexilic period during the time of Ezra and Nehemiah because of its focus on legal, priestly, and ritual matters and because of its lack of reference to an anointed monarch. But even Wellhausen held that the legal materials of Lev 1–7, 11–15, and 17–26 had to be considered as later additions to the fundamental P narratives.[4] Contemporary scholars have noted that the prophet and priest Ezekiel, who lived during the late monarchic and early exilic period in the late seventh and early sixth centuries BCE, cites the holiness code in his discussion of moral responsibility in Ezek 18.[5] Recent studies, however, have begun to argue that Lev 1–16 also cites from P material, which suggests that it may have been written during the late monarchic period from Hezekiah's reforms of the late eighth century BCE through the reign of King Josiah during the late seventh century BCE.[6] Cultic centrality in Lev 1–16, which would accept only one temple as the proper site for the worship of YHWH, also plays an important role in arguments that Lev 1–16 should be placed in relation to the reforms of Hezekiah and Josiah. Other studies argue that the holiness code cites and reinterprets material from the E and J strata of Exodus and Numbers and the D stratum of Deuteronomy.[7]

The present synchronic form of Leviticus is formulated as a narrative that reports YHWH's direct speeches to Moses in the tent of meeting, the holy of holies of the wilderness tabernacle, situated at Mount Sinai. YHWH's instructions to Moses call upon him to address the people of Israel or Aaron and his sons in order to convey YHWH's instructions to them. In some cases, the YHWH speech formula may also introduce supplemental instruction concerning the main topics of the subunit, such as the instructions concerning the sin/purification offering (*khatta't*) and the guilt/reparation offering (*'asham*) in Lev 4:1-5:13 that is followed by supplemental instruction in Lev 5:14-19 and 5:20-26. In others, such as Lev 8:1–10:20, the narrative unit also presents an account of the events that follow from YHWH's instructions. In yet other cases, such as Lev 13:1 and 15:1, YHWH addresses both Moses and Aaron, in the first instance to convey instructions that are directed to priestly practice and in the second to convey instructions to the people of Israel at large. Insofar as the narrative setting presupposes that YHWH speaks to Moses in the tent of meeting, Lev 13:1 and 15:1 emphasize that Moses must convey these instructions to the named parties in each instance.

Leviticus 1:1–27:34 constitutes an account of YHWH's instructions to Moses from the tabernacle concerning the sanctity of Israel. Each speech account constitutes a subunit of this text, introduced by the YHWH speech formula, "and YHWH spoke to Moses, saying," and its variations in Lev 13:1 and 15:1 noted above. The following structure diagram conveys the arrangement of the narrative subunits that constitute the text as a whole:

Account of YHWH's Instructions to Moses from the Tabernacle Concerning the Sanctity of Israel	Lev 1:1–27:34
I. YHWH's Instructions to Moses Concerning the Whole Burnt Offering (*'olah*), the Grain Offering (*minkhah*), the Wellness Offering (*zebakh shelamim*)	1:1–3:17
A. Concerning the Whole Burnt Offering	1:1-17
B. Concerning the Grain Offering	2:1-16
C. Concerning the Wellness Offering	3:1-17

II. YHWH's Instructions to Moses Concerning the Sin/Purification Offering (*khatta't*) and the Guilt/Reparation Offering (*'asham*) 1:1–3:17	4:1–5:26
A. Concerning the Sin/Purification and the Guilt/Reparation Offering	4:1–5:13
B. First Supplemental Instruction Concerning the Guilt/Reparation Offering	5:14-19
C. Second Supplemental Instruction Concerning the Guilt/Reparation Offering	5:20-26
III. YHWH's Instructions Summarizing the Offerings of Israel	6:1–7:38
A. Concerning the Entirely Burnt Offering and the Grain Offering	6:1-11
B. Concerning the Anointment Offering by Aaron and His Sons	6:12-16
C. Concerning the Sin/Purification Offering, the Guilt/Reparation Offering, and the Wellness Offering of Well-Being	6:17–7:21
D. Concerning the Treatment of Fat	7:22-27
E. Concerning the Treatment of the Well-Being Offering by Aaron and His Sons	7:28-36
F. Summary Statement	7:37-38
IV. YHWH's Instructions Concerning the Ordination of Aaron and His Sons as Priests	8:1–10:20
A. Concerning the Ordination Proper	8:1-36
B. Concerning the Proper Service of Aaron and His Sons	9:1–10:20
V. YHWH's Instruction Concerning the Proper Treatment of Animals	11:1-47
VI. YHWH's Instruction Concerning Childbirth	12:1-8
VII. YHWH's Instruction Concerning Skin Diseases	13:1–14:57

A. YHWH's Instruction Concerning Diagnosis and Treatment	13:1-59
B. YHWH's Instruction Concerning Purification Rituals	14:1-32
C. YHWH's Instruction Concerning Analogous Cases: Mildew, Mold, and So On	14:33-53
D. Summary-Appraisal	14:54-57
VIII. YHWH's Instruction Concerning Bodily Discharges	15:1-33
IX. YHWH's Instructions Concerning the Scapegoat Offering on Yom Kippur	16:1-34
X. YHWH's Instructions Concerning the Sanctity of Blood	17:1-16
XI. YHWH's Instructions Concerning Sexual Conduct	18:1-30
XII. YHWH's Instructions Concerning Holy Conduct	19:1-37
XIII. YHWH's Instructions Concerning Unholy Conduct	20:1-27
XIV. YHWH's Instructions Concerning the Conduct and Ideal Status of Priests	21:1-24
A. YHWH's Instructions Concerning the Conduct of Priests	21:1-15
B. YHWH's Instructions Concerning the Ideal Status of Priests	21:16-24
XV. YHWH's Instructions Concerning the Offerings of the People	22:1-33
A. YHWH's Instructions Concerning Vows	22:1-16
B. YHWH's Instructions Concerning Vows and Free-Will Offerings	22:17-25
C. YHWH's Instructions Concerning Specialized Offerings	22:26-33
XVI. YHWH's Instructions Concerning Holidays and Observances	23:1-44

A. YHWH's Instructions Concerning Shabbat and Passover	23:1-8
B. YHWH's Instructions Concerning Shavuot	23:9-22
C. YHWH's Instructions Concerning Rosh haShanah and Yom Kippur	23:23-32
D. YHWH's Instructions Concerning Succoth	23:33-44
XVII. YHWH's Instructions Concerning the Sanctuary and Blasphemy of the Divine Name	24:1-23
XVIII. YHWH's Instructions Concerning the Jubilee Year	25:1–26:46
XIX. YHWH's Instructions Concerning Vows, Temple Tax, and Tithes	27:1-34

Leviticus is organized to convey the various instructions concerning the sanctity of Israel, beginning with the offerings presented at the sanctuary and continuing through the ordination of Aaron and his sons as priests and the various practices of the people concerning personal purity and conduct. Several key observations follow.

First, the instructions concerning the *'olah*, or entirely burnt offering, in Lev 1 do not provide full instruction concerning all aspects of the disposal of the entrails of the animal to be offered. Instead, Lev 1 provides an overview—or a prescription—concerning the offering of the *'olah*.[8] Such instruction is not directed to the priests; it is directed to the people who must provide the animals to be offered and who need rationale concerning their offerings.

Second, the priesthood as envisioned in Leviticus includes only Aaron and his sons, not the whole tribe of Levi. Insofar as Aaron's descendants appear to serve only in the central sanctuaries of Israel, beginning with the wilderness tabernacle (Exodus–Numbers) followed by Shiloh (1 Sam 1–3) and later at Jerusalem (1 Kgs 2; 7–8), Leviticus presupposes centralized worship only at these sites. The priesthood at Shiloh was ultimately supplanted (1 Sam 2) by that of Jerusalem (1 Kgs 2), and the sanctuary at Shiloh was ultimately destroyed according to Jeremiah (Jer 7), leaving only Jerusalem as the site for centralized worship in Israel/Judah. The Aaronide priesthood, based especially in Jerusalem, would have composed Leviticus.

A number of the instructions in Leviticus have multiple texts devoted to them, such as the instructions concerning the *'olah*, *minkhah*, and *zebakh shelamim* offerings in Lev 1–3 and the *khatta't* and *'asham* offerings in Lev 4–5 that are followed by a distinctive set of instructions concerning these offerings in Lev 6–7. Instructions concerning the *khatta't* and *'asham* offerings in Lev 4–5 include supplementary sections in Lev 5:14-19 and 5:20-26. Other examples of such supplementary sections appear throughout Leviticus, such as sexual and holy conduct in Lev 18; 19; and 20 or the instructions concerning the different types of vows in Lev 22, which suggests that the book went through a number of stages of expansion following the time of its initial composition as later writers sought to explain or develop elements that were unclear or insufficient. Even the holiness code in Lev 17–26 may well be an expansion on earlier teachings in Lev 1–16, 27. One might posit a process of composition that began in the late monarchic period and continued through the reforms of Nehemiah and Ezra in the fifth through fourth centuries BCE as the Jerusalem temple and YHWH's Torah emerged as the central institutions of Judaism. By the time of Nehemiah and Ezra, the need for instruction of the people concerning their sanctification in relation to the temple would have been especially important to garner popular support. The final form of Leviticus—and indeed of the Torah or Pentateuch as a whole—would have emerged during Nehemiah's and Ezra's reforms.

II

We now turn to the accounts of YHWH's instructions concerning the sanctity of Israel.

The first speech by YHWH appears in Lev 1–3, which presents instruction concerning the so-called "gift offerings": the *'olah*, or whole burnt offering, in Lev 1; the *minkhah*, or grain offering, in Lev 2; and the *zebakh shelamim*, or well-being sacrifice, in Lev 3. Each of these offerings is given daily to YHWH by Israel, and each has a distinctive function.

The Jerusalem temple functions as YHWH's house, which symbolizes YHWH's role as the master of creation. The temple therefore serves as an idealized home for YHWH that ensures the stability of creation when properly maintained. Insofar as YHWH is conceived as the king of creation, YHWH's house is built on the pattern of a royal palace.[9] The offerings are presented as idealized meals for YHWH. YHWH does not need to eat, but the offerings honor and thank YHWH for providing the nation with stability in creation and food for its support.

Leviticus 1 presents instructions concerning the *'olah*, or whole burnt offering, presented daily to YHWH by individuals or by the nation as a whole. This offering is called the *'olah*, or whole burnt offering, because the entire animal is burned on the altar so that it "goes up" (*'olah* means, "that which goes up [in smoke]"). None of it is eaten by the priests or people. The animal may be chosen from the herd (cattle), the flock (sheep or goats), or birds (turtledoves or pigeons). In the case of the herd or the flock, it is to be a male without any blemish; only healthy animals without any indication of wounds, sickness, or deformity may be offered to YHWH to express the ideal nature of the divine and the creation that human beings are expected to maintain. Insofar as the offerings are drawn from those animals that would be suitable for food for the people, they would appear in Lev 11. When presenting the animal for an offering, it is slaughtered with a sharp knife to ensure that the animal suffers no pain and the blood vessel is opened so that the animal bleeds to death. The reason for the draining of the blood is because blood represents the sanctity of life and humans are granted only limited capacity to shed blood (Gen 9:1-6). The blood is dashed against the altar so that it returns to the earth. The animal is flayed and cut up, and its entrails are removed and washed as if they were to be eaten. The whole body is placed upon the altar and burned entirely as a daily gift offering for YHWH.

The instructions for the *minkhah*, or grain offering, appear in Lev 2. The *minkhah* is a gift offering that accompanies the sacrificial animal, whether that animal is used for an *'olah* or any other sort of offering. The *minkhah* may therefore be eaten by the priests when the offering is something other than the *'olah*. The conceptualization of the *minkhah* is based on a meal; meat should be eaten with bread to constitute a meal. The *minkhah* is unleavened bread, much like a pita, or a cake that is made with fine flour, oil, and frankincense. The cakes may be baked in an oven or prepared with oil on a griddle. Leavened flour is not permitted because leavening changes the grain by initiating a process of decomposition, and it therefore interferes with the ideal nature of the grain. Salt is included to impede fermentation and decomposition.

Leviticus 3 presents the instructions for the *zebakh shelamim*, "the sacrifice of well-being." The term is also translated as "peace offering" insofar as *shelamim* is a plural form of the term that refers to peace or well-being. There is no specific occasion for the *zebakh shelamim*, although it functions as a celebratory offering from which the priests and the people may eat. It is given in thanks to YHWH and to YHWH's priests for their service at the sanctuary. The *zebakh shelamim* may be an animal from the herd or the flock, again without blemish, illness, or deformity. Birds are not specified for the *zebakh shelamim*. Birds are an offering given by those who cannot offer the more expensive animals of the herd and the flock, and so the offering represents a sacrifice beyond that which is minimally required. Like the *'olah*, the animal is slaughtered, its blood is drained and dashed against the altar, its body is cut up, and its entrails are washed. Unlike the *'olah*, the *zebakh shelamim* is not entirely consumed on the altar. The entrails and hind quarters are burned on the altar. The breast and right thigh are granted to the priests (Lev 7:11-36). The presenter and the other people may eat the rest.

YHWH's second instruction speech appears in Lev 4:1–5:13, which takes up the *khatta't*, "sin or purification offering," and the *'asham*, "guilt or reparation offering." Such offerings are made when a person violates one or more of the instructions given in YHWH's Torah. These offerings may also be made when the nation as a whole violates YHWH's instruction. Such violation constitutes a disruption of the ideal nature of the created world, and the *khatta't* and *'asham* offerings represent repentance by those who have violated YHWH's instructions.

Leviticus 4:3-12 takes up the case in which "the anointed priest," the high priest of the sanctuary (Lev 21:10; Num 35:25), unintentionally commits a sin in carrying out his sacred duties. The anointed priest is ultimately responsible for the sanctity of the people and the temple, and an error on his part would then compromise the sanctity of the temple as the holy center of creation and thereby compromise the sanctity of creation at large. Upon recognizing his sin, the priest is required to bring a bull, which would be the largest and most expensive of the animals that would qualify for a *khatta't* offering, to present at the altar as part of his efforts to purify himself and the sanctuary from his transgression. He must sprinkle the blood of the *khatta't* before the holy of holies of the sanctuary, the incense altar, and the sacrificial altar to purify each of these elements of the sanctuary from the desacralizing effects of his erroneous action. The bull is flayed; its entrails are removed and burned on the altar. The body of the animal is not to be eaten; instead it is taken to a place outside of the sanctuary and city, where it is burned in its entirety so as not to provide cause for a festive meal.

Leviticus 4:13-21 presents instruction when the sin has been committed unintentionally by the entire nation. The presentation of this *khatta't* is similar to that of the high priest, although the text prescribes sprinkling the blood of the bull only before the holy of holies and upon the sacrificial altar. The animal is flayed, its entrails are removed, and the priest burns them on the altar in order to purify the nation and the sanctuary from the sin that they had committed. The carcass of the bull is burned outside of the sanctuary like that of the *khatta't* for the high priest.

Leviticus 4:22-26 takes up the *khatta't* offering of a *nasi'*, a tribal chieftain or leader of the people who unintentionally commits a sin that compromises the sanctity of the people, the sanctuary, and creation at large. The animal for this form of the *khatta't* is a goat, which suggests that the sin committed by a *nasi'* is less severe than that of the priest or the nation or that the *nasi'* will not have the means available to the priest and nation at large. The presentation of the offering does not call for any blood to be sprinkled inside the sanctuary; rather it is poured out at the altar like the others and its entrails are burned on the altar.

Leviticus 4:27-31, which takes up the *khatta't* of an individual who has inadvertently committed a sin, calls for the offering of a female goat. A female offering indicates that the individual will also lose the capacity of the goat to give birth to future generations that might increase the herd and its milk that might further support the family. A male goat can impregnate many females, but a female goat gives birth only to one kid at a time; hence, females would be more valuable. Leviticus 4:32-35 presents instruction concerning the offering of a female sheep as the *khatta't* offering for an individual. The *khatta't* in and of itself does not purify the person in question; such purification comes from YHWH following the repentance of the wayward party.

Leviticus 5:1-13 concludes the instructions concerning the *khatta't* offerings by discussing cases in which an individual might have sinned, in most cases inadvertently, and then the sin becomes known to him. Examples include declining to testify under oath even when he might have knowledge of the matter at hand, inadvertently coming into contact with something unclean such as a carcass, coming into contact with some sort of human uncleanness, or failing to act upon an oath. Again, the text calls for the presentation of a female sheep or goat from the flock as a *khatta't* offering. Should the individual in question not have the means to provide a female goat or sheep, the text prescribes alternatives, such as turtledoves, pigeons, or fine flour.

YHWH's third instruction speech appears in Lev 5:14-19, which takes up the presentation of the *'asham*, "the guilt offering" or the "reparation offering." The *'asham* is presented in cases in which an individual has committed some wrongdoing and seeks to make restitution. The *'asham* differs from the *khatta't* insofar as the *'asham* is offered for restoration or reparation, whereas the *khatta't* provides a means for purification. The *'asham* covers violations associated with the sacred things of YHWH, which would refer to offerings devoted to the temple, implements, fixtures, and so on, that someone might damage or render impure by negligent or improper action. Such restitution is presented either for YHWH or for an individual, which suggests improper action that compromises someone else's sacred offerings to YHWH. The *'asham* calls for a ram from the flock, without any blemish, defect, or disease, or its equivalent in cash and the addition of a fifth part of its value in the case of the holy things of YHWH.

YHWH's fourth speech in Lev 5:20-26 builds upon the preceding instruction by specifying the actions committed by one individual against another that would call for an *'asham* as well as the means to resolve the issues. Such acts include deliberate actions, such as deceit in deposits or pledges, robbery, fraud, lying about lost property, or swearing falsely. The present text recognizes the deliberate commission of wrongdoing and may well represent an expansion of the earlier instruction to cover the cases of inadvertent acts mentioned above. The procedure calls for the restoration of what was lost to the victimized party plus an additional one-fifth of the value lost. The offending party then presents a ram or its equivalent in cash as an *'asham*.

Leviticus 6–7 presents five instruction speeches by YHWH concerning the offerings discussed in Lev 1–3 and 4–5, including the *'olah*, the *minkhah*, the *zebakh shelamim*, the *khatta't*, and the *'asham*. These instructions add additional information and, in some cases, reconceptualize the offering in question. Such changes suggest that these texts presuppose a process of reflection on the earlier texts and updating of their contents in order to address issues that had arisen in the application of the earlier instruction.

Leviticus 6:1-11 takes up the *'olah* and the *minkhah*. The text adds instructions concerning the need to keep the fire on the altar for the *'olah* burning all night until morning as well as the wearing of vestments by the priest during the course of the entire ritual. The text specifies that the priests must offer a portion of the *minkhah* together with the appropriate spices on the altar for YHWH. The rest they may eat as unleavened bread within the sanctuary.

Leviticus 6:12-16 focuses on the offering due to YHWH from the sons of Aaron on the occasion of their anointing as priests. It builds upon the treatment of the *minkhah* in Lev 6:1-11. The offering calls for the presentation of one-tenth of an ephah of fine flour cooked with oil on a griddle, half in the morning and half in the evening. It is burned on the altar as an offering to YHWH in thanks for what will be provided to the newly ordained priests.

Leviticus 6:17-23 focuses on the *khatta't* from which the priests did not eat in Lev 4:1–5:13. The present text indicates that the priests may indeed eat of the *khatta't*, and it specifies issues of purity pertaining to the holiness of the *khatta't*. The *khatta't* is holy, and anything that touches it becomes holy. Garments and copper vessels coming into contact with the *khatta't* must be properly washed, and earthenware vessels must be broken. Any blood must be burned.

Leviticus 7:1-10 takes up the *'asham*, which is treated much like the *khatta't*. Again, the priests may eat of the *'asham*, and the priest who performs the offering on behalf of an individual may keep the skin of the *'olah* and eat of the *minkhah* offered with the *'asham*.

Leviticus 7:11-21 focuses on the *zebakh shelamim* by clarifying the distinctions between those offered as thanksgiving offerings and those offered as votive or voluntary offerings. Those offered for thanksgiving may be eaten in part by the priest who makes the offering. Those offered as votive offerings may be eaten on the day of the offering or on the day following, but any leftovers are burned on the third day. If it touches anything unclean, it becomes unclean. Anyone who is not sanctified who eats from the offering is expelled from the people.

Leviticus 7:22-27 specifies the unclean things that people may not eat, such as the suet or hard fat or animals that died on their own or were killed by other animals. Anyone who eats these things is considered unclean. Likewise, anyone who eats blood is considered unclean.

Leviticus 7:28-36 grants to the priests the breast of the *zebakh shelamim* as a *tenuphah*, or elevation offering, and the right thigh of the animal as a *terumah*, or gift offering.

The summary statement in Lev 7:37-38 concludes the instructions in Lev 6–7.

YHWH's third major instruction speech appears in Lev 8:1–10:20, which takes up the account of YHWH's instruction to ordain Aaron and his sons in Lev 8:1-3, Moses's compliance with YHWH's instruction in Lev 8:4-36, and a narrative account of the proper and improper discharge of the sacred duties of the priests in Lev 9:1–10:20.

Leviticus 8:1-3 provides only a perfunctory account of YHWH's instruction to Moses to ordain Aaron and his sons as priests. The reason for the brevity of the narrative is because Exod 29:1-46 already presents YHWH's detailed instructions concerning the ordination of Aaron and his sons as priests. Moses's compliance with YHWH's instruction in Lev 8:4-36 actually summarizes much of YHWH's detailed instructions from Exod 29. Leviticus 9:1–10:20 then follows with accounts of the proper and improper discharge of priestly duties. Leviticus 9:1-24 presents an account of the proper presentation of the *'olah*, *khatta't*, and *zebakh shelamim* offerings by Aaron and his sons. But Lev 10:1-20 provides an account of the deaths of Aaron's sons, Nadab and Abihu, when they offered a "strange fire" (Heb., *'esh zarah*), apparently a reference to an unauthorized form of incense. Such instruction highlights the necessity of proper observance of the holy and the profane and the clean and the unclean by the priests and people.

A key issue in interpretation is the fact that Aaron and his sons have not yet been selected as the priests of Israel. Their selection as priests actually takes place in Num 17–18 during the wilderness period, so that the present narrative must anticipate the selection of Aaron and his sons as priests. Although the present narrative (and

Exod 29) focuses only on Aaron and his sons, the narratives in Num 8 and 17–18 expand upon the conceptualization of the priesthood to present one based not only on Aaron and his sons, but one based on the entire tribe of Levi as well. First Samuel 1–3 and 1 Kgs 2 portray only descendants of Aaron as priests, that is, Eli and his family at Shiloh and Zadok and his family at Jerusalem, but Josiah's reform calls for the priests who served sanctuaries in the countryside to come to Jerusalem to serve in the temple. Many interpreters note the correlation of the dead sons of Aaron (Nadab and Abihu) with the sons of the first king of northern Israel, Jeroboam ben Nebat (Nadab and Abijah), and suggest that Lev 10 presents a veiled critique against northern Israel for improper worship. Jeroboam figures prominently in the Deuteronomistic History (Joshua–Kings), which highlights the sins of northern Israel, initiated by Jeroboam, as the cause for northern Israel's destruction.[10] Such an accusation supported Josiah's calls for proper worship of YHWH (2 Kgs 22–23).

Such a scenario suggests that the P texts concerning the ordination of the Aaronic priesthood, Exod 29 and Lev 8–10, are earlier texts that have been recontextualized by the EJ material in Num 8 and 17–18 that allow for the recognition of all Levites as priests. Such a scenario presupposes that the P texts actually do derive from an earlier period when Aaronide priests served in the temple, for example, during the reign of Hezekiah, and that the EJ stratum was introduced during the reign of Josiah to allow for the inclusion of all the Levites in the priesthood of the Jerusalem temple so that the Jerusalem temple could serve as the holy center of a reunited people, Israel and Judah. When read in its present context, however, Lev 8–10 calls upon the Aaronide priests to observe their charge to function properly as priests, teaching the people by example to distinguish between the sacred and the profane and the clean and the unclean. When read in relation to the reforms of Nehemiah and Ezra, such a charge would provide the foundation for all Israel to function as a holy people or kingdom of priests.

Leviticus 11–27 continues with a sequence of YHWH speeches that give instruction on various aspects of purity and holiness.

Leviticus 11:1-47 takes up human consumption of meat. This is particularly important insofar as the eating of meat entails the shedding of blood, and the shedding of blood, within which life resides, disrupts the sanctity of creation with the contamination of death. The shedding of blood, together with the intermarriage of divine and human beings, was the key cause for the flood narrative in Gen 6–9, which was heavily edited by the P stratum. Genesis 9:1-6 allowed the shedding of blood on a limited basis to provide an outlet for the violence of human beings under the condition that human beings would not consume blood nor would they shed the blood of a human being without cause. Leviticus 11 builds on the instructions of Gen 9:1-6 by limiting the ability of human beings to shed blood. Leviticus 11 defines those animals that may be eaten by humans to be just a few of the animals in creation, that is, those with a cleft hoof, those who chew the cud, fish with fins and scales, and winged swarming things that have jointed legs and walk on all fours.

All other creatures are prohibited to humans as food in order to limit the violence of bloodshed that desecrates creation at large.

Leviticus 12:1-8 takes up the purification of a woman following childbirth. The birth of a child renders a woman unclean insofar as she discharges blood as well as the placenta from her body during the birth of the child. The blood and the placenta are living substances while inside her body, but they die as a result of their discharge, rendering her impure. In the case of a baby boy, the woman is impure for the first seven days following childbirth, after which time the baby boy is circumcised, and she remains impure for another thirty-three days for a total of forty days. In the case of a baby girl, the woman is impure for fourteen days on analogy with her menstruation and an additional sixty-six days following for a total of eighty days.

Leviticus 13–14 presents three successive YHWH speeches which present instruction concerning impurities caused by skin diseases. Many interpreters understand the Hebrew term, *tsera'at* as a reference to leprosy. But the symptoms described in these texts do not correspond to the symptoms of Hanson's disease, which is the contemporary medical designation for leprosy. Although each of the speeches begins with its own YHWH speech formula, they function as a unit insofar as they take up the various aspects of diagnosing and treating the affliction. Thus, Lev 13:1-59 takes up the basic diagnosis and treatment of the skin diseases addressed here. Leviticus 14:1-32 takes up the various rituals that purify someone who has been cured of the disease in question. Leviticus 14:33-53 takes up analogous infections, mold and mildew, which might defile the walls of a house. Leviticus 14:54-57 then concludes the sequence with a summary-appraisal statement concerning the nature of the preceding instructions.

Leviticus 15:1-33 takes up the issue of personal purity as it relates to bodily discharges from both men and women. In the case of a man, the instruction focuses on a seminal discharge or an infection. The basis for considering such discharges as unclean is that semen or other discharges, such as pus and the like, were originally living substances that die following discharge from the body. Such a discharge entails death, which is the ultimate impurity in priestly thought. In the case of a woman, the discharge is presumed to be menstrual blood or other blood discharges that a woman might experience in the case of a miscarriage or the like.[11]

Leviticus 16 focuses on the purification of the sanctuary at Yom Kippur, which is observed on the tenth day of the seventh month (see Lev 16:29-31; also Exod 30:10; Lev 23:26-32). YHWH's speech begins with reference to the deaths of Aaron's sons Nadab and Abihu for desecrating worship of YHWH with strange fire (Lev 10). Although the intervening instructions have all dealt with issues of purity and holiness that would potentially compromise the sanctuary, this instruction is the only one that takes up the sanctuary per se. It deals with any lingering defilement to ensure that the sanctuary will begin the year pure. The text stipulates that once per year only the high priest may enter the holy of holies behind the curtain where the ark of the covenant resides. Insofar as the ark functions as YHWH's throne on earth, the holy of holies functions as the sacred place where the priest representing humankind may directly encounter the divine presence of YHWH. The text underscores this point by emphasizing that YHWH appears at this place. The encounter therefore becomes a visionary experience like that described in 1 Sam 3; Isa 6; Ezek 1; Dan 7; 1 Enoch 14; and the rabbinic Heikhalot literature. In rabbinic tradition, the priest invokes the name of YHWH as part of the ritual to request atonement for the people of Israel (m. Yoma 3:8). Because of the power of the divine name, this is the only time and circumstance in which the divine name is uttered. The priest offers a bull as a *khatta't* offering for himself and his family and a goat as a *khatta't* offering for the people. He then lays hands upon a second goat to "ordain" it for holy service symbolically to carry the sins of the sanctuary out into the wilderness to Azazel, an ancient demon figure.

Leviticus 17 takes up the treatment of blood. Scholars have already noted that Lev 17 begins the holiness code, in Lev 17–26, an exilic-period text apparently known to Ezekiel (see Ezek 18) that is concerned with maintaining the sanctity of the nation. When viewed in relation to its synchronic literary context in Leviticus, however, Lev 17 continues the concerns with purity—and therefore holiness—that appear beginning in Lev 11. The focus on blood builds upon concerns in Gen 9:1-6, which limits the ability of human beings to shed blood and stipulates the conditions under which it may be done, and Lev 7:26-27, which forbids human consumption of blood. Leviticus 17 holds that cattle, sheep, and goats slaughtered outside of the camp must be brought to the meeting tent (tabernacle) or temple to be presented as an offering to YHWH. This stipulation contextualizes the instructions in Deut 12:20-27 that allow for animals to be slaughtered outside of the temple provided that their blood is returned to the ground, whereas sacred offerings must be presented at the temple. Leviticus 17 summarizes the proper procedures for the offerings but stipulates that Israel and immigrants may not eat blood.

Leviticus 18 takes up proper sexual practices as understood in the text. Although the text attributes practices such as incest, sexual relations with a woman during her menstrual period (due to the flow of blood), adultery, specific acts of male intercourse with another male, and bestiality to the Egyptians and Canaanites, there is no evidence that these peoples engaged in such practices any more than any other nation. A variety of concerns come to the forefront, all of which are understood in the text to protect the natural order and sanctity of creation. The prohibitions of intercourse with family members, including direct female relatives and those married to male relatives, are designed to protect against incest. Those concerned with a menstruating woman are concerned with blood and personal purity. Those concerned with adultery are designed to protect social order and the descendants of the family in question. The prohibitions against offering children to Molech, the Moabite god, are concerned with apostasy. The prohibition against lying with a man prohibits a specific sexual act, though the text was written at a time when homosexuality was understood to be the result of human choice and not one's creation. The prohibition against bestiality is designed to protect creation.

Leviticus 19 takes up laws concerning holy human conduct in what contemporary society would consider to be a combination of ritual and secular action. No such differentiation was made in ancient Judah or Israel. YHWH's instruction begins in Lev 19:2b-3 with instructions to be holy and to observe the Shabbat as a means to highlight the sanctity of the people and creation as the motivating factor behind the instructions listed herein. Topics include the prohibition of idolatry, proper offerings at the sanctuary, gleaning in the fields, a brief synopsis of instruction from the Ten Commandments, proper economic conduct, care for the deaf and blind, judicial integrity, proper mating of animals to ensure the integrity of creation, proper clothing for men and women to aid in preserving gender identification and roles, improper relations with slave women, the planting of trees, prohibitions against eating blood, divination and other actions associated with idolatry and foreign religious practice, allowing a daughter to become a harlot, keeping the Shabbat, deference to the old, the proper treatment of strangers, and proper measurements.

Leviticus 20 builds upon the concerns with divination and proper sexual conduct in the preceding chapters by providing further definition or by stipulating punishments.

Leviticus 21 takes up issues concerning the sanctity of the priests. Because death is the ultimate defilement, the text makes sure to limit the contact that a priest might have with the dead. Such a concern presupposes that family members bury their own dead and therefore must handle the body of the dead relative before they prepare it for burial. Consequently, priests are only allowed to handle the bodies of dead parents, siblings, and children, all of whom are blood relatives. A priest may not defile himself for a relative by marriage, including his wife and any in-laws. The reason for such limitation is that the priest is expected to be holy to YHWH; therefore, contact with the dead must be limited. He may not engage in practices associated with idolatry and foreign worship, such as shaving portions of the head or beard or by gashing his body. These practices are mourning practices for dead fertility gods, such as Baal in Canaanite culture or Tammuz/Dumuzi in Mesopotamian culture. He may not marry women who have slept with other men, including harlots and women who are divorced. The text does not mention widows. If his daughter becomes a harlot, she forfeits her life. The high priest has even higher expectations. He may not defile himself by contact with the dead even for his parents. He does not bare his head or go outside the sanctuary because he is the one who must enter the holy of holies at Yom Kippur (Lev 16). He may only marry a virgin of his own kin; not even a widow is permitted for him. The instruction ends with stipulations that the priests must be free of any defects. Insofar as the temple represents the ideals of creation, so the priesthood must represent the ideals of humanity. Anyone who suffers a disability may not serve as a priest in the temple, either in the holy of holies or at the altar, although he may eat of the priestly portions of food.

Leviticus 22:1-16 builds upon the concerns with the sanctity of the priesthood expressed in Lev 21 by focusing on who is eligible to eat from the sacred offerings assigned to the priests. The text builds on prior statements of personal and priestly purity. Thus a priest from the sons of Aaron who is impure may not eat. Such impurity might include a man who has had a skin disease (Lev 14), touches a dead body

(Lev 21), has a seminal emission (Lev 15:1-18), comes into contact with unclean animals, or eats anything unclean (Lev 11). He must first purify himself before eating of the priestly fare. No outsiders or persons hired by the priests may eat of the food, but persons born into the families of the priests may eat, including a daughter who had married but is now a widow or divorced without children. If an unauthorized person mistakenly eats, he repays the food with an additional 20 percent of its value.

Leviticus 22:17-33 specifies that animals offered at the altar must be without blemish, disease, or defect, again to emphasize the ideal nature of creation and to prevent Israelites from finding a convenient way to dispose of their flawed animals. Other specifications include the requirement that a calf, a sheep, or a goat must stay with its mother for eight days after it is born before it can be used as an offering. A mother and its calf cannot be sacrificed on the same day.

Leviticus 23:1-8, 9-22, 23-25, 26-32, 33-44 present YHWH's speeches concerning the sacred Judean calendar. Time is also holy in ancient Judean thought, and its sanctity must be observed, beginning with the Shabbat, which serves as the foundation for creation in P and the final form of the Pentateuch as a whole (Gen 1:1–2:3). Although some argue that Shabbat is a postexilic observance, the appearance of this instruction in the exilic holiness code and its relation to the late-monarchic material in Exod 25–30; 35–40; Lev 1–16; 27 indicates that it is much earlier (Isa 1:10-17). Insofar as it is an Aaronide calendar, Lev 23 presents a distinctive perspective in relation to earlier calendars (Exod 23; 34; Deut 16); it highlights the principle of Shabbat, or the seven-day observance, to demonstrate how Shabbat stands as the foundation of the agricultural observances that follow. The text presupposes that this calendar is operative in Israel, but 1 Kgs 12:32-33 suggests that northern Israel may have used a different calendar.

YHWH's first speech, in Lev 23:1-8, begins with instruction in v. 3 to observe the Shabbat as the foundation for observance of the holy times in the calendar. The following instruction concerning the observance of Pesach (Passover) and the seven days of Matzot beginning respectively on fourteenth and fifteenth days of the first month (Nisan, March–April) likewise builds upon the seven-day principle of Shabbat. Pesach marks the offering of the Passover sacrifice and Matzot marks the seven-day period for eating unleavened bread. Passover is one of the three major holidays in which all men are to appear at the temple with their offerings (cf. Exod 23:14-15, 17; 34:18-20, 23; Deut 16:1-8, 16-17). Although these holidays are known for their celebration of the exodus from Egypt, they are also agricultural holidays that celebrate the firstborn of the herd and flock (Pesach) and the firstfruits of the harvest (Matzot).

YHWH's second speech, in Lev 23:10-22, focuses especially on the offering of the first sheaf (*'omer*) of grain as an elevation offering (*tenuphah*) to celebrate the seven-week period for the counting of the Omer, or the harvest of grain, that will culminate in the festival of Shavuot, "Weeks," in the third month (Sivan, May–June). Shavuot is not named (see Deut 16:9; cf. Num 28:26, which refers to it as the day of firstfruits as well as Shavuot, "weeks"), but the reference to the fiftieth day of the counting of the Omer would refer to the holiday. Shavuot celebrates the revelation of

Torah at Sinai in rabbinic tradition (Exod 19:1), but here the agricultural dimensions are emphasized as the holiday celebrates the conclusion of the grain harvest prior to summer. It is one of the three required holidays in which all men bring their offerings to the temple (cf. Exod 23:16-17; 34:22-23; Deut 16:9-12, 16-17).

YHWH's third speech, in Lev 23:23-25, presents a brief instruction concerning Rosh haShanah on the first day of the seventh month (Tishri, September–October). The observance is not identified here as the New Year (see Ezek 40:1, which uses the term Rosh haShanah, "beginning of the year"), but simply presupposes that it is a Shabbaton, a day of rest remembered with trumpet blasts, that marks the beginning of the agricultural year.

YHWH's fourth speech, in Lev 23:26-32, presents instruction concerning the observance of Yom Kippur (Day of Atonement or Day of Reconciliation) on the tenth day of the seventh month (Tishri, September–October). The text defines Yom Kippur as a Shabbat Shabbaton or a Sabbath of Full Rest on which the people do no work and afflict themselves with fasting and self-denial.

Finally, YHWH's fifth speech, in Lev 23:33-44, presents instruction on the observance of the festival of Succoth, "Booths," beginning on the fifteenth day of the seventh month (Tishri, September–October). Succoth commemorates the period of the wilderness journey in rabbinic thought, but here it celebrates the conclusion of the fruit harvest prior to the onset of the fall rains when the people lived in *succoth*, or small huts, out in the fields and orchards to bring in the crop before rain made the harvest impossible. Succoth is a seven-day observance with a Shabbaton on the first day and on the eighth day at the conclusion of the festival. Succoth is the third of the major holidays in which men bring offerings to the temple (Exod 23:16-17; 34:22-23; Deut 16:13-17).

Leviticus 24:1-23 presents instruction on the need to sanctify the sanctuary and the divine name of YHWH in addition to the observance of Shabbat and the holidays. Verses 1-4 call for the collection of olive oil to supply a menorah that will burn continuously as *a ner tamid*, "continuous light," in the sanctuary. The second instruction in vv. 5-9 calls for the presentation of twelve *challot* (singular, *challah*, "braided loaf of bread") on the table before the holy of holies (Exod 27:20-21). The *challot* represent a symbolic meal offering on behalf of the twelve tribes of Israel to YHWH. Verses 10-23 present the third instruction concerning desecration of the holy name of YHWH, which is not to be pronounced (Exod 3; 20:7; Deut 5:11). The narrative describes such blasphemy as a capital offense and concludes with a statement of the legal principle of "an eye for an eye" and so on. This principle is not understood literally but refers to the notion that punishment must be commensurate with the crime.

Leviticus 25:1–26:46 concludes the holiness code with one continuous speech by YHWH in which YHWH gives instruction concerning the sanctity of the land of Israel and the lives of the people who live in it. The Aaronide preoccupation with the sanctity of the Shabbat stands as the basis for the instructions presented concerning the ownership of land and the treatment of persons who must sell their land and their own labor in times of economic adversity. Insofar as these laws are designed to protect the rights of the original tribal owners of the land as well as their personal status, the application of the Shabbat principle to these questions functions as a means to restore the place of Israel within the land as a facet of creation.

The laws concerning land in Lev 25:2b–26:2 begin in vv. 2b-7 with a restatement of the need to provide the land with a Shabbat rest every seventh year. This instruction builds upon the earlier instruction in Exod 23:10-11 by specifying that slaves, laborers, and animals may all share in the produce of the land during the seventh year, in which it lies fallow. Verses 8-22 build upon this concern for the support of the poor by calling for the observance of a Jubilee year in which land sold in times of economic distress will return to its original owners. Again, the Shabbat principle is operative here in that the Jubilee year is calculated by counting seven weeks of years, or forty-nine years, with the Jubilee (*yovel*) to be observed in the fiftieth year beginning on Yom Kippur. The Jubilee year is a year of release (*deror*), which builds upon concerns expressed in the sabbatical instructions addressed in vv. 2b-7 and the laws concerning debt slavery in Exod 21:2-11. When a man went into debt in the ancient world, he could sell his land and his own labor to become a debt slave to work for his creditor for specified periods of time. The debt slavery law does not take up the question of land ownership, but it does allow for a man to serve as a slave forever. The present law addresses those issues by allowing for the return of land, with appropriate adjustment for the number of years that the land was transferred to a creditor, and the return of the man to his land. The law does not address the issue of women who were sold insofar as Exod 21:2-11 considers them as wives in the creditor's family. Deuteronomy 15, which originated in King Josiah's reign, allows for the release of debts and debt slaves, both men and women, with greater rights, but the law in Lev 25:8-22 extends this principle to allow for the return of land.[12] The instructions in Lev 25:25-28 obligate a relative to redeem land that has been sold. The exception is Lev 25:29-34, which exempts a house in a walled city from redemption after one year, but houses in unwalled towns and the open country are to be redeemed during the Jubilee. The Aaronides recognize the rights of the Levites to redeem their houses, but it presumes that they live in levitical cities and that their land cannot be sold. Verses 35-46 build upon Exod 22:24 and Deut 23:20-21 by prohibiting interest to be charged to a kinsman. The kinsman will not be treated as a slave but will be treated as a hired laborer. Verses 47-55 call for a kinsman to redeem an Israelite who sells himself to an immigrant. Finally, Lev 26:1-2 prohibits idolatry and calls for the observance of YHWH's Shabbats and veneration of YHWH's sanctuary to ensure the holiness of the land and the people.

The second part of YHWH's speech in Lev 26:3-46 stipulates blessings and curses that are tied to the people's observances of YHWH's instructions. Like the blessings and curses of Deut 28–30, they are modeled on the blessings and curses that appear as part of Assyrian and Babylonian suzerain-vassal treaties so that YHWH appears in the present text like a suzerain king who promises blessings for his subjects if they observe his commands and curses for them if they fail to do so. But the present text makes it clear that it is dealing with YHWH as the master of creation and of human events. If the people obey, creation will respond with rains and food and the people will have peace. If they fail to observe YHWH's instructions, the people will suffer loss of rain and food and invasion by their enemies. The divine element becomes clear when YHWH states in vv. 11-13 that the temple will be established in the midst of the people and employs the covenant formula to guarantee the covenant. The Shabbat principle comes into play when YHWH states that periods of exile will be considered as Shabbat years so that the land might renew itself. This is not a statement of a conditional covenant in that vv. 39-44 promise restoration when the people repent.

Leviticus 27 concludes Leviticus with a last speech by YHWH that focuses on solomn promises made by the people for the support of the temple. This text is not a part of the holiness code, but it is a part of the P legislation in Lev 1–16. The text may well date to the late monarchic period, as this was the time when a cash economy began to emerge in the ancient Near East. The solemn promise serves as a temple tax on the people of Jerusalem, or Judah, and they are valued according to age and gender. Adult males, aged twenty to sixty years, pay the most at fifty shekels of silver because they are the ones who own land and presumably have the greatest income. Adult females pay less at thirty shekels because their income potential is lower. Children, aged five to twenty years, pay twenty shekels for a boy and ten for a girl. Infants and toddlers from one month to five years pay five shekels for a boy and three for a girl. Persons sixty years and older pay fifteen shekels for a man and ten for a woman. If someone cannot pay the determined rates, the priests will make a determination of their tax based on their ability to pay. If animals, land, produce, houses, and so forth, are presented, their value is calculated. Leviticus 27 calls for a tax beyond the festival offerings that ensure that the temple will serve as the holy center of creation.

Numbers

I

Numbers is perhaps the least understood book of the Pentateuch.[1] Numbers, however, deserves close attention. It is not simply about the journey from Sinai to the promised land; it is fundamentally concerned with the character of Israel and its relationship with YHWH during the course of the journey. Numbers portrays serious tensions in the relationship between Israel and YHWH insofar as Israel questions YHWH's intentions in bringing them into the wilderness where they might die. There are also tremendous tensions between YHWH and Moses, especially when Moses stands up to YHWH in an effort to prevent the destruction of Israel in the wilderness. There are tensions between Moses and the people, including his own sister, Miriam, and his brother, Aaron, as they both question Moses's leadership. In the end, YHWH destroys the wilderness generation, with the exception of Caleb and Joshua, to purge Israel of a rebellious population born to slavery before they will enter the promised land of Israel. Even Moses, Miriam, and Aaron are forbidden to enter the promised land, and they all die in the wilderness instead. Clearly, important theological and historical issues are at stake in the book, and interpreters must continue in their efforts to understand them.[2]

In order to understand fully the concerns expressed in Numbers, we must begin by considering the formal literary structure of the book. The final form of the Pentateuch is constituted as a sequence of narratives that present the generations of the heavens and the earth from creation in Gen 1:1–2:3 through the generation of Aaron and Moses in Num 3:1–Deut 34:12. Thus, the account of the census of Israel in Num 1–2 actually forms the conclusion of the generations of the twelve tribes of Israel in Gen 37:2–Num 2:34 by depicting the organization of Israel around the tabernacle prior to their departure from Sinai. Numbers 3:1–Deuteronomy 34:12 then form the concluding segment of the Pentateuch by portraying the history of Israel under the guidance of the Levites led by Aaron and his sons. Although composed independently of the final form of the P edition of Genesis–Numbers, Deuteronomy is subsumed structurally under Num 3:1–36:13 in the final synchronic literary structure of the Pentateuch. The formal structure of Num 3:1–Deut 34:12 appears as follows:[3]

XII. History of Israel under Guidance of Levites, Led by Aaron and Sons	Num 3:1–Deut 34:12
A. Sanctification of the People Led by the Levites	3:1–10:10
1. Introduction: Identification of the Levites as Those to Be Ordained to Priesthood	3:1-4
2. Commission of the Levites to Serve as Priests in Place of Oldest Male Child	3:5–4:49
3. Instruction Account Concerning Purification of the People Israel in Preparation for Journey through Wilderness to Promised Land	5:1–6:27
4. Instruction Account Concerning Purification of the Tabernacle and Levites in Preparation for Journey through Wilderness to Promised Land	7:1–10:10
B. From Sinai to Wilderness of Paran: Rebellion in the Wilderness	10:11–19:22
1. Departure from Sinai	10:11-27
a. Date of Departure: Second Year, Second Month, Twentieth Day	10:11
b. Itinerary: From Sinai to Paran	10:12
c. Organization of the March: Tribes Arrayed around Tabernacle with Judah in the Lead	10:13-27
2. Journey by Stages	10:28–19:22
a. Introduction to Journey by Stages	10:28
b. Journey by Stages Proper	10:29–19:22

	1) Preliminary Issue: Account of Contract with Hobab to Serve as Guide	10:29-32
	2) Initial Three-Day Journey by Stages	10:33–11:34
	a) Programmatic Statement: Three-Day Journey with Ark/ Cloud in the Lead	10:33-34
	b) Movement of Ark	10:35-36
	c) Complaints of People	11:1-34
	i. At Taberah: General Portrayal of Complaints by People and Divine Retaliation	11:1-3
	ii. At Kibroth-hataavah: Food and Community Authority/ Leadership	11:4-34
	3) Journey from Kibroth-hataavah to Hazeroth: Challenge to Moses by Miriam and Aaron	11:35–12:15
	4) Journey from Hatzeroth to Wilderness of Paran	12:16–19:22
	a) Narrative Introduction	12:16
	b) Spy Narrative: Rebellion Resolved by YHWH's Decision to Destroy Wilderness Generation	13:1–14:49
	c) Instruction Account Concerning the Sanctification/ Purging of the People	15:1-41
	d) Account of Failed Rebellion by Korah and the Reubenites	16:1–17:15
	e) Selection of Aaron and Sons as Priestly Line amidst Levites	17:16–18:32

f) Instruction Account Concerning Ritual of Purification Following Contact with the Dead	19:1-22
C. From Paran to Wilderness of Zin/Kadesh: Water from the Rock; Condemnation of Moses and Aaron; Edom's Refusal to Grant Passage	20:1-21
D. From Zin/Kadesh to Mount Hor: Death of Aaron; Conflict with Arad	20:22–21:3
E. From Mount Hor to Edom/Moab: Defeat of Sihon and Og	21:4-35
F. Arrival at Moab: Balaam, Census and Organization of People Prior to Entry into Promised Land	22:1–36:13
1. Arrival at Aravot Moab Opposite Jericho	22:1
2. Balaam Account: Blessing for Israel	22:2–24:25
3. Account of Incident at Baal of Peor/Shittim: Phinehas ben Eleazar ben Aaron Granted Perpetual Covenant of Priesthood	25:1-18
4. Census at Shittim: New Generation	26:1-65
5. Account of Organizational Issue: Inheritance by Women	27:1-11
6. Account of Joshua's Selection to Succeed Moses as Leader	27:12-23
7. Instruction Account Concerning Offerings at Festivals	28:1–30:1
8. Instruction Account Concerning Solemn Promises by Women	30:2-17
9. Account of Holy War against Midian	31:1-54
10. Obligation to Be Part of Israel	32:1-41
11. Summation of Israel's Journey through the Wilderness	33:1-49

12. Final Instruction Account Concerning Apportionment of Land	33:50–36:13
G. Moses's Final Address to Israel: Repetition of Torah	Deut 1:1–34:12

Numbers is fundamentally concerned with establishing proper leadership for the nation of Israel. Specifically, it is concerned with portraying the role of the Levites alongside Aaron and his sons as the priesthood of Israel that will replace earlier reliance on oldest male children. The narrative thereby authorizes Aaron and his sons together with the Levites to guide Israel in YHWH's teachings and thereby to avoid the disasters that had plagued Israel's history and disrupted its national life.

Numbers is based in part on the itineraries of the ancient Near Eastern kings who would march out following the completion of the harvest to collect tribute from their vassals.[4] But the itineraries are heavily influenced by the pilgrimage pattern identified in Exodus, insofar as the people are marching toward the promised land with the tabernacle in hand in order to establish YHWH's sanctuary in the land of Israel.[5] Numbers must be considered generically as an account of Israel's pilgrimage from Sinai to the land of Israel insofar as the military imagery of the march derives from the role of the Levites as the guardians of the sanctity of the tabernacle, the temple, and Israel as a whole.

The interest in the role of the Levites together with the Aaronide priests would have begun with King Josiah of Judah's program of religious reform and national restoration in the late seventh century BCE when he invited the countryside priests to serve in Jerusalem together with the Aaronide priests of the Zadokite line. It reached its culmination in the fifth- through fourth-century reforms of Nehemiah and Ezra who restored the role of the temple under the supervision of the Aaronide priests and Levites as the central institution of Jewish life in the aftermath of the Babylonian exile. Such concerns were expressed in the D stratum (Deuteronomy) as well as the P redaction of the EJ narratives in the book of Numbers. Thus, the final form of Numbers is a P-stratum composition that has taken up the earlier EJ narrative of the wilderness tradition and pointed to Aaron and the Levites as the proper leadership of Israel. Past scholarship accepted the roles of the Aaronide and levitical priests as part of the P-stratum agenda, but the service of the Aaronide priests in Jerusalem throughout the period of the Davidic monarchy suggests that the Aaronide priests are a J-stratum concern.

II

We may now turn to a detailed discussion of the book.

The account of the census of Israel presented in Num 1–2 concludes the account of the generations of Jacob in Gen 37:2–Num 2:34. This segment serves as a presentation of the early history of the twelve tribes of Israel from the lifetime of Jacob's favored son Joseph through the exodus from Egypt and the revelation of YHWH's Torah at Sinai. The census functions as a means to assess the current numbers, strength, and organization of the twelve tribes of Israel at Sinai prior to their departure into the wilderness. Most interpreters fail to note the structural significance of the reference to the generations of Aaron and Moses in Num 3:1 and the implications of this notice that much of Numbers is actually concerned with YHWH's choice of the Levites in place of the oldest male children of Israel to serve as priests alongside the Aaronide priests who will ensure Israel's sanctity.

Numbers 1–2 makes its concern with both the census of Israel and the role of the Levites clear. It is a P-stratum composition that presents an overview of the numbers of Israel, 603,550 according to Num 2:32, but the text stipulates that the Levites have not been included in the census because of YHWH's decision to place them in charge of the tabernacle in Num 1:47-53 and 2:33-34. Thus, Num 1–2 signals YHWH's special plans for the Levites which will be emphasized throughout the next major unit of the Pentateuch, in Num 3:1–Deut 34:12.

Numbers 3:1–Deuteronomy 34:12 constitutes the twelfth and final unit within the synchronic literary structure of the Pentateuch. The introductory *toledoth* formula, "And these are the generations of Aaron and Moses on the day that YHWH spoke with Moses on Mount Sinai," has been largely overlooked.[6] Although Deuteronomy clearly has its own distinctive diachronic compositional history, it is subsumed structurally to the narrative in Num 3:1–36:13 as an account of Moses's last speeches to Israel in Moab on the banks of the Jordan River prior to Israel's entry into the promised land. Otherwise, the synchronic literary structure of Num 3:1–Deut 34:12 is defined by the itinerary formulae.[7] The result is a literary structure determined by the stopping points in Israel's journey from Sinai to Moab. Numbers 3:1–10:10 relates the Levites' sanctification of Israel at Sinai; Num 10:11–19:22 recounts Israel's journey through the wilderness from Sinai to Paran, including Israel's rebellion against YHWH and Moses; Num 20:1-21 recounts Israel's journey from Paran to the Wilderness of Zin/Kadesh, including accounts of the water from the rock, the condemnation of Moses and Aaron, and Edom's refusal to grant passage to Israel; Num 20:22–21:3 recounts Israel's journey from Zin/Kadesh to Mount Hor, including the death of Aaron and the conflict with Arad; Num 21:4-35 recounts Israel's journey from Mount Hor to Edom/Moab, including the defeat of Sihon and Og; Num 22:1–36:13 recounts Israel's arrival at Moab, including the Balaam narrative and the census and organization of people prior to entry into the promised land of Israel; and Deut 1:1–34:12 recounts Moses's final addresses to Israel prior to Israel's entry into the promised land.

The sanctification of the people led by the Levites at Sinai in Num 3:1–10:10 presents the last events at Sinai prior to Israel's departure into the wilderness on their journey to the land of Israel. It comprises four basic parts, including an introduction in Num 3:1-4 that identifies the Levites as those to be ordained to the priesthood, an account of the commission of the Levites to serve as priests in place of oldest male children in Num 3:5–4:49, an account of the instruction concerning the purification of Israel in preparation for their journey through the wilderness in Num 5:1–6:27, and the account of the instruction concerning the purification of the tabernacle and the Levites in preparation for journey through the wilderness in Num 7:1–10:10.

Numbers 3:1-4 identifies Aaron and Moses as the key leaders of the people in an account that will authorize their tribe, the Levites, as the party that will sanctify the people and the tabernacle during the wilderness journey. The passage is careful to identify the sons of Aaron and their respective fates. It first references Aaron's older sons, the firstborn Nadab and his brother Abihu, who died at Sinai in Lev 10 for offering strange fire, or improper incense, before YHWH. The younger sons, Eleazar and Ithamar, will become the ancestors of Israel's two major priestly lines. Eleazar is the father of Phinehas, who will be granted a covenant of eternal priesthood in Num 25, which will include the Zadokite priestly line of the Jerusalem temple. Ithamar will also become the ancestor of a line of priests, including Eli, Abiathar (who was expelled from the Jerusalem temple by Solomon in 1 Kgs 2), and Jeremiah, the priest and prophet from Anathoth, to which Abiathar was expelled.

Numbers 3:5–4:49 is a key text in Numbers. It presents YHWH's instructions to Moses to commission the tribe of Levi to serve in place of the oldest male children of Israel as attendants for Aaron and his sons. This P composition serves two agendas in relation to the compositional strata of the Pentateuch. It justifies the replacement of the firstborn of Israel by the Levites and thereby undercuts E's earlier understanding that the firstborn of Israel would serve as the priesthood of northern Israel. It also supplements J's view and the P view of Leviticus that Aaron and his sons alone would serve as the priesthood of Israel. Numbers 3:5–4:49 thereby serves P's agenda to ensure that the Levites were assigned various holy duties in keeping with the portrayal of the role of the Levites in the reforms of Nehemiah and Ezra, that is, the Levites will serve alongside the sons of Aaron in ensuring the sanctity of Israel, the tabernacle and eventually the temple.

Numbers 3:5–4:49 serves this purpose by presenting YHWH's instructions to Moses to bring near the tribe of Levi for holy service alongside the sons of Aaron. Whereas Aaron and his sons have responsibility for the offerings of Israel, the Levites will have responsibility for the tabernacle and the meeting tent. YHWH notes in Num 3:11-13 and 3:40-51 that in the past, the firstborn of Israel had served in this capacity, but now the Levites would take the place of the oldest male children. The role of the firstborn apparently represents northern Israelite practice. Such a practice apparently informs the charges in 1 Kgs 12:31 that King Jeroboam ben Nebat of Israel sinned by appointing priests who were not of levitical descent at Bethel, Dan, and elsewhere. YHWH's instructions to Moses to record the Levites by their ancestral clans includes the Levites in the census of Israel and signals their distinctive status. Each clan—the family of Gershon, the family of Kohath, and the family of Merari—was numbered and assigned to guard the western, southern, and the northern sides of the tabernacle respectively. Each clan has special responsibility for tabernacle furnishings, that is, Gershon oversees the flexible fixtures of the meeting tent; Kohath oversees the ark, the table, the menorah, the altar, and the utensils; and Merari oversees structural fixtures of the tabernacle. Moses, Aaron, and Aaron's sons would then lead the procession on the east side of the tabernacle.

Numbers 4:1-49 presents YHWH's instructions to Moses to take separate censuses of the families of Kohath, Gershon, and Merari, including all men from the age of thirty to fifty, in order to assign their respective functions in setting up the tabernacle when the people stop in the wilderness. Insofar as Moses and Aaron and his sons are from the family of Kohath, they are responsible for the sacred equipement, the lighting of oil and incense, the meal offering (Lev 2), and the anointing oil of the tabernacle. The Gershonites carry the cloth coverings of the tabernacle, and the Merarites carry the structural components of the tabernacle.

Numbers 5:1–6:27 then turns to the instructions concerning the purification of the people in preparation for their journey through the wilderness. This textual component begins in Num 5:1-31 with instructions on how to deal with those who have become defiled in one manner or another. Such persons must be expelled from the people in order to prevent the nation as a whole from becoming defiled, and they must be purified from their malady. Issues here include the removal of those who were defiled by eruptions or discharges from the body, those who have come into contact with a corpse, those who have wronged another person, and married women who have allegedly cheated on their husbands. Those with bodily discharges or corpse contamination are removed from the camp until they have been purified, and those who have wronged someone must confess the wrong, restore what was taken plus an additional 20 percent, and present the appropriate guilt offering (*'asham*, cf. Lev 5). In the case of a woman who has allegedly cheated on her husband, a lengthy and intimidating ritual is imposed as a result of her husband's suspicions. If she has what amounts to a miscarriage,[8] she is cursed for adultery. If she remains unaffected by the ritual, she is considered innocent.

Numbers 6:1-27 then takes up the case of a Nazirite vow of a person who dedicates him- or herself to a period of priestly service to YHWH. The Nazirite vow calls for abstinence from wine or any other form of alcoholic drink, refusal to shave the head for the duration of the vow, and avoidance of contact with the dead. All of these features suggest an interest in forming the Nazir as an ideal human being, like the first humans from creation. A person who takes a Nazirite vow commits to a period of holy life as defined in relation to these practices, but such practices do not ensure a period of priestly practice. Samson is an example of a Nazirite (Judg 13–16), but despite his vow he appears to be quite a rambunctious fellow who has little use for holy practice but a great interest in fighting and foreign women. In the end, he proves to be a tragic figure, especially because he is never able to control his desires. Indeed, he does come into contact with the dead and holds a drinking feast (Judg 14:8-10). Samson ends up as one of the few suicides in the Bible when he collapses a temple upon his Philistine captors, who had gouged out his eyes and put him to work like an ox pushing millstones to grind grain. Samuel also appears to be a Nazirite insofar as his mother, Hannah, vows his service to YHWH (1 Sam 1:11). When the Nazirite completes the period of the vow, Num 6 specifies the offerings that the Nazir must present at the temple. Numbers 6:22-27 continues the emphasis on holy service to YHWH by presenting the priestly benediction by which the priests bless the people.

Numbers 7:1–10:10 then completes the account of Israel's sojourn at Sinai with an instruction account concerning the purification of the tabernacle and Levites in preparation for their journey through the wilderness to the promised land.

Numbers 7:1-88 begins with an account of the offerings made by the chieftains of each tribe to support the tabernacle and the Levites who would serve it. Each tribal chieftain presents a cartload of offerings for the new tabernacle, and Moses divides them for each of the levitical families according to their service. Thus, the sons of Gershon received two cartloads of goods and four oxen to carry them, and the sons of Merari received four cartloads of goods and eight oxen to carry them. Both these families were placed under the supervision of Ithamar ben Aaron. The sons of Kohath received no goods because they were required to carry the tabernacle components on their shoulders through the wilderness. Each tribal chieftain brought their offerings on successive days for a total of twelve days.

Numbers 7:89 notes that Moses would hear the voice of G-d from above the covering of the ark and between its two cherubim when he entered the meeting tent.

Numbers 8:1-4 presents YHWH's instruction to Moses concerning the raising of the menorahs, or lampstands, in the tabernacle. Unlike contemporary Hanukkah menorahs that have nine lights, the temple menorah has only seven. Rabbinic tradition precludes replicating temple fixtures, and so the Hanukkah menorah includes two additional lamps to mark the eight days of the festival and one to serve as the *Shamas*, "Caretaker," to light the others.

Numbers 8:5-22 presents YHWH's instructions to Moses to anoint the Levites for service in the wilderness tabernacle. The ordination ceremony differs from that of the ordination of the priests recounted in Exod 28–29 and Lev 8. They are ordained by the people of Israel and designated by Aaron as an elevation offering (*tenuphah*) before YHWH. They then present their *'olah* and *khatta't* offerings as atonement so that the Levites may serve as attendants to Aaron and his sons in the sanctuary. Numbers 8:13-19 makes it clear that the Levites serve in place of the oldest male children of Israel.

Numbers 8:23-26 presents YHWH's instructions concerning the duration of levitical service from the age of twenty-five through the age of fifty, whereas the priests serve from the age of thirty through the age of fifty.

Numbers 9:1-14 presents additional instruction concerning the offering of the Passover sacrifices. The passage specifies the date of the Passover offering on the fourteenth day of the first month. The instruction to allow persons unclean due to contact with a corpse to present the Passover offering in the second month is a concession to ritual impurity. The passage may well represent the influence of an older festival calendar observed in northern Israel. According to 1 Kgs 12:32, Jeroboam called for the celebration of Succoth on the fifteenth day of the eighth month, one month later than the observance of Succoth in Judah on the fifteenth day of the seventh month.

Numbers 9:15-23 signals the impending departure from Sinai by noting the movements of the cloud symbolizing the divine presence over the tabernacle. When the cloud rises from the tabernacle, it is ready to move. When it rests upon the tabernacle, it stays in place.

Finally, Num 10:1-10 completes the Sinai pericope with a notice concerning the manufacture of two silver trumpets that will be blown to summon the people of Israel and set them in motion as they embark on their journey from Sinai through the wilderness to the promised land. The passage also notes that the trumpets will be used to summon the people to war and to signal the onset of the holidays.

III

Numbers 10:11–19:22 constitutes the account of the first stage of Israel's journey through the wilderness from Sinai to the Wilderness of Paran. This unit resumes the concern with Israel's rebellion in the wilderness in Exod 14–15; 16–18; and 32–34, and thereby signals the text's interest in correlating Israel's rebellion with the ultimate downfall of the northern kingdom of Israel in 722–721 BCE. Although there is significant P-stratum material in this unit, the concern with rebellion as an expression of northern Israel's demise is a mark of the J stratum of the late monarchic period. A part of the solution to the problem will be the ordination of the Levites to serve together with the Aaronide priests to ensure the sanctity of the people of Israel. The narrative thereby supports the efforts of King Josiah of Judah to explain Israel's downfall as a result of inadequate priestly supervision of the sanctuaries at Bethel and Dan and to prepare for the reinstitution of Davidic rule over the territory of the former northern tribes. A key element in this narrative is the ordination of the Levites to serve together with Aaron and his sons as priestly assistants, which is consistent with Josiah's call for the priests of the shrines of Judah to serve at the Jerusalem temple (2 Kgs 23:8-9), which in turn developed into the P-stratum view that the Levites, formerly the priests of the countryside shrines, would serve together with Aaronide priests in the Jerusalem temple from the time of Nehemiah and Ezra on.

Numbers 10:11-27 is a P-stratum text that recounts the departure from Sinai, including the date, that is, the twentieth day of the second month of the second year in Num 10:11; the itinerary of the journey from Sinai to Paran in Num 10:12; and an account of the organization of the march in which the tribes of Israel are arrayed around the tabernacle with Judah in the lead in Num 10:13-27.

The main account of the journey by stages from Sinai to Paran then follows in Num 10:28–19:22, beginning with a brief superscription in Num 10:28, which introduces the account. The account of the journey proper appears in Num 10:29–19:22, beginning with preliminary issues in Num 10:29-32, that is, the contract with Hobab ben Reuel, the Midianite father-in-law of Moses, who will serve as Israel's guide. Martin Noth views the designation of Hobab ben Reuel as a J-stratum harmonization of the names applied to Moses's father-in-law, including Reuel, the priest of Midian, in Exod 2:16-21 and Hobab in Judg 4:11. The E stratum identifies

Moses's father-in-law as Jethro, the priest of Midian in Exod 18 (cf. Exod 3:1).[9] The P stratum will later reject Moses's and Israel's association with Midianite women in Num 12 and 25. The following J-stratum reference in Num 10:33-36 indicates that YHWH, represented by the ark of the covenant and the cloud, will serve as the true guide for Israel (cf. Num 9:15-23; 10:11-12).

Numbers 10:33–11:34 relates the initial three-day journey of Israel through the wilderness by stages. This section includes the above-noted reference to the ark and the cloud as symbols of YHWH's presence and guidance through the wilderness in Num 10:33-34 and the formulaic reference to the movement of ark in Num 10:35-36. The J-stratum narrative of Israel's rebellion in the wilderness begins in Num 11:1-34 with an account of the complaints of the people concerning several issues. Insofar as the narrative refers to the seventy elders, which some see as a northern Israelite institution,[10] it would appear that J's purpose in this passage is to make a polemic against the northern kingdom of Israel by portraying it as an unruly and rebellious mob in order to justify the Assyrian destruction of the kingdom in 722–721 BCE as an act of punishment by YHWH. The passage begins in Num 11:1-3 with a general portrayal of complaints by the people and divine retaliation by fire that had to be quelled by Moses's appeal to YHWH. The place was named Taberah, which means "burning," to commemorate the incident. A second incident takes place in Num 11:4-34 at Kibroth-hattaavah, where the people rebelled once again concerning the provision of food and issues concerning community authority and leadership. In the first instance, in vv. 4-15, the people complained concerning the lack of meat that they claimed to have enjoyed in Egypt while in slavery. The text indicates that they were tired of manna. There is a certain element of irony here in that it is difficult to understand how the Israelites could have enjoyed meat while in slavery and would then refuse the manna provided by YHWH. When Moses complains to YHWH about the burden of meeting the demands of the people, YHWH proposes that he gather seventy elders of Israel who would serve as elders and officers and thereby share his burden of leadership. Many interpreters have seen the association between the seventy elders and prophecy as a sign of northern Israelite, or E-stratum, composition.[11]

Even with the addition of the seventy elders, the crowd continues to get out of hand. Two men, Eldad and Medad, then claim to be prophets. When Joshua ben Nun calls upon Moses to restrain them, Moses cries out in frustration that he cannot control the people. YHWH's ironic solution likewise demonstrates divine frustration, namely, YHWH brings so much quail that the people could not even finish their meal before YHWH struck them down, naming the place Kibroth-hattaavah, "the Graves of Craving."

Numbers 11:35–12:15 then recounts the journey from Kibroth-hattaavah to Hazeroth, where a challenge to Moses by Miriam and Aaron takes place. Miriam and Aaron object to Moses's marriage to a Cushite woman. There is a question of the woman's identity. Cush normally indicates an Ethiopian identity, and such an identification would suggest that the reference to Moses sending away his wife, Zipporah, in Exod 18:2 indicated that he had divorced her and married another wife from Ethiopia.[12] The understanding that Exod 18:2 indicates Moses's divorce of Zipporah is uncertain, however, and the parallel between the tents of Cushan and pavilions of the land of Midian in Hab 3:7 suggests to some that Cushite is an alternative reference to Midianite. If this is the case, there is no need to postulate that Moses divorced Zipporah or that he married an Ethiopian woman. But even if Zipporah is indeed Midianite, she is not Israelite, and therefore Miriam and Aaron have a legitimate question concerning the propriety of Moses's marriage to a foreign woman. The issue is settled, however, when YHWH insists that Moses is YHWH's choice as leader of Israel, insofar as YHWH speaks with Moses face-to-face in simple words and not in riddles. To emphasize the point, YHWH afflicts Miriam with a skin disease, requiring her to remain outside the camp for seven days until she is purified. The text provides no explanation as to why Aaron is not similarly afflicted. The marriage of Israelite men to Midianite women remains an issue, however, as Num 25:10-18 rewards Phinehas ben Eleazar ben Aaron, the grandson of Aaron, with a covenant of eternal priesthood for killing an Israelite man and a Moabite woman for engaging in illicit, sexually-based worship. Phinehas's covenant of eternal priesthood would then identify his descendants as the Zadokite line of priests that later served in the Jerusalem temple, beginning during the reign of Solomon (1 Kgs 2:26-27, 35). Moses's line, by contrast, disappeared forever.

Numbers 12:16–19:22 presents a detailed account of Israel's journey from Hazeroth to the Wilderness of Paran in a series of six subunits, which includes the narrative introduction concerning the journey from Hazeroth to Paran in Num 12:16; the spy narrative in Num 13:1–14:49; an instruction account concerning the sanctification or purging of the people in Num 15:1-41; an account of the failed rebellion by Korah and the Reubenites in Num 16:1–17:15; an account concerning the selection of Aaron and his sons as the priestly line amongst the tribe of Levi in Num 17:16–18:32; and instruction concerning rituals of purification concerning those who come into contact with the dead in Num 19:1-22. Overall, the choice of Aaron and sons among the Levites to serve as priests brings order and leadership back into the camp.

The spy narrative in Num 13:1–14:49 brings the rebellion motif to its culmination with YHWH's decision to destroy the wilderness generation of Israel for its failure to hold faith in YHWH's promise to them of the land of Israel. The account is fundamentally a J-stratum narrative in Num 13:17b-20, 20-24, 26-31; Num 14:1b, 4, 11-25, 39-45, with a P-stratum redactional overlay in Num 13:17a, 21, 25-26, 32, 33; Num 14:1a, 2-3, 5-10, 26-38. The J-stratum narrative is designed to show that the northern tribes of Israel are unworthy of possession of the promised land of Israel due to their lack of faith in YHWH's promises, whereas Judah, led by Caleb, is indeed worthy. The P stratum adds details concerning the identities of the spies, and it accentuates the conflict between Moses and YHWH to highlight the question of divine punishment of Israel in the aftermath of the Babylonian exile. When the people arrive along the southern borders of Canaan, Moses chooses twelve spies to scout out the land. When the spies return with reports of the great bounty of the land

and the power of the people who live there, the people are both awed by the richness of the land of Israel and afraid of the giants who live there. Only two of the spies, Caleb ben Jephunneh of Judah and Hoshea ben Nun of Ephraim, renamed by Moses as Joshua ben Nun (Num 13:6) had enough faith to believe that they would be able to take the land as promised by YHWH. The people refuse to believe that they can take the land despite the promises of YHWH that they can do so. The people's rebellion sparks the conflict between YHWH and Moses once again, but the anger and emotions portrayed in Num 13–14 far exceed those of the earlier conflict between YHWH and Moses concerning the gold calf in Exod 32–34. When YHWH becomes angered at the people's rebellion and proposes to kill all of them so that Moses might become the basis of a great nation, Moses responds that YHWH's reputation will be ruined. The nations will believe that YHWH was powerless and brought the people into the wilderness only to kill them. Moses, in Num 17–18 (see Exod 33:6-33), also repeats portions of the formula for YHWH's capacities for mercy and judgment before imploring YHWH to spare the people. But YHWH does not relent as in Exod 32–34; YHWH instead grants pardon by killing off the wilderness generation, except Caleb ben Jephunneh of Judah and Joshua ben Nun of Ephraim, thereby allowing only those who were born in the wilderness and who did not know slavery to enter the promised land after forty years of wandering.

Numbers 15:1-41 follows with instruction concerning the sanctification or purging of the people. The passage outlines instructions for the offering of the *'olah*, or entirely burnt offering, (Lev 1), the *minkhah*, or grain offering, (Lev 2), a *terumah*, or gift offering—which appears to be derived from the *zebakh shelamim*, "peace offering" (Lev 3)—and the *khatta't*, sin or purgation offering (Lev 4:1–5:13). As the parallels to Lev 1–5 indicate, the passage appears to be analogous to the instruction in Leviticus, although the *'asham*, guilt offering, (Lev 5:14-26) is missing. Whereas Lev 1–5 presents instruction for the priests on the presentation of offerings intended to sanctify or purge the people, Num 15 presents instruction for the people concerning their sanctification and purging from the effects of wrongdoing. A paragraph in Num 15:32-36 emphasizes the importance of Shabbat observance by decreeing a death penalty against a man who desecrated the Shabbat by working to gather sticks for a fire. Another paragraph in Num 15:37-41 calls upon Israelites to wear tasseled garments with blue threads as a reminder of their obligation to observe YHWH's commandments. Such a garment signified Israel as a kingdom of priests (Exod 19:6), insofar as blue thread was a mark of royalty. The tasseled garments became the basis for the *tallit*, the prayer shawl worn by Jews at times of prayer and public worship.[13]

Numbers 16:1–17:15 presents the account of the failed rebellion of Korah and his Reubenite supporters. The narrative appears to have originated as a J-stratum narrative in Num 16:1-2, 12-15, 25, 26, 27b-32, 33, 34 overlaid by a P-stratum redaction in Num 16:1-11, 16-24, 27a, 35-50; Num 17:1-13.[14] The J-stratum narrative was concerned with the rebellion of Dathan and Abiram from the tribe of Reuben, who did not wish to join the other tribes in completing the conquest of the land of Canaan. Many interpreters maintain that the Reubenites's hesitance is based in attempts by the Transjordanian tribes to rebel against Moses by declaring their freedom from the rest of Israel (cf. Josh 22).[15] An alternative explanation is that the narrative reflects the conquest of the Transjordanian tribes by the Arameans and their Moabite allies in the late ninth to early eighth century BCE when the House of Omri was overthrown by Jehu and the Arameans proceeded to dismember northern Israel as indicated in the Tel Dan, Deir Alla, and Moabite inscriptions.[16] Such readings suggest the potential for E-stratum material from the northern kingdom of Israel in these narratives. The P narrative redirects the issues to the rebellion of Korah, the ancestors of a well-known family of levitical singers who composed numerous psalms, to challenge the leadership of the Aaronide priesthood. The challenge failed, and the Korahites were pushed out of power as a result of their failed bid. The narrative emphasizes that Aaron stood between the living and the dead that resulted from YHWH's judgment against Korah's supporters and thereby quelled the plague that threatened the lives of the nation of Israel. Aaron was an ambiguous figure in the gold calf episode of Exod 32–34, but here he shows himself as a true priest and leader of Israel who is qualified to stand before YHWH.

Numbers 17:16–18:32 recounts the selection of Aaron and sons as a priestly line among the Levites. Most interpreters view this section as a P work because of its interest in the priestly leadership of Israel, but there are actually two issues here. The first is the selection of Aaron and his sons as the priesthood of Israel, and the second is the selection of the Levites as their support staff. The Aaronide priesthood was hardly a postexilic phenomenon as proponents of assigning this text to P would maintain. Aaronide priests had served in the sanctuary at Shiloh during the premonarchic period (1 Sam 1–3) and as the priests of the Jerusalem temple during the reign of Solomon (1 Kgs 2:26-35). The Levites, however, only emerged as potential candidates for service in the Jerusalem temple when King Josiah invited the priests of the countryside to serve in Jerusalem. The book of Deuteronomy, written during his reign, emphasizes the obligation to care for the Levites as part of the poor of the land.[17] The Levites only appear in service at the Jerusalem temple during the careers of Nehemiah and Ezra. Such a concern with the appointment of both the Aaronides and the Levites to holy service suggests an early J text concerned with the appointment of Aaron and sons as the priests of Israel and Judah that has been overlaid and rewritten by a P text concerned with the appointment of the Levites. J material pertaining to the Aaronides appears in Num 17:16-28; 18:1-5, 8-20, and P material pertaining to the Levites appears in Num 18:6-7, 21-32. The Aaronide priests are assigned oversight of the meeting tent, the holy of holies, and the altar (Num 18:1-5). They receive the *terumah*, gift or elevation offerings; the most holy of the fire offerings, including the *'olah, minkhah, khatta't,* and *'asham* offerings; all the *tenuphah*, the gift or wave offerings; and the firstfruits offerings. The Levites perform the service of the meeting tent under the supervision of the Aaronides (Num 18:6-7), and they receive the tithes of Israel for their service (Num 18:32). The Levites in turn present a tenth part of their tithes as a *terumah*, or gift offering, to the Aaronide priests.

Numbers 19:1-22 presents instruction concerning the ritual of purification following contact with the dead. Numbers 19:1-10 presents instruction concerning the purification of the meeting tent with the ashes of a fully red heifer that has no blemish. The red heifer is also necessary for the purification of the site of the desecrated sanctuary and is therefore a necessary element in the restoration of the temple. Numbers 19:11-22 presents instruction for the purification of someone who has come into contact with the dead. It functions in relation to the narrative context in that Moses and Aaron fail to purify themselves following the burial of Miriam when they serve as priests before YHWH to produce water from the rock in Num 20. Numbers 19 is a key element of the P narrative concerning YHWH's decision to forbid Moses and Aaron to enter the land because they failed to observe their priestly duties following their designation as priests.

Numbers 20:1-21 presents the account of Israel's journey from Paran to the Wilderness of Zin where Israel encamps at Kadesh. The first narrative element appears in Num 20:1-13, which relates the death and burial of Miriam and the incident of the water at the rock. Miriam's death and burial are briefly mentioned in v. 1, and the main focus of the narrative of the incident at the rock appears in vv. 2-13. The people lack water and so they complain to Moses and Aaron to find them some in a classical example of the wilderness rebellion motif. Moses and Aaron appear before YHWH in the meeting tent, and YHWH instructs them to take their rod, assemble the people, and order the rock to produce water for the people to drink. They do so and provide water for the people when Moses strikes the rock twice with the rod. As a result, YHWH accuses both Moses and Aaron of failing to show proper trust in YHWH so that they might affirm YHWH's sanctity. YHWH therefore decrees that they will never enter the land of Israel, and names the place "the Waters of Meribah (Rebellion)." Interpreters have struggled since antiquity to explain YHWH's decision.[18] Moses and Aaron had just buried their dead sister, Miriam, and they did not purify themselves following their contact with her corpse. Instead, they appeared before YHWH in the holy meeting tent in an impure state. Their action is striking because Num 19 had specified that purification was necessary following contact with the dead, and Moses and Aaron had just been designated as priests in Num 17:16–18:32. All are obligated to observe YHWH's instructions, even Moses and Aaron.

Numbers 20:14-21 presents the account of Edom's refusal to grant Israel passage through their land. The account is an E-stratum text that has been supplemented by J materials in vv. 19, 20, and 21a. It illustrates Edom's enmity toward Israel and Israel's refusal to be drawn into a fight. The passage presupposes the Jacob narratives in Gen 25–35 in which Jacob and Esau, the eponymous ancestors of Israel and Edom, are fraternal twin brothers who are in conflict but go their separate ways to avoid continuing their hostilities. Edom was an early vassal of King David according to 2 Sam 8:13-14, but Edom broke away from Judean control during the wars with Aram in the late ninth through the early eighth centuries BCE according to 2 Kgs 8:16-22.

Numbers 20:22–21:3 recounts Israel's journey from Kadesh in the Wilderness of Zin where Mount Hor is located. This brief P narrative relates the death and burial of Aaron and the succession of his son, Eleazar, as the high priest of Israel. Numbers 21:1-3 relates Israel's conflict with Arad in the (southern) Negev wilderness. Israel vowed to destroy the people of Arad if YHWH would give them into their hand. YHWH did so, and Arad was destroyed. Arad is a known city site in the Negev wilderness with an interesting example of a three-room sanctuary with a *matzevah* or pillar for the worship of a deity in its holy of holies. The site shows little evidence of having been destroyed, but it would have been banned during King Josiah's reforms.

Numbers 21:4-35 relates Israel's journey from Mount Hor to Edom and Moab where they defeated Kings Sihon and Og. The narrative relates Israel's final approach to the promised land by circumventing Edom following Edom's refusal to grant passage. The J narrative in Num 21:4-9 presents the final example of the rebellion motif in which YHWH releases serpents called *seraphim* against the people as punishment. Such snakes are revered in the ancient world as gods of healing, but here they afflict the people by biting their heels much like the snake is to bite the heels of the descendants of Eve in Gen 3:15. YHWH commands Moses to make a *saraph* figure and mount it on a standard so that the people might look upon it and be healed. Such a figure likely represents an etiological account of the Nehushtan, a snake figure removed from the Jerusalem temple in King Hezekiah's reform in 2 Kgs 18:4. Numbers 21:10-20 is a non-source text that simply completes the itinerary of the journey through the wilderness to Moab, and Num 21:21-35 presents a number of E-stratum narratives that relate Israel's defeat of the Amorite King Sihon of Heshbon and King Og of Bashan. Sihon controlled a kingdom that ranged north from the Wadi Arnon, the northern border of Moab to the Wadi Jabbok, which formed the border with the Ammonites. This territory would later be settled by the tribe of Reuben, although the Moabites conquered it at the time of the Aramean defeat of Israel during the late ninth and early eighth centuries BCE. The present text thereby presents Israel's claim to this territory with a threat against the Moabites who took it from them. The account of the defeat of King Og of Bashan in vv. 33-35 serves a similar purpose insofar as Bashan constituted the territory of the tribe of Gad, which was likewise displaced when Aram defeated Israel.

Numbers 22:1–36:13 then constitutes the final unit of the book of Numbers with an account of Israel's arrival at Moab that combines E, J, and P elements. The introductory notice in Num 22:1 is a P itinerary formula that signals Israel's arrival at the plains of Moab across the Jordan River from Jericho. It thereby establishes the setting for the eleven narrative units that follow through to the end of Numbers as well as for the book of Deuteronomy.

Numbers 22:2–24:25 relates the Balaam narrative in which Balaam ben Beor, a well-known Aramean prophet, was hired by Balaak ben Zippor, the King of Moab, to curse Israel. But because Balaam could only speak the words that YHWH placed in his mouth, Balaam could only bless Israel. The narrative is a combination of E and J elements with the E layer comprising Num 22:2-3a, 9-12, 20, 38, 41; 23:1-27, 29, 30, and the J layer comprising Num 22:3b-8, 13-19, 21-37, 39-40; 23:28; 24:1-25. Past scholarship viewed this model as a J composition expanded by the addition of

E material, but the current redating of J calls for a model in which the foundational E narrative has been edited and expanded by the J stratum. The current form of the narrative is clearly fictionalized insofar as it features Balaam's talking donkey who is able to see the angel of YHWH blocking their path whereas the great seer, Balaam, does not. The narrative presents a caricature of Balaam in order to show that the famous seer of Aram was entirely under the control of YHWH, leaving him unable to say or see anything unless YHWH permitted him to do so. Balaam ben Beor, the great Aramean seer, ultimately blesses Israel.

The reason for such literary characterization is that Balaam ben Beor is a known historical figure whose prophecy concerning Israel was discovered in excavations at Deir Alla, a Transjordanian site located about halfway between the Sea of Galilee and the Dead Sea just across the Jordan River from the Israelite highlands.[19] The Aramaic text of Balaam's prophecy was written in ink on the plastered wall of a building situated at the top of the tel where it could be seen from Israel across the Jordan River. The text is fragmentary, and only the first part of it is preserved. It dates to the late ninth and early eighth century BCE, which would be the years when Israel lost the Transjordan to the Arameans during the reign of King Jehu of Israel (842–815 BCE), who had overthrown the Omride dynasty due to dissatisfaction with Israel's failure to defend itself against Aramean advances. Upon Jehu's ascent to the throne, the Arameans were able to overrun Israel, leaving it virtually defenseless.[20] Israel's fortunes did not improve until the reign of Jehu's grandson, Jehoash (Joash) ben Jehoahaz (801–786 BCE) and his great grandson, Jeroboam ben Joash (786–746 BCE), when Israel regrouped and reestablished mastery over Aram. The remains of Balaam's prophecy indicate a vision that portrays a crisis in which the Aramean gods will need to intervene. The second part of the prophecy is not extant, but such a text would be inevitably followed by an account of what the gods will do to bring the world back into order. Balaam's prophecy would have functioned as a prophecy against Israel and supported Aramean efforts to defeat Israel and conquer the Transjordanian territories of the tribes of Manasseh, Gad, and Reuben. The Tel Dan Inscription indicates success in such an endeavor, and the Moabite Stone likewise indicates the success of King Mesha of Moab in reclaiming the territories of Reuben and Gad and slaughtering their inhabitants.[21]

Balaam ben Beor appears as a typical Mesopotamian *baru*-priest, which was a professional class of oracle givers or diviners common in ancient Babylonia, Assyria, and Aram. *Baru*-priests were exceptionally literate so that they could record their oracles, and they were trained in the various techniques of oracular inquiry.[22] Following his arrival in Moab, he goes about his business by setting up seven altars, apparently to read the smoke patterns from the fires as the basis for his oracular inquiry. The altars were accompanied by the offerings of seven bulls and seven rams to ensure the cooperation of the gods. The introductions to his oracle employ typical oracular language; see for example, Num 24:15b-16, "The utterance of Balaam the son of Beor, and the oracle of the man whose eye is open/closed. The utterance of the one who hears the words of G-d and who knows the knowledge of the most high, who envisions the vision of Shaddai, falling down with his eyes uncovered." The formula portrays ecstatic prophecy by an expert. Balaam attempts to curse Israel four times, but each time he blesses Israel in accordance with the will of YHWH. The comical aspects of the narrative continue beyond Balaam's conversation with his donkey who can see better then he when YHWH wills it insofar as Balaam and Balak argue throughout the narrative because Balak is angry at not getting the curses for which he had paid Balaam so handsomely. In the end, Balaam returns home after having blessed Israel repeatedly and predicted its ultimate victory over Balak and Moab.

The foundational E stratum of Num 22–24, caricatures of Balaam and Balak, and the discovery of the Deir Alla Inscription suggest that Num 22–24 was composed as Israel's response to the Balaam prophecy posted at Deir Alla. Whereas the Deir Alla Inscription is designed to curse and undermine Israel in an effort to portray Aram's seizure of Israelite territory in the Transjordan, Num 22–24 is designed to respond that Israel will indeed be blessed by Balaam ben Beor himself, that it will achieve victory over Moab and Edom following the rise of a new Israelite monarch, and that it will flourish along the Jordan Valley as described in the biblical text. The reference to the support given to Israel from the Kittim in Num 24:24, often understood as a reference to the Assyrians, signals Israel's alliance with the Assyrians beginning with the reign of King Jehu and continuing throughout the course of the Jehu dynasty, which was a key factor in enabling Israel to retake the Transjordan and subjugate Aram. Numbers 22–24 would therefore have been written initially in northern Israel during the reign of either Jehoash ben Jehoahaz, who reestablished Israel's control over the Transjordan, or Jeroboam ben Joash, who ruled in peace over the great empire that his father had established. The J redaction of Num 22–24 would have taken place during the late monarchic period when King Josiah of Judah attempted to reestablish Judean mastery over the older Solomonic empire, including the former territory of northern Israel and the Transjordan in anticipation of Assyria's demise.

Numbers 25:1-18 presents incidents of apostasy by the Israelites with foreign women at Baal of Peor and Shittim while Israel is encamped in Moab along the Jordan River. Numbers 25:1-5 is a J text that recounts how Israelite men joined Moabite women in the worship of their foreign god, here named as Baal of Peor, that is, the Baal-deity of Peor. This narrative functions as another example of the rebellion motif requiring Moses to order the execution of the apostate men in order to prevent any such recurrence. Numbers 25:6-18 must be judged as part of the J-stratum narrative. The text describes the action of Phinehas ben Eleazar, the grandson of Aaron, in impaling an Israelite man and a Midianite woman who had gone into the meeting tent to desecrate the sanctuary. Insofar as Phinehas was able to kill them both with one thrust of his javelin, the act was likely sexual in nature. Phinehas is rewarded for his action with a covenant of peace and a covenant of eternal priesthood, which establish Phinehas as the ancestor of the Zadokite priestly line that would serve in Jerusalem. The identification of the woman as a Midianite would constitute a swipe at Moses, whose wife Zipporah was a Midianite, and thereby hinder the claims of his levitical line to be recognized as a legitimate priestly family.

The census of Israel in Num 26:1-65 must be recognized as a P text that plays off of the census in Num 1:1-54. It accentuates the theme of the death of the old generation of Israel in the wilderness and the birth of the new generation that will enter the promised land of Israel.

Numbers 27:1-11 takes up the case of the daughters of Zelophehad, a man from the tribe of Manasseh who died leaving no sons and five daughters. The focus on the tribe of Manasseh suggests that this text may have originated as an E-stratum text from the northern kingdom of Israel. The issue at hand is the inheritance of Zelophehad's land, insofar as land passes to male heirs, but not to female heirs. The decision here is that daughters may inherit their father's estate when there are no sons. If there are no daughters, then the text specifies other male relatives who would then inherit the dead man's property. The issue will be revisited in Num 36:1-12.

Numbers 27:12-23 relates the account of Joshua's selection to succeed Moses as leader. The text is a P composition as indicated by the role that the high priest, Eleazar ben Aaron, plays in the transfer of leadership to Joshua and because of the dependence of this narrative on that of Moses's and Aaron's failure to sanctify YHWH at the rock in Num 20:2-13. This narrative presupposes the spy narrative in Num 13–14 in which Joshua ben Nun was one of the two spies who were willing to accept YHWH's promise of the land of Israel to the people. The narrative appears to presuppose an earlier stratum, insofar as Moses, a Levite, is to be succeeded by Joshua ben Nun, an Ephraimite. Insofar as Ephraim was the dominant tribe of the northern kingdom of Israel, it may well be that an earlier form of the narrative played a role in the E stratum of the Pentateuch. Joshua is portrayed elsewhere in prophetic terms as "an inspired man" (Num 11:10-25), although other elements suggest a quasi-priestly role, for example, the laying on of hands in v. 18, his exhortations to observe Torah (Josh 1), and his reading Torah to the people at Shechem (Josh 8:30-35). Northern Israel was known for its non-levitical priests (1 Kgs 12:31), and so it is possible that Joshua was understood to have a priestly role.

Numbers 28:1–30:1 presents instruction concerning the offerings at festivals. This text is understood as a non-source text (i.e., not J, E, D, or P), although it is concerned with the presentation of offerings at the temple altar. It specifies public offerings for each day (28:3-8); the Shabbat (28:9-15); Passover and the seven-day festival that follows (28:16-25); Shavuot, or Weeks (28:26-31); Rosh haShanah, or the New Year (29:1-6); Yom Kippur (29:7-11); and Succoth (29:17-38). Earlier scholarship might have seen this text in conflict with the festival calendar of Lev 23, but we should note that the instructions in Num 28:1–30:1 are directed to the people to specify what they should present at the altar on each of the holy occasions in the festival year. Leviticus 23, however, was concerned with instructions as to how Aaron and his sons should prepare and offer the sacrifices of Israel at the altar. Numbers 28:1–30:1 surely fits into the P concern with the offerings at the temple, but instruction to the people—and not the priests—suggests that this text might be earlier. The covenant code in Exod 20–23 already presents instruction concerning the observance of the festivals in the E stratum of the Pentateuch. Numbers 28:1–30:1

builds upon the covenant code to specify the offerings for each occasion, indicating that it is a J-stratum text.

Numbers 30:2-17 presents instruction concerning solemn promises made by women. It follows on the preceding text insofar as it ended with vows and other offerings in Num 29:29–30:1. The concern with the status of women suggests that Num 30:2-17 could be associated with the earlier text in Num 27:1-11 concerning the daughters of Zelophehad which has possible E roots. Should the woman be married or an unmarried girl still in her father's house, the husband or father is given final authority as to whether the solemn promise is valid or not. If the husband or father objects on the day that he hears about the vow, it is invalid. But if he does not object on that day, it is valid.

Numbers 31:1-54 presents a P account of a holy war against Midian. This narrative builds upon earlier narratives concerned with the Midianites, including Num 12:1-16, which was concerned with Moses's Cushite wife (understood as a reference to Midian; cf. Hab 3:7), and Num 25:6-18, in which Phinehas ben Eleazar killed an Israelite man and a Midianite woman who desecrated the meeting tent with an apparently illicit sexual act. Underlying issues for the tensions with Midian may lie in conflict with Midian during the course of Israelite history. The Aramean prophet, Balaam ben Beor, is also killed because of his association with the Midianites who joined Moab's King Balak ben Zippor in hiring Balaam to curse Israel (Num 22:4, 7).

Numbers 32:1-41 addresses the status of the tribes of Reuben and Gad in Israel. The status of Reuben and Gad in the Transjordan suggests that it is rooted in the E material and later edited by J. Questions of the status of Reuben and Gad among the tribes of Israel would be raised in Josh 22 as well, insofar as the Jordan River would form a natural boundary between Israel's highlands and Judah and the Transjordan. The setting would be linked to the Aramean conquest of the Transjordan and Israel's subsequent recovery of this territory in the late ninth through the early eighth century. The text focuses on the question of land holdings in the Transjordan for both tribes. The tribe of Manasseh is also noted in vv. 33-41, but Manasseh would possess land in both the Transjordan and the highlands of Israel. The instruction specifies that Reuben and Gad would be granted land in the Transjordan on condition that they join the other tribes in the conquest of Canaan. When read in relation to J, Num 32:1-41 would appear to lay claim to the Transjordan during the late Judean monarchy.

Numbers 33:1-49 summarizes the journey from Egypt through the wilderness to Moab prior to entry into the land of Israel. This is the basis for P's itinerary through the wilderness.

Numbers 33:50–36:13 contains the final instructions concerning the apportionment of the land of Canaan among the tribes of Israel. These texts appear to be a combination of E- and J-stratum material. Numbers 33:50-55 begins with instruction to destroy the Canaanites so that they do not become a source of idolatry and apostasy for Israel. The concern with the Canaanites as a source for leading Israel astray is emphasized in Exod 34:10-16 and Deut 7:1-7, both of which date to the late monarchic period reign of King Josiah. Exodus 34:10-16 was part of the J narrative concerning the gold calf and the rewriting of the earlier covenant code material, whereas Deut 7:1-7 was part of the book of Deuteronomy written during Josiah's reign. Numbers 34:1-29 defines the boundaries of the land and the process by which it shall be apportioned among the tribes. The definition of the land includes all of the territory settled by the tribes of Israel, including both Judah in the south and the Transjordan to the east, which suggests it derives from the E-stratum material that would have been completed during the reign of Israel's King Jeroboam ben Joash (786–746 BCE) and then later read in relation to the J stratum, which would have expressed King Josiah's ambitions to extend Davidic rule over the land. Numbers 35:1-8 takes up the responsibility of each tribe to apportion towns and land for levitical use. Numbers 35:9-34 defines the cities of refuge to which persons who have committed unintentional manslaughter might flee to save their lives. Those guilty of intentional homicide, however, remain subject to the death penalty. Numbers 36:1-12 returns to the question of the daughters of Zelophehad (cf. Num 27:1-11). This text considers a problem inherent in the earlier ruling of Num 27:1-11: What happens to tribal land if the women who inherited from their father marry men from another tribe? The present text therefore stipulates that women who inherit land because their fathers died without sons must marry within the clan of their father to retain control of the land, which will then pass to their sons. If such women marry outside of their own clans, they lose the right to land inherited from their father. The instruction is designed to maintain the integrity of tribal land holdings in Israel. Insofar as Num 27:1-11 is deemed to be E-stratum material, the present text would be a J-stratum revision of the earlier text. Numbers 36:13 then concludes this unit with a summary statement concerning the commands and regulations enjoined upon Israel by YHWH.

Deuteronomy

I

Deuteronomy is the last book of the Pentateuch. It constitutes the last major element of Israel's history under the guidance of the Levites in Num 3:1–Deut 34:12.[1]

Deuteronomy 1:1–34:12 is an account of Moses's last speeches to Israel on the last day of his life while encamped in Moab by the Jordan River. Moses's last words present a summary and review of YHWH's Torah that Israel is expected to observe when it begins its life in the land of Israel. But a close reading of Moses's instruction to Israel in Deuteronomy demonstrates that it is not simply a repetition or summation of previously presented material. Instead, Moses's speeches constitute reflection upon and rewriting of earlier instruction in Genesis–Numbers that addresses unanswered questions and that specifies and applies the earlier material to facilitate a holy, just, and viable society in Israel. Deuteronomy illustrates the self-reflective and evolving character of a living legal system that adapts to meet the needs of a changing and dynamic society.[2]

The synchronic literary structure of Deuteronomy includes two major elements. The first is the account of Moses's last four speeches to Israel in Deut 1:1–30:20, and the second is the account of Moses's transfer of leadership to Joshua immediately prior to Moses's death and burial in Deut 31:1–34:12. The account of Moses's first speech to Israel in Deut 1:1–4:43 is an exhortational résumé of Israel's journey from Horeb/Sinai through the wilderness that is designed to persuade the people to observe YHWH's Torah. The account of Moses's second speech in Deut 4:44–26:19 is an example of levitical Torah, or instruction, a sermonic form employed by the Levites and priests to teach divine expectations to the people.[3] It includes an introduction in Deut 4:44-49 that defines the setting of the speech in Beth-peor across the Jordan River in Moab, identifies Moses's speech as YHWH's Torah, and presents an account of the speech itself in Deut 5:1–26:19. The account of Moses's levitical sermon proceeds with a brief speech formula in Deut 5:1aα^{1-2}, which identifies Moses as the speaker, followed by Moses's speech per se, including his introductory exhortation to observe YHWH's Torah in Deut 5:1aα^{3-6}–11:32 and the Torah proper in Deut 12:1–26:19, which lays out in detail YHWH's statutes and cases. The account of Moses's third speech, in Deut 27:1–28:69, recounts the blessings and curses that follow either from Israel's observance of the covenant or its failure to observe the covenant with YHWH. The account of Moses's fourth speech, in Deut 29:1–30:20, presents Moses's final exhortation to observe the covenant with YHWH. The synchronic literary structure of Deuteronomy may be outlined in detail as follows:

Narrative Account of Moses's Last Addresses to Israel: Deuteronomic Torah

Deut 1–34

I. Narrative Account of Moses's Last Speeches to Israel	1:1–30:20
A. Account of Moses's First Speech: Exhortational Résumé of Israel's Journey	1:1–4:43
B. Account of Moses's Second Speech: Exhortational Summary of YHWH's Torah	4:44–26:19
1. Introduction: Setting of Speech and Identification as Torah	4:44-49
2. Report of Speech Proper: Levitical Torah	5:1–26:19
a. Speech Formula	5:1aα^{1-2}
b. Speech Proper: Levitical Torah	5:1aα^{3-6}–26:19
1) Introductory Exhortation	5:1aα^{3-6}–11:32
2) Torah Proper: Statutes and Cases	12:1–26:15
a) Superscription	12:1
b) Statutes and Ordinances Proper	12:2–26:15
i. Concerning Cultic Differentiation from the Nations	12:2–13:19
aa. Instructions Concerning Exclusive Worship at YHWH's Chosen Altar	12:2-31

bb. Cases Concerning Cultic/National Apostasy	13:1-19
ii. Concerning Holy Conduct of Treasured People	14:1–26:15
aa. Basic Instruction: Holiness of People	14:1-2
bb. Specific Instruction	14:3–26:15
i) Eating of Meat	14:3-21
ii) Tithes	14:22-29
iii) Debt Issues	15:1-18
iv) Offering of Firstborn	15:19-23
v) Observance of Holidays	16:1-17
vi) Judicial and Political Authority	16:18–17:20
vii) Religious Authority	18:1–19:13
viii) Territorial /Boundary Issues	19:14–21:23
ix) Treatment of What Pertains to Others	22:1-8
x) Mixing What Does Not Belong Together	22:9-29
xi) Impurities	23:1-15
xii) Improper Transactions with Human Beings	23:16–24:5
xiii) Improper Financial/Lending Transactions	24:6-13
xiv) Justice to the Poor	24:14–25:3
xv) Rights to Sustenance/ Continuation	25:4-12

xvi) Obligation to Give What Is Due	25:13–26:15
3) Concluding Exhortation	26:16-19
C. Account of Moses's Third Speech: Blessings and Curses	27:1–28:69
D. Account of Moses's Fourth Speech: Final Exhortation to Observe Covenant	29:1–30:20
II. Account of Moses's Transfer of Leadership to Joshua and Moses's Death	31:1–34:12

Historical scholarship maintains that—with the exception of minor elements from the account of Moses's death and burial in Deut 34:1aα, 7-9,[4] Deuteronomy comprises the D stratum of the Pentateuch.[5] Most interpreters maintain that an early form of the book of Deuteronomy is to be identified with the Torah scroll found in the temple during the reign of Judah's King Josiah ben Amon (who ruled 640–609 BCE), which provided the basis for King Josiah's program of religious reform and national restoration.[6] Many earlier interpreters argue that Deuteronomy was originally written in northern Israel, perhaps by prophetic circles that promoted religious reform in the northern kingdom of Israel, and that it was later brought south where it would form the basis for Josiah's reform efforts.[7] Much of the reason for this view was that Deuteronomy addresses all Israel, lacks reference to Davidic royal ideology, and emphasizes the northern site of Shechem as the gathering point for the tribes of Israel in Deut 27. But more recent scholarship maintains that Deuteronomy's emphasis on a single site for the worship of YHWH—in contrast to northern Israel which recognized multiple sites in Bethel, Dan, and elsewhere—indicates that Deuteronomy was produced in Judean circles to support Josiah's reform.[8]

Deuteronomy constitutes an attempt to revise earlier instructions applied in Israel and Judah, particularly the E-stratum covenant code of Exod 20–23,[9] in order to correct problems that had emerged in the application of the earlier laws. Deuteronomy continues to employ the forms of Assyrian suzerain-vassal treaties to depict YHWH as the suzerain monarch of Israel and Israel as the vassal of YHWH.[10] Key among Deuteronomy's concerns is the interest in giving greater rights to the poor farming classes known as the *'am-ha'aretz* or the people of the land—the very constituency that placed Josiah on the throne following the assassination of his father, Judah's King Amon ben Manasseh (who ruled 642–640 BCE).[11] The instructions in Deuteronomy paid particular attention to addressing the rights and needs of women because they were a major element of the poor.[12] Deuteronomy also called upon the people to support the Levites, who were not entitled to own land. Deuteronomy functions as the introduction to the Deuteronomistic History, or Former Prophets, in

Joshua, Judges, Samuel, and Kings, insofar as it lays out the theological foundations of the covenant between YHWH and Israel that is featured throughout the history.[13]

II

The account of Moses's first speech to Israel in Deut 1:1–4:43 constitutes an exhortational summary of Israel's journey from Mount Horeb (the alternative name for Mount Sinai in D) through the wilderness. Moses's summation of the journey reminds the people of YHWH's role in leading Israel to the promised land and sustaining them in the wilderness. The account of Moses's first speech begins with a narrative introduction in Deut 1:1-5, which states the location and the date of Moses's speech together with the speech itself in Deut 1:6–4:40, which includes the historical review in Deut 1:6–3:29 and the exhortation to observe YHWH's instruction in Deut 4:1-40. The narrative concludes with an account in Deut 4:41-43 of Moses's actions in which he incorporates the Transjordan into the administrative and judicial structure of the land of Israel. The synchronic literary structure of the account appears as follows:

The Account of Moses's First Speech to Israel: Exhortational Summary of Israel's Journey from Horeb/Sinai to Moab	Deut 1:1–4:43
I. The Account of Moses's Speech	1:1–4:40
A. Narrative Introduction: Place and Date of Speech	1:1-5
B. Moses's Speech Proper	1:6–4:40
1. Historical Review of Israel's Journey from Horeb to Moab	1:6–3:29
2. Exhortation to Observe YHWH's Torah	4:1-40
II. The Account of Moses's Actions Following the Speech: Establishment of Cities of Refuge in the Transjordan	4:41-43

The introduction to Moses's first speech in Deut 1:1-5 identifies the location and date of Moses's speech. The location is identified as "the other side of the Jordan" in Moab. This statement prompted the medieval Spanish Rabbinic commentator, R. Abraham Ibn Ezra (1089–1167 CE), to recognize that the narrative framework could not have been written by Moses. This statement presupposes a perspective from a writer who was situated inside the land of Israel rather than Moses, who never entered the land of Israel during his lifetime. The reference to the fortieth year since the departure from Horeb/Sinai highlights the conflict between Israel and YHWH in the wilderness that called for a forty-year journey so that the entire slave generation would die in the wilderness prior to entry into Israel (Num 13–14). The use of the term *be'er*, "to expound, to make plain," to describe Moses's presentation of the Torah to Israel emphasizes the role of the Levites in teaching and explaining YHWH's Torah (cf. Lev 10:10-11).

The account of Moses's speech in Deut 1:6–4:40 begins with the historical review in Deut 1:6–3:29 in which Moses recounts Israel's forty-year journey from Mount Horeb to Moab where the people will prepare to enter the land of Israel. The historical review emphasizes a combination of YHWH's acts of mercy on behalf of Israel in the wilderness and Israel's complaints against YHWH and Moses that led to YHWH's decision to kill off the wilderness generation. Deuteronomy thereby offers a theodicy, that is, it asserts that YHWH is present, powerful, righteous, and merciful. Israel's suffering is not due to YHWH's absence, weakness, immorality, or unwillingness to protect Israel as many might claim in a time of disaster. Rather, Israel's rebellion causes YHWH to inflict judgment as a means to bring Israel in line with YHWH's expectations. In short, Deuteronomy defends YHWH against charges of neglect, absence, impotence, and immorality in a time of disaster for Israel by charging that Israel is to blame for its own suffering. This theological viewpoint is deeply questioned in the aftermath of the Shoah (Holocaust) in which six million Jews were murdered during World War II, not because they had sinned against G-d but because they were Jewish.[14]

The historical review begins with instances of tension or rebellion within Israel. For example, it refers to the need to appoint judges (chieftains) to resolve problems within Israel. It also refers to Israel's refusal to enter Canaan despite YHWH's promises of well-being; the people's refusal is based on the reports brought back by the spies who searched out the land and reported that the Canaanites were too powerful for Israel to overcome. Such lack of confidence in YHWH in turn prompted YHWH's decision to kill off the wilderness generation before they could enter the land. But the review also turns to YHWH's acts of mercy and protection for Israel during the wilderness journey, such as the journey through Edom and Moab where YHWH protected the people from attacks by the various kings of the region.

The portrayal of YHWH's mercy and judgment prepares the reader for the exhortational material in Deut 4:1-40. This portion of Moses's speech emphasizes the experience of divine revelation at Mount Horeb/Sinai in which YHWH revealed the Torah to Israel in order to provide the social and legal foundations for Israel's life in the land. The exhortational speech combines warnings of punishment for failure to observe YHWH's Torah and promises of divine compassion in response to the observance of the Torah.

Finally, the narrative account in Deut 4:41-43 of Moses's establishment of three cities of refuge in the Transjordan formally binds the Transjordan into the administrative structure of Israel. Such an account emphasizes that the Transjordan is indeed a part of Israel. Historically, it would counter claims by Aram to the land and support the efforts of King Josiah to reestablish Davidic rule over the Transjordan as well as the rest of the former northern kingdom of Israel.

III

The account of Moses's second speech, in Deut 4:44–26:19, is the longest of his four speeches to Israel, and it presents the fundamental core of legal instruction to Israel in the book of Deuteronomy. It is formulated as a levitical sermon or instruction speech that presents YHWH's Torah in detail and attempts to persuade the people to observe it. We have already noted that it does not simply repeat the earlier legal instruction of Exodus–Numbers; instead, it reflects upon, develops, reformulates, and specifies the earlier material to provide a basis for both the relationship between YHWH and Israel and the foundations for a holy, just, and viable society in the land of Israel. Many interpreters view Moses's second speech, which includes the law code in Deut 12–26, as the original core of Deuteronomy found in King Josiah's renovation of the Jerusalem temple (2 Kgs 22–23).[15]

The account begins in Deut 4:44-49 with a brief introduction that identifies the following material as the Torah, or instruction, that Moses presents to Israel, the location of Moses's speech at Beth-peor in Moab, and the circumstances of the journey from Egypt to Moab. The emphasis given to the Transjordan aids in claiming the region as part of the land of Israel. Such a claim is especially important in the aftermath of Aramean attempts to seize the Transjordan in the late ninth and early eighth centuries BCE as well as King Josiah's attempts to extend Davidic rule over the Transjordan in the late seventh century BCE.

The account of the speech proper appears in Deut 5:1–26:19. After the speech formula in Deut $5{:}1a\alpha^{1\text{-}2}$, the speech follows in Deut $5{:}1a\alpha^{3\text{-}6}$–26:19. The speech includes two major portions: the introductory exhortation to observe YHWH's Torah, in Deut $5{:}1a\alpha^{3\text{-}6}$–11:32, and the instruction proper, in Deut 12:1–26:19, which lays out the statutes and cases to be observed.

Moses's introductory exhortation in Deut $5{:}1a\alpha^{3\text{-}6}$–11:32 is an elaborate sermon that is designed to persuade the Israelites and its reading audience to observe YHWH's Torah:

- It identifies YHWH as Israel's G-d, benefactor, and partner in a covenant relationship.
- It states the basic ideal principles that are articulated throughout the Deuteronomic Torah (Deut $5{:}1a\alpha^{3\text{-}6}$-30).
- It clearly states that loyalty to YHWH alone as G-d is an absolute requirement of the covenant relationship (Deut 6:1-25).
- It warns of the consequences to be suffered by the people should they engage in actions that would compromise their loyalty to YHWH, such as intermarriage with the pagan peoples of the land and adherence to other gods (Deut 7:1-11).

- It reminds the people that YHWH provides the benefits of living in the land (Deut 7:12–8:20)
- It reminds the people that their choice by YHWH to live in the land is not due to any special merit on their part, as their rebellions in the wilderness amply illustrate (Deut 9:1–10:11).
- It concludes with a renewed call to observe YHWH's Torah with clear reminders of YHWH's actions on behalf of Israel, YHWH's promises to the ancestors of Israel, the benefits to be enjoyed by observing YHWH's Torah, and the curses to be suffered should Israel fail to observe YHWH's Torah (Deut 10:12–11:32).

The formal literary structure of Moses's introductory exhortation appears as follows:

I. Moses's Introductory Exhortation to Observe YHWH's Torah	Deut 5:1a$\alpha^{3\text{-}6}$–11:32
A. Exposition of the Ideal Principles Underlying YHWH's Torah	5:1a$\alpha^{3\text{-}6}$-30
B. Exhortation to Observe YHWH's Torah	6:1–11:32
1. Requirement of Absolute Loyalty to YHWH as Sole G-d	6:1-25
2. Consequences of Failure to Show Loyalty to YHWH	7:1-11
3. Benefits of Living in the Land Provided by YHWH	7:12–8:20
4. Choice by YHWH Not Due to Special Merit	9:1–10:11
5. Renewed Call to Observe YHWH's Torah	10:12–11:32

The exposition of the ideal principles underlying YHWH's Torah in Deut 5:1a$\alpha^{3\text{-}6}$-30 begins once again with a presentation of the Ten Commandments from Exod 20 in modified form. The passage makes it clear that these principles are the essential core of YHWH's expectations of Israel in its covenant relationship with YHWH and that they were conveyed directly to Moses face-to-face at Mount Horeb (Sinai).[16] As we saw in the discussion of Exod 20 above, the Ten Commandments cannot be considered as law per se, insofar as they cannot be adjudicated in a court of law due to the absence of any means to correct or resolve the violations that they address. Rather, their instructive and imperative or prohibitive forms require that they be understood as statements of the basic principles that underlie the specific statutes and cases that appear in the Deuteronomic Torah.

The sequence of the instructions in Deut 5 is basically the same as that in Exod 20, but individual instances differ due to the specific concerns of Deuteronomy over against Exodus. Deuteronomy 5:6 identifies YHWH as Israel's one and only G-d who brought the nation out of Egyptian bondage. Deuteronomy 5:7-10 prohibits the worship of other gods and the making of any images of the gods. Deuteronomy 5:11 prohibits making false solemn pledges in the name of YHWH. Deuteronomy 5:12-15 calls upon the people to observe the Shabbat, but this command differs slightly from Exod 20:8-11, which calls upon Israel to "remember" the Shabbat. The difference is crucial in understanding the distinctive theological viewpoints of Deuteronomy and Exodus. The Deuteronomic version represents a stronger statement of action, but it also provides a different rationale. Whereas Exod 20:8-11 explains the basis of the command as YHWH's role as creator of the world in six days, Deut 5:12-15 explains it as a result of YHWH's role as deliverer of Israel from Egyptian slavery. Deuteronomy 5:12-15 also extends the command for Shabbat observance to the animals of the household as well as to the humans mentioned in Exod 20:8-11. Deuteronomy 5:16 commands the people to honor their parents, which plays a role in ensuring social stability through family structure in ancient Israelite and Judean society. Deuteronomy 5:17 presents the prohibitions against murder,[17] adultery, theft, and false witness against a neighbor. Deuteronomy 5:18 prohibits coveting a neighbor's house, wife, slaves, animals, and possessions. The following statements make it clear that the Ten Commandments were spoken publically to Israel at Horeb but that Moses remained behind to receive the entire body of legal statutes and cases that comprise YHWH's Torah revealed at Mount Horeb/Sinai.

The rest of Moses's exhortation in Deut 6:1–11:32 turns to the exhortation per se.

The requirement of absolute loyalty to YHWH is a fundamental condition of the covenant relationship between YHWH and Israel. Deuteronomy 6:4-5 constitutes the basic statement of the Shema, that is, "Hear (Heb., *shema*) O Israel, the L-rd is our G-d, the L-rd is One." The Shema is the fundamental statement of Jewish adherence to YHWH as sole G-d, which is read as an essential element of every Jewish worship service and which is expected to be the last statement that a Jew speaks prior to death. Verses 6-9 are also read as part of the Shema in the Jewish worship service together with Deut 11:13-21 and Num 15:37-41. Traditional Jews pray daily with tefillin, small pouches containing miniature manuscripts of the Shema affixed to the head and arm in keeping with the commandments in Deut 6:6-9. Ancient tefillin were found at Qumran together with the Dead Sea Scrolls in the second century BCE, and silver amulets with the Shema inscribed upon them to be affixed to the doorposts (mezuzah) of houses are known from as early as the seventh and sixth centuries BCE. Such amulets function in Jewish tradition as a means to establish the sanctity of the home.

Deuteronomy 7:1-11 turns to the consequences of Israel's failure to show full and unconditional loyalty to YHWH by worshipping other gods. This concern is expressed through a prohibition against intermarriage with seven nations that once lived in the land of Canaan. The rationale for such a prohibition is the concern that these nations would lead Israel to abandon YHWH by engaging in the worship of foreign gods. Deuteronomy envisions that *gerim*, "resident aliens" (or "immigrants") might also join Israel in the land. The *gerim* are understood in Rabbinic tradition to be converts to Judaism.

Deuteronomy 7:12–8:20 focuses on the benefits of living in the land provided by YHWH, and it therefore begins with statements of blessing that will follow from adherence to YHWH's Torah. YHWH's role as creator comes forward as the blessings include agricultural abundance, fertility in herd and flock, the birth of children, and the absence of illness. YHWH's role as deliverer of Israel also comes into play as the text emphasizes that YHWH will protect Israel from enemies, just as YHWH delivered Israel from the Egyptians.

Deuteronomy 9:1–10:11 focuses on the question of Israel's status as chosen people of YHWH. Moses's speech makes it very clear that YHWH did not choose Israel as a result of any special merit of the people. Indeed, his rehearsal of the bitter conflicts between YHWH and Israel in the wilderness demonstrates that Israel lacks any special merit. Modern readers must again observe that such a portrayal of Israel is an expression of theodicy, that is, an attempt to protect the moral integrity and power of YHWH by charging that the people—and not YHWH—were at fault when they suffer reversal. Insofar as YHWH's commitment to the covenant with Israel's ancestors would come into question, Moses's speech stresses that YHWH's commitment to the solemn pledge sworn to Abraham, Isaac, and Jacob explains YHWH's decision to bring the people into the promised land of Israel and not to destroy them in the wilderness.

Finally, Deut 10:12–11:32 concludes Moses's exhortation with a renewed call to observe YHWH's Torah. Moses now comes to the major point, that is, the attempt to persuade the people (and the readers of the text) to observe YHWH's Torah and thereby to uphold the covenant that brings them into the promised land of Israel. Including the references to Mount Gerizim and Mount Ebal, the passage anticipates the blessings and curses that appear following the exposition of Deuteronomic Torah in Moses's third and fourth speeches, in Deut 27:1–28:69 and 29:1–30:20.

Moses's exhortation speech shows striking affinities with the preambles of Assyrian vassal treaties from the eighth and seventh centuries BCE, in which the Assyrian monarch states the expectations that his vassal must observe, generally in the form of commands and prohibitions like those of the Ten Commandments. The Assyrian king thereby attempts to persuade the vassal monarch to accept the terms of the treaty by pointing to the benefits of acceptance and the consequences of refusal.[18] Such treaties were well-known to Judah and Israel in the eighth and seventh centuries

BCE and played an influential role in Deuteronomy and other literary works that portray YHWH as a suzerain deity who enters into a relationship with the vassal people Israel.[19] Such a rhetorical strategy enabled ancient Judah to think of YHWH as a monarch more powerful than the Assyrian—and later Babylonian and Persian—monarchs. Such a strategy enabled ancient Judah to view YHWH as the ultimate monarch of the universe.

IV

The account of Moses's Torah, or instruction speech proper, in Deut 12:1–26:19 presents the statutes and cases that constitute YHWH's Torah in Deuteronomy. Most interpreters believe that this law code contains the original core of Deuteronomy that was discovered in Josiah's temple renovation.[20] The account begins with a superscription in Deut 12:1 that identifies the following material in Deut 2:2–26:19 as *hakhuqqim*, "the statutes," and *hammishpatim*, "the (legal) cases," in YHWH's Torah. The distinction between "the statutes" and "the cases" is crucial for understanding the generic character and organization of Deut 12:2–26:19 as legal instruction. "The statutes" refer to those legal paragraphs that include commands and prohibitions concerning specific actions that Israel might undertake. Although such commands and prohibitions appear frequently in biblical law, more recent scholarship recognizes that such statements do not constitute law at all because they cannot be adjudicated in a court of law. Such statutes or apodictic "laws" therefore constitute statements of legal principle that underlie and inform the Israelite law codes, which are in turn designed to implement those principles in actual court settings. "The cases," however, do constitute laws that can be adjudicated in court insofar as they begin by positing a hypothetical set of circumstances, generally beginning with a circumstantial clause introduced by *'im*, "if"; *ki*, "when/if"; *'asher*, "when," and so on, that is followed by statement as to how the case is to be resolved. Such legal paragraphs have been identified in modern scholarship as "casuistic laws" or "case laws," insofar as they state a set of circumstances together with a statement of resolution. Interpreters have noted for over two thousand years that the laws of the Bible cannot possibly constitute a comprehensive catalog of every legal case that might arise in Israelite/Judean society. But the work of J. J. Finkelstein on the goring-ox laws of the Bible and the Mesopotamian law codes demonstrates that the legal paragraphs in biblical law must be understood as examples of the resolution of legal cases. Each case law states a set of facts and a resolution for the case, but the facts may vary in any given case that might come before a court. The court judge or judges would have to study the legal precedent stated in the case law, take account of any variables in the circumstances of the court case at hand, determine the legal principle that applies to the case at hand, and then come to a decision concerning the means to resolve the case. The same presuppositions and procedures apply in contemporary American law from the local courts all the way to the U.S. Supreme Court. Such a model apparently explains the functions of both ancient Near Eastern and biblical law codes in general as well as the origins of the

Rabbinic concept of oral Torah, in which a case had to be studied in order to apply it to different and newer sets of circumstances, thereby revealing the divine intent or oral Torah that is inherent in the specific case of written Torah. In this manner, Rabbinic law determines how to ensure that justice is done in Jewish society.

Study of the interrelationship between the statutes and cases of Deuteronomic Torah indicates that the Deuteronomic Torah is organized according to a pattern of initial "statutes" that state the fundamental legal theme or principle, followed by a series of "cases" that takes up the same legal theme or principle and applies it to the resolution of selected legal cases. As we have seen in the structure of Deut 12–26, these concerns include an initial section concerning Israel's and Judah's religious differentiation from the nations in Deut 12:2–13:9, followed by a detailed discussion of specific legal instruction concerning Israel's or Judah's holy conduct in Deut 14:1–26:15. Following an introductory statement concerning the holiness of the people in Deut 14:1-2, the sixteen specific concerns addressed include: (1) the eating of meat (Deut 14:3-21); (2) tithes (Deut 14:22-29); (3) debt issues (Deut 15:1-18); (4) the offering of the oldest male child (Deut 15:19-23); (5) the observance of holidays (Deut 16:1-17); (6) judicial and political authority (Deut 16:18–17:20); (7) religious authority (Deut 18:1–19:13); (8) territorial and boundary issues (Deut 19:14–21:23); (9) treatment of what pertains to others (Deut 22:1-8); (10) mixing what does not belong together (Deut 22:9-29); (11) impurities (Deut 23:1-15); (12) improper transactions with human beings (Deut 23:16–24:5); (13) improper financial and lending transactions (Deut 24:6-13); (14) justice due to the poor (Deut 24:14–25:3); (15) rights to sustenance and continuation (Deut 25:4-12); and (16) the obligation to give what is due (Deut 25:13–26:15). A concluding exhortation to observe YHWH's Torah in Deut 26:16-19 closes Moses's speech.

A close reading of the Deuteronomic Torah indicates that many of the legal topics have been previously addressed in the law codes of Exodus–Numbers.[21] In many instances, the Deuteronomic instruction revises legal cases from earlier law codes in order to address problems or gaps that would have arisen in the earlier formulations of law. The Deuteronomic Torah demonstrates a heightened concern with the rights and welfare of the poor, particularly women, immigrants, and Levites. At the synchronic level, such revision and concern represent an attempt to present an unfolding of Israel's legal system by addressing the expanding circumstances and applications of legal instruction in relation to the earlier law codes, that is, statements in Deuteronomy would repeat earlier law to a certain extent, but they would also take up dimensions of a given law that were not made explicit in the earlier forms of law in Exodus–Numbers. At the diachronic level, such revision reflects the setting of the composition of Deuteronomic Torah in the court of Judah's King Josiah (who ruled 640–609 BCE), who was placed on the throne by "the people of the land," the farming class of ancient Judah, who put down a revolt against the house of David. The "people of the land" represented the poorer agricultural class that had to be rebuilt following the Assyrian invasions of Judah in the late eighth century BCE. Women, immigrants, and Levites would all have been important constituents of the lower economic echelons of ancient Judean society insofar as they were not able fully to own or control land which served as the economic basis for an agricultural society. The socioeconomic aspects of Josiah's reforms were meant to address the needs of these groups and thereby secure their support of the throne. Such efforts would be similar to the enactment of new laws in modern society that are designed to assist the needy or to redress obstacles and discrimination faced by disadvantaged racial, ethnic, gendered, and religious groups.

The initial subsection in Deut 12:2–13:19 focuses especially on Israel's/Judah's religious differentiation.[22] This subsection thereby establishes the foundations for the following topics addressed in the Deuteronomic Torah insofar as it portrays Israel/Judah as a distinctive people among the nations. The text begins with a series of statutes or commands in Deut 12:2-28 that command the destruction of foreign worship sites throughout the land (Deut 12:2-3), the prohibition against worshipping YHWH anywhere except for the one site where YHWH chooses to manifest the divine name or presence (Deut 12:4-7), the commands to bring all offerings to the one place where YHWH chooses to manifest the divine name or presence (Deut 12:8-16), the commands to eat all offerings in the one place where YHWH chooses to manifest the divine name or presence (Deut 12:17-27), and a concluding command to observe YHWH's commandments and not to follow in the practices of the foreign nations (Deut 12:28–13:1). The cases then follow in Deut 13:2-19, including instructions to adhere only to prophets of YHWH and to put foreign prophets to death (Deut 13:2-6), to put to death those who would lead the people into the worship of foreign gods (Deut 13:7-12), and to destroy any town in Israel that engages in the worship of foreign gods (Deut 13:13-19). Fundamentally, this subunit is concerned with the exclusive worship of YHWH in Israel/Judah, and it emphasizes that worship must be carried out only at the one sanctuary or temple site where YHWH chooses to manifest the divine name or presence. This overriding concern with cultic centralization differs from Exod 20:19-23, which calls for the worship of YHWH but allows for the building of altars in every place where YHWH's presence might be manifested. Synchronically, the enactment of Deuteronomy's law allows for only one temple site in Israelite religion, generally understood as a reference to the Jerusalem temple, although Jerusalem is never mentioned. Diachronically, it points to Josiah's concern to centralize worship in Jerusalem in contrast to northern Israel, which permitted multiple sanctuaries.

Deuteronomy 14:1-2 introduces the paragraphs concerned with the holy conduct of the people by instructing them to refrain from the foreign practices of gashing oneself or shaving the front of one's head, which were employed as mourning practices on behalf of the dead.

The first major legal paragraph, in Deut 14:3-21, takes up the eating of meat. This section appears only in the form of statutes or apodictic instruction that prohibits the eating of anything abhorrent. It then goes on to define those animals, fish, birds, and insects that may be eaten over against those that are unfit for human consumption (Deut 14:4-21). These instructions expand upon Exod 22:30, which prohibits the consumption of meat from animals that have been killed by beasts in the wild.

Deuteronomy 14:22-29 focuses on the requirement for the tithe in ancient Israel and Judah. The tithe is a form of income tax that calls for one-tenth of each Israelite's income to be presented as offerings at the sanctuary. The tithe is well-known in Israel from early times (see Gen 14:20; 28:22; 1 Sam 8:15, 17). Deuteronomy 14:22-29 updates and specifies the earlier law in Exod 22:28-29 that requires Israelites to bring offerings to the sanctuary without specifying any quantity or percentage, and Deut 14:22-29 states that such tithes are to support the poor, including the Levites, widows, and orphans (cf. Exod 23:10-11).

Deuteronomy 15:1-18 takes up debt issues. Deuteronomy 15:1-8 begins with statutes that call for the remission of debt in every seventh year (Deut 15:1-3) and that prohibit poverty among the people (Deut 15:4-6). Specific cases then follow, including the requirement to lend to the poor even when the seventh year of remission approaches (Deut 15:7-11) and specifications concerning the terms of service for debt slavery (Deut 15:12-18). The standard six-year term of service for debt slavery is already well-known in Exod 21:1-11, but Deut 15:12-18 corrects some of the problems inherent in the Exodus law by stipulating that the freed slave be granted a portion of the master's income to help ensure that he will not go back into debt. Deuteronomy 15:12-18 also requires that female slaves be freed on the same basis as male slaves, thereby providing greater incentive to a male slave who is married during the term of his service to choose to be freed as he will be able to leave with his wife.

Deuteronomy 15:19-23 discusses the offering of the oldest male offspring from herd and flock that are to be consecrated to YHWH. The basic statute appears in vv. 19-20, but the following case in vv. 21-23 stipulates that defective animals are not offered to YHWH but are to be slaughtered and eaten in the villages and towns. This statute differs from earlier cases in Exod 13:1-2, 11-16; 22:28-29; and 34:19-20, which call for the offering of the firstborn to YHWH. The Deuteronomic instruction allows the people living in the countryside to keep and eat a greater share of their herds and flocks.

Deuteronomy 16:1-17 focuses on observance of the three major pilgrimage festivals in ancient Israel in which all males are to appear at the sanctuary to make the offerings required for each festival.[23] The pilgrimage festivals include Pesach (Passover), Shavuot (Weeks), and Succoth (Booths). This section provides detailed instruction concerning the observance of each festival, thereby elaborating and expanding upon Exod 23:14-18; 34:18-26.

Deuteronomy 16:18–17:20 focuses on the questions of judicial and political authority in ancient Israel, including the appointment of judges and tribal officials as well as the selection of a king.[24] The statutes that appear in Deut 16:18–17:2, which command the appointment of judges and tribal officials, call for the practice of justice in all judicial proceedings, forbid the installation of *'asherot* (sacred posts) or *matzevot* (sacred pillars) that are identified with Canaanite religious practice, and prohibit the sacrifice of defective animals at the altar. The case laws appear in Deut

17:2-20, which define the judicial procedure for executing someone who commits religious apostasy, call for the submission of difficult cases to the Levites and judges, and define the procedure and qualifications for selecting a king in Israel. This section systematizes and clarifies procedures for the appointment of judges in Exod 18 and the various judicial instructions in Exod 23:1-3, 6-9, 13.

Deuteronomy 18:1–19:13 deals with the questions of religious authority in ancient Israel and Judah, particularly the rights and responsibilities of the Levites and the prophets. Apodictic instruction or statutes appear in Deut 18:1-5 and stipulate that the Levites will possess no land in Israel, but they will instead be supported by offerings from the people. The cases appear in Deut 18:6–19:13, which enable the Levites to live in the central sanctuary of the land, call for the appointment of prophets to speak on behalf of YHWH, and institute cities of refuge where someone who commits manslaughter may flee for protection from blood vengeance by the family of the victim. The instructions concerning YHWH's prophets indicate that the criterion for identifying a true prophet of YHWH is whether or not the prophet's words will come to pass. Such a principle apparently provides effective criteria when the prophet's words are fulfilled in a short period of time, but it poses problems when the prophet's words are not fulfilled for longer periods, such as years, centuries, and even millennia. The role of the Levites presupposes the narratives of Num 17–18, which identify the Levites as the priestly tribe and defines their ritual rites and responsibilities.[25] Likewise, the question of the prophets presupposes Num 11, in which all of the elders of Israel prophesy.[26] The prohibition of Canaanite practice presupposes Exod 23:24; 34:11-16. Numbers 35:9-34 provides detailed discussion of cities of refuge and the treatment of those who commit manslaughter.

Deuteronomy 19:14–21:23 focuses on questions related to territorial boundaries and judicial oaths. The apodictic instructions appear in Deut 19:14-15, including the prohibition against moving territorial boundary markers and the requirement that two witnesses are necessary to convict an accused person in a court of law. The statutes include a statement of the *lex talionis* (cf. Exod 21:23-25; Lev 24:17-21). The cases then follow in Deut 19:16–21:23, including procedures for trying a case in court and engaging in war. Instruction concerning the procedure for war includes the role of the priests in blessing the army, the question of those who might be exempt from military service, instructions concerning the acceptance of surrender, instructions concerning the need to destroy a town that does not surrender, the treatment and use of trees in an enemy nation, procedures for making decisions concerning the discovery of a corpse in the land, instructions concerning the marriage of Israelite men to captive foreign women, the designation of a man's legal heirs, the treatment of a defiant son, and the disposition of the body of a man executed for a capital offense. In addition to the alternative versions of the *lex talionis* mentioned above, this section elaborates and expands upon laws concerned with warfare in Exod 23:23-33; 34:11-16; and Num 34:50-56; questions of murder and corpse contamination in Num 35:16-24; and questions not treated in the earlier law codes.

Deuteronomy 22:1-8 focuses on the treatment of property and social relationships or boundaries, that is, what pertains to others. The section begins with statutes in vv. 1-5 which present instruction concerning the return of a neighbor's ox, ass, garment, or other property and a prohibition against cross-dressing. These instructions develop and expand upon earlier instruction concerning the return of property in Exod 23:4. The cases in vv. 6-8 prohibit the taking of a mother bird together with her eggs, since the parent and offspring should not die together, and the requirement to build a parapet on the roof of a house to prevent fatal accidents. The case of the birds echoes the concern with boiling a kid in its mother's milk in Exod 23:19; 34:26 (cf. Lev 22:28). The concern with personal liability takes up Exod 22:28-36.

Deuteronomy 22:9-29 focuses on the prohibition against mixing things that do not belong together, which pertains to issues of agriculture, clothing, social identity, and marital relations. The statutes in vv. 9-12 take up various concerns, including the mixing of seed in a field, plowing with an ox and an ass together, wearing clothing made of mixed fiber, and the instruction to affix tassels on a garment to identify oneself as an Israelite. Such instructions are likely intended to protect against diluting agricultural produce with a cheaper seed, protecting animals with very different capabilities, and diluting clothing with cheaper fabric. The principle extends to social identity, insofar as v. 12 calls for distinctive clothing for Judeans. Tassels were known to be worn by monarchs and other members of higher social classes in the ancient Near Eastern world, and the fringe of a garment often functioned as an indication of legal signature, that is, in ancient Mesopotamian practice, one might send a piece of the fringe from one's garment to verify the signature. The following cases then extend the principle into cases of sexual relations, including the protection of a newly married woman against charges of promiscuity, the condemnation of adulterers, and the treatment of unmarried women who have relations with a man. These cases are designed to protect the woman in question if she does not consent to relations with the man. If she is raped by a man, the requirement that he marry her without the possibility of divorce is designed to ensure her economic support for life. The earlier law in Exod 22:15-16 required that the man marry her or at least pay the bride price, but it did not protect her from subsequent divorce.

Deuteronomy 23:1-15 develops the concern of the previous section by delving more deeply into forbidden mixing or social relations of various types. The statutes in vv. 1-9 prohibit marriage to the wife of one's father and prohibit the entry into the congregation of Israel of various classes of persons who would worship in the sanctuary. Those prohibited include those with damaged reproductive organs rendering them unable to father children, persons born of prohibited marriages (for example, incest), and Ammonites and Moabites because of their past treatment of Israel in the wilderness period. Descendants of the Edomites and the Egyptians are permitted, however, presumably due to Edom's status as descendants of Jacob's brother Esau and Egypt's status as a source for the mixed multitude that accompanied Israel through the wilderness. The case in vv. 10-15 takes up issues of purity in a military camp.

Deuteronomy 23:16–24:5 extends the concern for mixing what does not belong together by focusing on the questions of improper transactions between human beings. The statutes in vv. 16-21 include prohibitions against turning over an escaped slave who seeks refuge, prohibitions against working at sacred shrines to other deities, the use of income derived from prostitution, and prohibitions against charging interest to fellow Israelites or Judeans. The cases in Deut 23:22–24:5 call for the fulfillment of solemn promises, eating of produce in a fellow Israelite's or Judean's vineyard or field (but harvest is not allowed), and a ban on remarrying a former wife after she has married another man. Such laws protect the poor and women, that is, Israelites are given privileges that will carry them through times of need, and women are protected from abuse in fraudulent marriage schemes concocted by their husbands.

Deuteronomy 24:6-13 takes up improper financial transactions. The statutes in v. 6 forbid taking hand mills and upper millstones in pawn because the implements necessary for grinding grain are essential for the preparation of food. The cases in vv. 7-13 call for a death penalty for kidnappers, special care in the treatment of skin disease, and the proper treatment of items given in pledge for a loan. All of these cases are concerned with the sustainability of life on behalf of the poor and develop and expand upon principles stated in Exod 22:24-26.

Deuteronomy 24:14–25:3 focuses on justice for the poor. The statutes in vv. 14-18 include prohibitions against abusing the poor, holding parents and children accountable for each other's deeds, and subverting the rights of foreigners, orphans, and widows. The cases call for agricultural practice that will leave food for the poor at harvest time, and they stipulate limits on punishment to be rendered in legal disputes. This section develops Exod 21:16; 22:20-26.

Deuteronomy 25:4-12 takes up concerns with the sustainability of life. The statute in v. 4 prohibits muzzling a threshing ox, so that the ox can eat and sustain itself while working. The following cases develop this principle by calling for a levirate marriage procedure by which the brother (or other male relative; for example, Ruth's marriage to Boaz) of a man who dies childless will father a child with the widow to ensure the continuity of the dead man's house and name. Likewise, a woman who tries to crush the genitals of an opponent loses her hand because her act threatens the future descendants of the man so affected.

Deuteronomy 25:13–26:15 takes up obligations to give what is due. The statutes in vv. 13-19 call for the use of just weights for calculating measures in financial transactions, and they remind the reader of Amalek's attempts to destroy Israel when it was defenseless. The case in Deut 26:1-15 calls for the presentation of tithes due to YHWH as obligatory offerings at the sanctuary, given in return for YHWH's grant of land to Israel. The case develops the obligation to bring offerings previously discussed in Exod 23:14-19; 34:18-26; and Deut 16:1-17, and it specifically notes that the tithe will help to support Levites, foreigners, orphans, and widows.

Finally, Deut 26:16-19 presents a concluding exhortation that persuades the people to observe YHWH's Torah in order to ensure Israel's status as a holy nation before YHWH.

V

Deuteronomy 27:1–28:69 presents the account of Moses's third speech to Israel prior to the nation's entry into the promised land. Moses now turns to the blessings and curses that will depend upon Israel's observance of YHWH's instructions. It emphasizes the curses of agricultural failure, invasion by foreign enemies, exile, and even the plagues visited on Egypt that will follow should Israel choose not to observe divine Torah. But the curses work together with the blessings and the portrayal of possible repentance and return from exile in the following account of Moses's fourth speech (Deut 29:1–30:20).

The result is a text that addresses the question of theodicy insofar as it attempts to account for both the realities of Israel's suffering due to foreign invasion by various enemies (e.g., the Egyptians, Arameans, Assyrians, Babylonians) and the possibilities of Israel's restoration in the aftermath of calamity. YHWH appears as a G-d who is capable of both justice and judgment and mercy (cf. Exod 34:6-7). Deuteronomy holds that YHWH is a moral deity whose morality calls for the punishment of YHWH's own people when they purportedly do wrong and for the blessing of the people when they purportedly do what is right.

But such a model of divine morality also raises problems. Insofar as the model presupposes that the experience of evil is necessarily rooted in the presumption of human wrongdoing and that the experience of blessing is likewise necessarily rooted in the presumption of human righteousness, it ultimately produces a model in which the victims of evil are charged with having committed some great sin that prompted the judgment realized against them. The problems with such a model of divine moral causation have become apparent in modern theological discussion of the Shoah, or Holocaust, in which theologians have come to recognize that the Shoah cannot be explained adequately—or even at all—as the result of Jewish wrongdoing, but the Shoah must be explained as the result of decisions made by the perpetrators of such murders, i.e., the Nazi government of Germany and its supporters in Europe and beyond. The Bible as a whole is also aware of this problem, for example, when Esther postulates a scenario of destruction in which YHWH is absent and when Job posits a scenario in which YHWH's morality comes into question.[27] Deuteronomy emerges as one portrayal of divine power and morality among the various portrayals offered throughout the books of the Bible.

When considered diachronically, Deut 27–28 clearly presupposes covenant or treaty making in the ancient Near Eastern world, particularly by the Neo-Assyrian empire. The Assyrian king appears as the suzerain monarch and the subject king as the vassal who must observe the suzerain's requirements in such treaties which call for blessings should the vassal obey and threaten punishment should the vassal fail to observe the suzerain's terms. YHWH here plays the role of suzerain, and Israel plays the role of a vassal subject to YHWH's requirements. King Josiah's conceptualization of Israel's relationship with YHWH, sovereign deity of all creation and humankind, would reflect its experience as a vassal of the Assyrian empire during the late eighth and seventh centuries BCE.

A particular problem in diachronic scholarship appears in the portrayal of the covenant cursing ceremony at Mount Ebal and Mount Gerizim in Deut 27. The chapter portrays the site of Shechem in central Israel, but Moses never entered the land of Israel, much less traveled to Shechem. The text very carefully portrays Moses as calling upon the people to perform this ceremony once they have taken possession of the land. The significance of this act must be traced to the role that Shechem plays in Israel's early history. Shechem is the site where the major north-south and east-west crossroads come together in northern Israel.[28] It also sits on the boundary of Ephraim and Manasseh, the two tribes that constitute the core of the northern kingdom of Israel. Shechem appears in biblical texts as a site where Israel comes together to undertake major actions and to make major decisions, such as the sealing of the covenant by Joshua in Josh 8:30-35; 24; the attempt to seize kingship in Israel by Abimelech in Judg 9; and the decision to reject the house of David and select Jeroboam ben Nebat as the first king of northern Israel in 1 Kgs 12. By placing the covenant cursing ceremony in Shechem, Deuteronomy deliberately appeals to the former northern kingdom of Israel to accept that its destruction by Assyria in 722–721 BCE was the result of YHWH's judgment for Israel's failure to observe divine Torah (cf. 2 Kgs 17).

VI

Deuteronomy 29:1–30:20 presents Moses's final exhortation to Israel on the plains of Moab to observe YHWH's Torah as the basis for its relationship with YHWH and its life in the land of Israel. Moses rehearses Israel's history, including elements of its journey through the wilderness as well as YHWH's promises to the ancestors and the exodus from Egypt. It is somewhat of a piecemeal history that hits many of the high points of YHWH's actions on behalf of Israel in an effort to remind Israel of the benefits of its relationship with YHWH.

Nevertheless, this speech presupposes the scenario of punishment laid out in the previous section and builds on that section by presenting a scenario for a future after punishment and exile, that is, the possibility that Israel might repent from wrongdoing and return to the land of Israel from foreign exile. Moses's fourth speech ultimately holds out the possibilities of repentance and restoration as a means to convince its audience that they should choose to observe divine Torah even in the aftermath of exile.[29]

Deuteronomy 29–30 presumes that wrongdoing on the part of Israel explains national disaster and observance of YHWH's Torah explains blessing and restoration. Such contentions are clearly challenged by the experience of the Shoah in modern times, namely, such a murderous event does not take place because the victim Israel brought suffering on itself by refusing to observe Torah but because a nation such as Germany chose to attack Jews to serve its own anti-Semitic understanding of the world. The situation is analogous to rape, that is, women and men are not raped because they deserve it; they are raped because the rapist choses to perpetrate a crime.

The emphasis on repentance and return from exile could serve the interests of the Josianic restoration, insofar as it attempts to convince northern Israelites to return to YHWH, the Jerusalem temple, and YHWH's anointed Davidic monarch in Josiah's Judah. Deuteronomy 29–30 may also be read in relation to the later Babylonian exile to provide a theological basis for YHWH's decision to restore Israel/Judah following the exile.

VII

Deuteronomy 31–34 closes both Deuteronomy and the Pentateuch as a whole with an account of Moses's death and burial, together with provisions for the transfer of leadership to Joshua and the promulgation of YHWH's Torah. The literary structure of this section appears as follows:

The Account of Moses's Transfer of Leadership to Joshua, Torah to the Levites, and Death and Burial in Moab	Deut 31:1–34:12
I. Moses's Provisions for Transfer of Leadership to Joshua and Torah to the Levites	31:1-13
II. YHWH's Provisions for Transfer of Leadership to Joshua and Torah to the Levites	31:14–32:47
III. Moses's Preparations for Death: Blessing for Israel	32:48–33:29
IV. Moses's Death and Burial	34:1-12

The account begins in Deut 31:1-13 with Moses's announcement to Israel that he is old and that YHWH has appointed Joshua ben Nun to serve as his successor as leader of the nation. Moses's charge to Joshua likewise stresses that YHWH will go before Israel into the land based on the promises made to the ancestors. Moses's writing of the Torah points to the traditional understanding that Torah is transmitted from YHWH to Israel through Moses, and his handing the Torah to the Levites ensures that the Levites will serve as the primary agents by which Torah is taught to Israel. Thus, Moses's leadership functions are divided insofar as Joshua, a man from the tribe of Ephraim, takes on the administrative and military role, like that of the kings of Israel, and the Levites take on the religious role, anticipating their function in the future temple. The selection of the Ephraimite Joshua as Moses's successor both coincides with earlier EJ tradition (see Num 13–14; 27:12-23) and provides a basis to appeal to former northern Israelites to identity with Deuteronomy's agenda. The instruction to read Torah before the people every seventh year, that is, the year of remission (Deut 15:1-11), at the Festival of Succoth, puts into place the liturgical structure by which this task is to be accomplished.

Deuteronomy 31:14–32:47 shifts to YHWH's provisions for the transfer of leadership to Joshua and the responsibility for teaching Torah to the Levites. YHWH's speech to Moses confirms the selection of Joshua as Moses's successor, but it also provides a rationale for the teaching of Torah by anticipating Israel's apostasy against YHWH. Such a statement is remarkable insofar as it once again offers a theodicy, namely, despite YHWH's roles as the author of creation and the master of human events, it asserts that the people will suffer because they will fail to adhere to YHWH or to observe YHWH's Torah. Such an assertion is designed to explain suffering even though Israel's G-d is the ultimate power in the universe who has made unconditional promises to Israel's ancestors.

The concern with Israel's suffering then explains Moses's writing of the Song of Moses in Deut 32:1-43 to rehearse YHWH's relationship with the people of Israel. Many modern interpreters assert that the song is based on the covenant lawsuit analogy employed by the prophets to portray YHWH's charges of apostasy against the people.[30] The poem takes up the themes of divine justice and mercy together with YHWH's roles as author of creation and deliverer of Israel. It asserts divine fidelity at the outset and calls upon its audience to remember YHWH's acts on behalf of Israel, particularly granting Jacob the land of Israel, from the beginning. But the poem explains Israel's setbacks by arguing that Israel/Jeshurun abandoned YHWH when it became fat and prosperous, which in turn provoked YHWH's anger and punishment. After asserting that YHWH will hide the divine presence from Israel, the poem turns to YHWH's decision to demonstrate fidelity to Israel and take vengeance against its/YHWH's enemies. The account concludes with statements of Joshua's/Hoshea's recitation of the words to the people and Moses's exhortation to the people to observe YHWH's words. The Song of Moses summarizes the theology of Deuteronomy and accounts for evil by asserting that it comes when the people abandon YHWH.

Although many argue that the Song of Moses presupposes the Babylonian exile, the reference to Hoshea ben Nun in Deut 32:44 suggests that the poem comes from a northern Israelite setting (see Num 13:8, 16, and the discussion of provenance there). The song just as easily addresses the problem of evil provoked by the collapse of the northern kingdom of Israel.

Deuteronomy 32:48–33:29 conveys Moses's preparations for death, including the blessing of Moses for the tribes of Israel. The account begins with YHWH's command to Moses to ascend Mount Nebo in Moab overlooking the Jordan River and the land of Israel, and it reiterates YHWH's decision that Moses would not enter the land due to his travesty at Meribath-kadesh in the Wilderness of Zin (Num 20). The blessing of Moses then follows in Deut 33:1-29 in the form of a blessing by a father over his sons prior to death (cf. Isaac's blessings of Esau and Jacob in Gen 27 and Jacob's blessing of his sons in Gen 49). The blessing begins with references to YHWH's revelation at Sinai and Seir in Edom and then turns to the individual tribes. It is noteworthy that Simeon is not included in the list, but Joseph's blessing refers to both Ephraim and Manasseh to account for a total of twelve tribes. Key elements in the blessing include hopes for the restoration of (the royal tribe) Judah, Levi's role in teaching Torah to Israel, Joseph's bounty and power, and Jeshurun's/Israel's security. The poem seems to presuppose a northern milieu given Joseph's power, but Judean concerns appear in the hope that Judah will be restored.

Finally, Deut 34:1-12 recounts Moses's death and burial on the summit of Pisgah on Mount Nebo in Moab. The narrative stresses Moses's view of the land of Israel and YHWH's promises to grant the land of Israel to the ancestors. It also makes sure that Moses's burial spot remains unknown, in part to ensure that it would not become a shrine. The narrative concludes with Joshua's assumption of power as the leader of Israel and an assessment of Moses's life identifying him as an incomparable prophet who spoke with YHWH face-to-face and who carried out the manifestations of YHWH's power in delivering Israel from Egypt.

Deuteronomy concludes the Pentateuch with Israel poised in Moab on the east bank of the Jordan River, ready to begin the conquest of Canaan under the leadership of Joshua. Deuteronomy thereby points to the fulfillment of the promises of YHWH to the ancestors of Israel and introduces the former prophets, Joshua, Judges, Samuel, and Kings, which recount the conquest of the land of Canaan and Israel's life in the promised land.

Conclusion

The Pentateuch—or the Torah as it is known in Judaism—provides the foundations for Jewish identity from biblical times through the present. It presents the basic narrative of Jewish origins from creation through the eve of the entry into the promised land of Israel, and it includes the basic law codes of ancient Israel and Judah that are designed to enable Israel and Judah to realize a just and holy society that will achieve divine purpose and ensure the security and well-being of the people. In presenting the early history and laws of the nation, the Torah aids Jews in understanding who they are in the world, what they must do to ensure the vitality, moral ideals, sanctity, and sense of purpose for the nation, and how they relate to G-d.

The synchronic or final literary form of the pentateuchal narrative is the form in which Jews and Christians have read the Torah narrative since antiquity. Its use of the *toledoth* formulas to establish its literary structure points to an interest in tracing the history of Israel from creation, the lives and challenges of the first human beings on earth, the ancestors of ancient Israel and Judah, the formation of Israel as a nation through its experience of deliverance from Egyptian bondage, the revelation of YHWH at Mount Sinai, and the challenges of the journey through the wilderness until Israel emerges as a holy nation, led by the Levites, Moses, and Aaron and prepares to enter the promised land of Israel.

The synchronic form of the Torah narrative shows both the positive and the negative dimensions of Israel's early history and its relationship with YHWH. We see YHWH's mercy in bringing about the creation of the world based upon the principle of the Shabbat and in granting life to the first human beings. We see YHWH's mercy once again with the blessings granted to the first ancestors of Israel, Abraham and Sarah, Isaac and Rebekah, Jacob, Leah, and Rachel, and the twelve sons of Jacob, who will go on to become the ancestors of the twelve tribes of Israel. We see YHWH's mercy in delivering the people from Egyptian bondage, in revealing the Torah to Israel at Mount Sinai, and in guiding the people through the wilderness to the borders of the promised land of Israel. We see Moses, a leader of Israel, who navigates between the demands of a G-d who both delivers the people and imposes punishment upon them and a people who constantly challenge his leadership and that of YHWH as well. And we see YHWH carefully burying Moses at the end of his life in a location where he will never be disturbed again after a lifetime of turbulence, conflict, and service both to G-d and to Israel.

But we also see YHWH's judgment against Adam and Eve when they eat from the forbidden fruit and are expelled from the garden of Eden. We see YHWH's judgment once again with the flood that destroys the world when human beings learn to shed blood and thereby desecrate YHWH's creation. We see doubts expressed about YHWH when it becomes unclear whether or not Sarah will ever bear a child, thereby ensuring the blessings that YHWH has promised. We see an immature Jacob who defrauds his brother Esau and who loses Rachel, the love of his life, and ultimately ends up as an exile in a foreign land. We see Joseph, who begins his life as a very spoiled young man who instills jealousy and anger in his brothers, but who through his own suffering matures to become a worthy leader of his own people. We see YHWH's judgment against Israel in both the gold calf and spy narratives when YHWH proposes to destroy the people and create a new nation from Moses. And finally, we see Moses denied entry into the promised land of Israel toward which he spent his life guiding his people.

Like the rest of the Hebrew Bible, the Torah shows us a realistic portrayal of both the strengths and weaknesses of human and divine character. The Pentateuch neither makes gods out of human beings in the way that Mesopotamian or Greek literature is wont to do, nor does it present G-d in purely loving terms when the realities of life in the world frequently include invasion, exile, murder, rape, and famine. In instilling in Israel and Judah their own sense of identity, the Pentateuch prepares the people for life in this world, including all of its challenges and blessings. The subsequent history of biblical Israel and Judah—and Judaism at large—bears out this agenda, insofar as they have suffered exile and destruction as well as restoration and blessing repeatedly throughout a long history from antiquity to the present.

The diachronic or the historical dimensions of the Pentateuch also have much to teach us. We have seen a process of formation that begins with the E, or Ephraimite, stratum of northern Israel in the ninth through eighth centuries BCE, a J, or Judean, redaction that edited and reread the narrative in relation to Judean interests in the late eighth through seventh centuries BCE, a D reworking of the covenant code in the seventh century BCE, and a P redaction and organization of the whole in the fifth through fourth centuries BCE. Altogether, the compositional history of the Pentateuch reconstructed here shows a combination of commitment to tradition together with the willingness to reflect upon that tradition and to expand upon it in order to meet the needs of the nation for the present and the future. The Pentateuch is the product of both the dynamism of a tradition that is designed to give expression to the changing views of the nation in relation to its historical experience as well as its stability that shows a deep commitment to learning from the past. Although some might see the Pentateuch only as a record of the past, it also functions as a blueprint for the present and future that must be critically analyzed in order to chart a course for times to come.

The institution of the final form of the Torah as the basis for Jewish life under Persian rule inaugurates a form of Jewish national life, which Joel Weinberg calls the Citizen-Temple Community, in which Jews enjoy local autonomy in governing their own affairs while simultaneously accepting the overall authority of the Achaemenid Persian empire.[1] This model ultimately developed into the Kehillah "community" system of Jewish local autonomy as political authority shifted to a succession of empires:[2] Alexander's Greek empire, the Hellenistic Ptolemaic and Seleucid empires, the Roman empire, the Byzantine empire, the Sassanian Persian empire, the Muslim empire, and on into the various European Christian and Middle Eastern Muslim kingdoms and nations that ruled over Jews throughout the world until Napoleon abolished the system in 1805 in an attempt to integrate Jews as citizens of modern France. Throughout that time, the Torah continued to serve as the foundation for Jewish identity as Judaism (a term derived from Judah which refers to the religion of Judah) developed the Rabbinic literature of the Talmuds; the Midrashic works; the Targums; the prayer book; Jewish Bible exegesis; Jewish philosophy; the various forms of Jewish mysticism, Kabbalah and Hasidism, Jewish Philosophy; modern Zionism as a form of Jewish political identity that called for the return of Jews to the promised land of Israel; and diaspora forms of Judaism, such as Reform, Conservative, and Orthodox Judaism.

Christians and Muslims also look to the Pentateuch as an element of their respective identities. Christianity views the Torah as the foundational document of the Bible, but revelation of Jesus in the New Testament has been read throughout Christian history as the inauguration of a new covenant with G-d in which the Gentiles are also included in the covenant by virtue of Jesus's crucifixion. Consequently, the Pentateuch and the rest of the Hebrew Bible become the Old Testament, or old covenant, that precedes the New Testament in documenting G-d's revelation to the world. Likewise, Islam views the Torah as the foundational document of G-d's revelation to the world. But Islam maintains the present form of the Torah is in error; the true form of the Torah resides with G-d, insofar as the revelation of the Quran through Muhammad constitutes the final and authoritative revelation of G-d's will for humankind. Both Christian and Muslim traditions maintain that they represent the true form of relationship with G-d. But when we consider G-d's eternal covenant with Israel and the world, we must recognize that G-d's covenant with Israel is still intact even as G-d expands the divine relationship to include the other nations of the earth as well, whether they practice Christianity, Islam, or even other traditions that recognize the divine. In all cases, the Pentateuch or Torah emerges as the foundational document concerning human identity in relation to G-d throughout the world.

Notes

General Preface

1. Chaim Potok, *In the Beginning* (New York: Fawcett Books, 1975), 3

Introduction

1. Magne Sæbø, ed., *Hebrew Bible/Old Testament: The History of Its Interpretation. Part III/1-2: The Nineteenth Century and the Twentieth Century* (Göttingen: Vandenhoeck & Ruprecht, 2013, 2015).

2. Ernest Nicholson, *The Pentateuch in the Twentieth Century: The Legacy of Julius Wellhausen* (Oxford and New York: Oxford University Press, 1998).

3. Julius Wellhausen, *Die Composition des Hexateuchs und der Historischen Bücher des Alten Testaments* (Berlin: Georg Reimer, 1889); Julius Wellhausen, *Prolegomena to the History of Israel* (Gloucester, MA: Peter Smith, 1973); Antony F. Campbell and Mark A. O'Brien, *Sources of the Pentateuch: Texts, Introductions, Annotations* (Minneapolis: Fortress, 1993).

4. Gerhard von Rad, "The Form-Critical Problem of the Hexateuch," in *The Problem of the Hexateuch and Other Essays*, trans. E. W. Trueman Dicken (London: SCM, 1984), 1–78.

5. Nicholson, *The Pentateuch*, 3–92.

6. Von Rad, "The Form-Critical Problem of the Hexateuch."

7. Martin Noth, *The Deuteronomistic History*, JSOTSup 15, trans. E. W. Nicholson (Sheffield: Sheffield Academic Press, 1981).

8. Martin Noth, *A History of Pentateuchal Traditions*, trans. B. W. Anderson (Englewood Cliffs, NJ: Prentice Hall, 1972). See now Rolf Rendtorff, *The Problem of the Process of Transmission in the Pentateuch*, JSOTSup 89, trans. J. J. Scullion

(Sheffield: Sheffield Academic Press, 1990); Erhard Blum, *Die Komposition der Vätergeschichte*, WMANT 57 (Neukirchen-Vlyun: Neukirchener Verlag, 1984); Erhard Blum, *Studien zur Komposition des Pentateuch*, BZAW 189 (Berlin and New York: Walter de Gruyter, 1990).

9. Thomas L. Thompson, *The Historicity of the Patriarchal Narratives*, BZAW 133 (Berlin and New York: Walter de Gruyter, 1974); John Van Seters, *Abraham in History and Tradition* (New Haven and London: Yale University Press, 1975); Nicholson, *The Pentateuch*, 132–60; Thomas B. Dozeman and Konrad Schmid, eds., *A Farewell to the Y-hwist? The Composition of the Pentateuch in Recent European Interpretation*, SBLSym34 (Atlanta: Society of Biblical Literature, 2006).

10. John Van Seters, *Prologue to History: The Y-hwist as Historian in Genesis* (Louisville: Westminster John Knox, 1992); John Van Seters, *The Life of Moses: The Y-hwist as Historian in Exodus–Numbers* (Louisville: Westminster John Knox, 1994); John Van Seters, *A Law Book for the Diaspora: Revision in the Study of the Covenant Code* (Oxford and New York: Oxford University Press, 2003); John Van Seters, *The Y-hwist: A Historian of Israelite Origins* (Winona Lake, IN: Eisenbrauns, 2013).

11. Hans Heinrich Schmid, *Der sogenannte J-hwist. Beobachtungen und Fragen zur Pentateuchforschung* (Zürich: Theologischer Verlag, 1976); Christoph Levin, *Der J-hwist*, FRLANT 157 (Göttingen: Vandenhoeck & Ruprecht, 1993).

12. Frank Moore Cross Jr., "The Priestly Work," in *Canaanite Myth and Hebrew Epic: Essays in the History of the Religion of Israel* (Cambridge, MA: Harvard University Press, 1973), 293–325.

13. Reinhard G. Kratz, "The Pentateuch in Current Research," in *The Pentateuch*, ed. Thomas B. Dozeman et al., FAT 78 (Tübingen: Mohr Siebeck, 2011), 31–61; David M. Carr, "Changes in Pentateuchal Criticism," in *Hebrew Bible/Old Testament*, 433–66.

14. David M. Carr, *Reading the Fractures of Genesis: Historical and Literary Approaches* (Louisville: Westminster John Knox, 1996).

15. Joel S. Baden, *J, E, and the Redaction of the Pentateuch*, FAT 68 (Tübingen: Mohr Siebeck, 2009); Joel S. Baden, *The Composition of the Pentateuch: Renewing the Documentary Hypothesis* (New Haven and London: Yale University Press, 2012); Joel S. Baden, *The Promise to the Patriarchs* (Oxford and New York: Oxford University Press, 2013).

16. David P. Wright, *Inventing G-d's Law: How the Covenant Code of the Bible Used and Revised the Laws of Hammurabi* (Oxford and New York: Oxford University Press, 2009).

17. Bernard M. Levinson, *Deuteronomy and the Hermeneutics of Legal Innovation* (Oxford and New York: Oxford University Press, 1997); Bernard M. Levinson, *Legal Revision and Religious Renewal in Ancient Israel* (Cambridge and New York: Cambridge University Press, 2008).

18. Jeffrey Stackert, *Rewriting the Torah: Literary Revision in Deuteronomy and the Holiness Legislation*, FAT 52 (Tübingen: Mohr Siebeck, 2007).

19. Jeffrey Stackert, *A Prophet Like Moses: Prophecy, Law, and Israelite Religion* (Oxford and New York: Oxford University Press, 2014).

20. See my study, "Hosea's Reading of Pentateuchal Narratives: A Window for a Foundational E Stratum," in *The Formation of the Pentateuch* (J. C. Gertz et al, eds.; FAT 111 (Tübingen: Mohr Siebeck, 2016), 851–71.

21. Marvin A. Sweeney, "Hosea" and "Amos," in *The Twelve Prophets*, Berit Olam (Collegeville, MN: Liturgical, 2000), 1–144 and 189–276.

22. Israel Finkelstein, *The Forgotten Kingdom: The Archaeology and History of Northern Israel* (Atlanta: Society of Biblical Literature, 2013).

23. Pritchard, *ANET*, 278–79.

24. Marvin A. Sweeney, *I and II Kings: A Commentary*, OTL (Louisville: Westminster John Knox, 2007).

25. Pritchard, *ANEP*, fig. 351.

26. S. Page, "A Stela of Adad Nirari III and Negal-ereš from Tell al Rimlah," *Iraq* 30 (1968): 139–53.

27. A. Biran and J. Naveh, "An Aramaic Stele Fragment from Tel Dan," *IEJ* 43 (1993): 81–98; A. Biran and J. Naveh, "The Tel Dan Inscription: A New Fragment," *IEJ* 45 (1995): 1–18.

28. Meindert Dijkstra, "Is Balaam also Among the Prophets?" *JBL* 114 (1995): 43–64; Jo Ann Hackett, *The Balaam Text from Deir ʿAllā,* HSM 31 (Chico, CA: Scholars Press, 1980).

29. Pritchard, *ANET*, 320–21.

30. Marvin A. Sweeney, "Form Criticism and the Endangered Matriarch Narratives of Genesis," in *Method Matters: Essays on the Interpretation of the Hebrew Bible in Honor of David L. Petersen*, ed. J. M. LeMon and K. H. Richards (Atlanta: Society of Biblical Literature, 2009), 17–38.

31. Ronald E. Clements, *Abraham and David* (London: SCM, 1967).

32. Jon D. Levenson, "The Temple and the World," *JR* 64 (1984): 275–98; Jon D. Levenson, *Sinai and Zion: An Entry into the Jewish Bible* (Minneapolis: Winston, 1985); Joel Rosenberg, *Kingship and Kin: Political Allegory in the Hebrew Bible* (Bloomington and Indianapolis: Indiana University Press, 1986).

33. Marvin A. Sweeney, "Samuel's Institutional Identity in the Deuteronomistic History," in *Constructs of Prophecy in the Former and Latter Prophets and Other Texts*, ed. L. L. Grabbe and M. Nissinen, ANEM 4 (Atlanta: Society of Biblical Literature, 2011), 165–74.

34. Marvin A. Sweeney, "Israelite and Judean Religions," in *The Cambridge History of Religions in the Ancient World. Volume 1: From the Bronze Age to the Hellenistic Age*, ed. M. Salzman et al. (Cambridge: Cambridge University Press, 2013), 151–73.

35. Marvin A. Sweeney, "The Wilderness Traditions of the Pentateuch: A Reassessment of Their Function and Intent in Relation to Exodus 32–34," in SBL *1989 Seminar Papers*, ed. D. Lull (Atlanta: Scholars Press, 1989), 291–99; Craig Evan Anderson, "The Tablets of Testimony and a Reversal of Outcome in the Golden Calf Episode," *Hebrew Studies* 50 (2000): 41–65.

36. Levinson, *Deuteronomy*.

37. Wright, *Inventing G-d's Law*; Van Seters, *A Law Book*.

38. D. J. Wiseman, "The Vassal Treaties of Esarhaddon," *Iraq* 20 (1958); Pritchard, *ANET*, 534–41.

39. Dijkstra, "Is Balaam"; Hackett, *The Balaam Text*.

40. Cross, "The Priestly Work."

41. Matthew A. Thomas, *These Are the Generations: Identity, Covenant, and the Toledoth Formulae* (New York: T and T Clark, 2011).

42. Marvin A. Sweeney, *Tanak: A Theological and Critical Introduction to the Jewish Bible* (Minneapolis: Fortress, 2012), 49–50.

Genesis

1. Cross, "The Priestly Work"; Thomas, *These Are the Generations*.

2. Sweeney, *Tanak*, 49–50.

3. For a translation of the Enuma Elish, see Pritchard, *ANET* 60–72, 501–3.

4. For a translation of the Baal Cycle, see Pritchard, *ANET* 129–42.

5. Levenson, *Sinai and Zion.*

6. Michael Fishbane, "Genesis 1:1–2:4a/The Creation," in *Text and Texture: Close Readings of Selected Biblical Texts* (New York: Schocken, 1979), 3–16.

7. For the source assignments of all Pentateuchal texts, see Campbell and O'Brien, *Sources.*

8. Jon D. Levenson, *Creation and the Persistence of Evil: The Jewish Drama of Divine Omnipotence* (San Francisco: Harper and Row, 1988).

9. Harry M. Orlinsky, *Notes on the New Translation of the Torah* (Philadelphia: Jewish Publication Society, 1969), 49–52.

10. Michael Fishbane, "Genesis 1:1–2:4a."

11. Ludwig Koehler and Walter Baumgartner, *Hebrew and Aramaic Lexicon of the Old Testament*, 5 vols. (Leiden: Brill, 1996), 460.

12. *HALOT*, 1190.

13. Ibid., 14.

14. Ibid., 1030.

15. Carol Meyers, *Discovering Eve: Ancient Israelite Women in Context* (New York and Oxford: Oxford University Press, 1988), 78–96.

16. M. Heerma van Voss, "Hathor," in *Dictionary of Deities and Demons in the Bible*, ed., K. van der Toorn et al (Leiden: Brill; Grand Rapids: Eerdmans, 1999), 385–86.

17. Pritchard, *ANEP*, 469–74.

18. W. G. Lambert and A. R. Millard, *Atra Ḫasis: The Babylonian Story of the Flood* (Oxford: Clarendon, 1969). For the Gilgamesh epic, see Pritchard, *ANET*, 72–99, 503–7.

19. Van Seters, *Abraham in History and Tradition*; Thompson, *The Historicity of the Patriarchal Narratives.*

20. For a translation of the Amarna Letters, see Pritchard, *ANET*, 483–90.

21. Marvin A. Sweeney, *Reading the Hebrew Bible after the Shoah: Engaging Holocaust Theology* (Minneapolis: Fortress, 2008), 23–41.

22. H. Tadmor, "The Campaigns of Sargon II of Assur: A Chronological-Historical Study," *JCS* 12 (1958): 22–40, 77–100.

23. Sweeney, "Form Criticism: The Question of the Endangered Matriarchs in Genesis."

24. Moshe Weinfeld, "Tithe," *EncJud* 15 (n.d.): 1156–62.

25. Marvin A. Sweeney, "Form Criticism," in *To Each Its Own Meaning: An Introduction to Biblical Criticisms and Their Application*, ed. S. L. McKenzie and S. R. Haynes (Louisville: Westminster John Knox, 1999), 58–89.

26. See the Sefire treaty, Pritchard, *ANET*, 659–61; Moshe Weinfeld, "The Covenant of Grant in the OT and in the Ancient Near East," *JAOS* 90 (1970): 184–203.

27. Pritchard, *ANET*, 172.

28. Ibid., 326.

29. Marvin A. Sweeney, "Puns, Politics, and Perushim in the Jacob Cycle: A Case Study in Teaching the English Hebrew Bible," *Shofar* 9 (1991): 103–118.

30. For the Tel Dan Inscription, see Biran and Naveh, "An Aramaic Stele Fragment from Tel Dan," 81–98; Biran and Naveh, "The Tel Dan Inscription," 1–18. For the Deir Alla Inscription, see Dijkstra, "Is Balaam," 43–64. For the Mesha Inscription, see Pritchard, *ANET*, 320–21.

31. For the Black Obelisk of Shalmaneser III, see Pritchard, *ANEP*, 351–55; for the vassal list of Adad Nirari III, see Page, "A Stela of Adad Nirari III and Negal-ereš from Tell al Rimlah."

32. Fishbane, "Genesis 25:19–35:22/The Jacob Cycle," in *Text and Texture*, 40–62; John E. Anderson, *Jacob and the Divine Trickster: A Theology of Deception and YHWH's Fidelity to the Ancestral Promise in the Jacob Cycle*, Siphrut 5 (Winona Lake, IN: Eisenbrauns, 2011).

33. Victor Avigdor Hurowitz, "Babylon in Bethel—New Light on Jacob's Dream," in *Orientalism, Assyriology, and the Bible*, ed. S. W. Holloway (Sheffield: Sheffield Phoenix Press, 2007), 436–48.

34. George W. Coats, *From Canaan to Egypt: Structural and Theological Context for the Joseph Story* (Washington, DC: The Catholic Biblical Association, 1976).

35. James L. Kugel, *In Potiphar's House: The Interpretive Life of Biblical Texts* (San Francisco: Harper and Row, 1990).

36. Sweeney, *1 and 2 Kings*, 152–86.

37. Pritchard, *ANET*, 23–25.

Exodus

1. Konrad Schmid, *Genesis and the Moses Story: Israel's Dual Origins in the Hebrew Bible*, Siphrut 3 (Winona Lake, IN: Eisenbrauns, 2010).

2. Sweeney, "Hosea's Reading of Pentateuchal Narratives"; Tzemach L. Yoreh, *The First Book of G-d*, BZAW 402 (Berlin and New York: Walter de Gruyter, 2010).

3. Cross, "The Priestly Work," 291–325, esp. 308–21.

4. Mark S. Smith, *The Pilgrimage Pattern in Exodus*, JSOTSup 239 (Sheffield: Sheffield Academic Press, 1997); Angela R. Roskop, *The Wilderness Itineraries: Genre, Geography, and the Growth of the Torah* (Winona Lake, IN: Eisenbrauns, 2011).

5. Levenson, *Sinai and Zion*.

6. Fishbane, "Genesis 1:1–2:4a," 12–13.

7. Sweeney, "Samuel's Institutional Identity in the Deuteronomistic History."

8. The Egyptian city of Pithom was only founded in the seventh century BCE. See T. F. Wei, "Pithom," in *ABD* 5:376–77.

9. See "The Asiatic Campaigning of Amen-Hotep II," in Pritchard, *ANET*, 247, where Amen-Hotep II claims to hold 3,600 Apiru slaves.

10. J. M. Weinstein and D. B. Redford, "Hyksos," in *ABD*, 3:341–48.

11. Pritchard, *ANET*, 376–78.

12. Ibid., 119.

13. Nahum Sarna, *Exodus*, JPS Torah Commentary (Philadelphia: Jewish Publication Society, 5751/1991), 14.

14. George W. Coats, *Exodus 1–18*, FOTL 2A (Grand Rapids and Cambridge: Eerdmans, 1999), 32–42, 174.

15. D. B. Redford, "Execration and Execration Texts," in *ABD*, 2:681–82.

16. Thomas B. Dozeman, *Exodus*, ECC (Grand Rapids and Cambridge: Eerdmans, 2009), 176–344.

17. Sweeney, "Samuel's Institutional Identity."

18. Sweeney, *1 and 2 Kings*, 161–86, 205–369.

19. Nahum Sarna, *Exploring Exodus: The Heritage of Biblical Israel* (New York: Schocken, 1986), 103–10.

20. Coats, *Exodus 1-18*, 117–21.

21. Ibid., 121–23.

22. Sarna, *Exodus*, 98.

23. Judith Baskin, *Pharaoh's Counsellors*, BJS 47 (Chico, CA: Scholars Press, 1983).

24. D. J. Wiseman, *The Vassal Treaties of Esarhaddon* (London: British School of Archaeology in Iraq, 1958).

25. Dennis J. McCarthy, *Old Testament Covenant: A Survey of Current Opinions* (Richmond: John Knox, 1972).

26. Wright, *Inventing G-d's Law*; Van Seters, *A Law Book*.

27. J. J. Finkelstein, *The Ox That Gored* (Philadelphia: The American Philosophical Society, 1981).

28. Sweeney, "The Wilderness Traditions of the Pentateuch."

29. Sweeney, *Reading the Bible after the Shoah*, 52–57, 67–72.

30. Sweeney, "The Wilderness Traditions."

31. Marvin A. Sweeney, *King Josiah of Judah: The Lost Messiah of Israel* (Oxford and New York: Oxford University Press, 2001), 137–69.

Leviticus

1. Mary Douglas, *Leviticus as Literature* (New York and Oxford: Oxford University Press, 1999).

2. For commentaries on Leviticus, see Baruch Levine, *Leviticus*, JPS Torah Commentary (Philadelphia: Jewish Publication Society, 5749/1989); Jacob Milgrom, *Leviticus 1–16*, AB 3 (New York: Doubleday, 1991); Jacob Milgrom, *Leviticus 17–22*, AB 3A (New York: Doubleday, 2000); Jacob Milgrom, *Leviticus 23–27*, AB 3B (New York: Doubleday, 2001).

3. Martin Noth, *A History of Pentateuchal Traditions* (Englewood Cliffs, NJ: Prentice-Hall, 1972), 8–9; Martin Noth, *Leviticus*, OTL (Philadelphia: Westminster, 1965), 9–10.

4. Nicholson, "The Priestly Source," *The Pentateuch*, 17–21; Wellhausen, *Die Composition des Hexateuchs*, 84.

5. Marvin A. Sweeney, "Ezekiel 18:1–19:14," *Reading Ezekiel: A Literary and Theological Commentary*, ROT (Macon, GA: Smyth and Helwys, 2013), 92–99.

6. Israel Knohl, *The Sanctuary of Silence: The Priestly Torah and the Holiness School* (Minneapolis: Fortress, 1995); Milgrom, *Leviticus 17-22*, 1319–67; Carr, "Changes in Penatateuchal Criticism," 460–64.

7. Stackert, *Rewriting the Torah*; Nihan, *From Priestly Torah to Pentateuch*.

8. Rolf P. Knierim, "The Purpose and Setting of the Text," *Text and Concept in Leviticus 1:1-9*, FAT 2 (Tübingen: Mohr Siebeck, 1992), 98–111.

9. Baruch Halpern, "The Palace," *The First Historians: The Hebrew Bible and History* (San Francisco: Harper and Row, 1988), 46–54.

10. Sweeney, "The Northern Kingdom of Israel," *King Josiah of Judah*, 77–93.

11. Deborah L. Ellens, *Women in the Sex Texts of Leviticus and Deuteronomy: A Comparative Conceptual Analysis*, LHBOTS 458 (New York: T and T Clark, 2008).

12. Stackert, *Rewriting the Torah*, 113–64.

Numbers

1. For commentaries on Numbers, see Martin Noth, *Numbers: A Commentary*, OTL (Philadelphia: Westminster, 1968); Jacob Milgrom, *Numbers*, JPS Torah Commentary (Philadelphia: Jewish Publication Society, 1990/5750); Baruch A. Levine, *Numbers 1–20*, AB 4 (New York: Doubleday, 1993); Baruch A. Levine, *Numbers 21–36*, AB 4A (New York: Doubleday, 2000); Rolf P. Knierim and George W. Coats, *Numbers*, FOTL 4 (Grand Rapids and Cambridge: Eerdmans, 2005).

2. For studies on Numbers, see George W. Coats, *Rebellion in the Wilderness: The Murmuring Motif in the Wilderness Traditions of the Old Testament* (Nashville: Abingdon, 1968); Dennis T. Olson, *The Death of the Old and the Birth of the New: The Framework of the Book of Numbers and the Pentateuch*, BJS 71 (Chico, CA: Scholars Press, 1985); Won W. Lee, *Punishment and Forgiveness in Israel's Migratory Campaign* (Grand Rapids and Cambridge: Eerdmans, 2003); Adriane

Leveen, *Memory and Tradition in the Book of Numbers* (Cambridge: Cambridge University Press, 2008); Roskop, *The Wilderness Itineraries.*

3. Sweeney, *Tanak*, 124–26.

4. Roskop, *The Wilderness Itineraries.*

5. Smith, *The Pilgrimage Pattern.*

6. Noth, *Numbers*, 4–5; see Thomas, *These Are the Generations*, who identified the structural role of the *toledoth* formula in Num 3:1.

7. Cross, "The Priestly Work," 293–325.

8. Levine, *Numbers 1–20*, 198, 200–212.

9. Noth, *Numbers*, 77–78; Campbell and O'Brien, *Sources*, 150.

10. Noth, *Numbers*, 88–90.

11. Baden, "A Complaint in the Wilderness" and "The E Source," in *The Composition of the Pentateuch*, 82–128.

12. Milgrom, *Numbers*, 93.

13. Ibid., 127–28.

14. Baden, "The Revolt in the Wilderness" and "The P Source," in *The Composition of the Pentateuch*, 149–92.

15. Levine, *Numbers 1–20*, 405–7.

16. For the Tel Dan stele, see Biran and Naveh, "An Aramaic Stele Fragment from Tel Dan"; Biran and Naveh, "The Tel Dan Inscription." For the Deir Alla Inscription, see Dijkstra, "Is Balaam." For the Mesha Inscription, see Pritchard, *ANET*, 320–21. For discussion of the historical background, see Sweeney, "1 Kings 16:29–2 Kings 15:16," in *1 and 2 Kings*, 202–372.

17. Sweeney, *King Josiah of Judah*, 137–69.

18. Milgrom, "Magic, Monotheism, and the Sin of Moses," *Numbers*, 448–56.

19. Levine, "The Balaam Inscriptions," *Numbers 21–36*, 263–75.

20. Dijkstra, "Is Balaam."

21. See Pritchard, *ANET*, 320–21; Sweeney, "1 Kings 16:29–2 Kings 15:16," in *1 and 2 Kings*, 202–372.

22. Frederick H. Cryer, *Divination in Ancient Israel and Its Near Eastern Environment: A Socio-Historical Investigation* (London: T & T Clark, 1962).

Deuteronomy

1. For commentaries on Deuteronomy, see Gerhard von Rad, *Deuteronomy: A Commentary*, OTL (Philadelphia: Westminster, 1966); Moshe Weinfeld, *Deuteronomy 1–11*, AB 5 (New York: Doubleday, 1991); Jeffrey H. Tigay, *Deuteronomy*, JPS Torah Commentary (Philadelphia: Jewish Publication Society, 5756/1996); Richard D. Nelson, *Deuteronomy*, OTL (Louisville: Westminster John Knox, 2002); Jack R. Lundbom, *Deuteronomy: A Commentary* (Grand Rapids and Cambridge: Eerdmans, 2013). For discussion of research, see R. E. Clements, *Deuteronomy*, OTL (Sheffield: Sheffield Academic Press, 1989).

2. Levinson, *Deuteronomy and the Hermeneutics of Legal Innovation.*

3. Von Rad, "Introduction," in *Deuteronomy*, 11–15; Sweeney, *King Josiah of Judah*, 142–43.

4. Campbell and O'Brien, *Sources*, 90; Anthony F. Campbell and Mark A. O'Brien, *Unfolding the Deuteronomistic History: Origins, Upgrades, Present Text* (Minneapolis: Fortress, 2000), 98–99.

5. Campbell and O'Brien, "Introduction" and "The Book of Deuteronomy," in *Unfolding the Deuteronomistic History*, 1–99; Moshe Weinfeld, *Deuteronomy and the Deuteronomic School* (Oxford: Oxford University Press, 1972); Moshe Weinfeld, "Introduction," in *Deuteronomy 1–11*, 1–84.

6. Mark A. O'Brien, "The Book of Deuteronomy," *CR:BS* 3 (1995): 95–128; Clements, *Deuteronomy.*

7. E. W. Nicholson, *Deuteronomy and Tradition: Literary and Historical Traditions in the Book of Deuteronomy* (Philadelphia: Fortress, 1967).

8. Ronald E. Clements, "Deuteronomy and the Jerusalem Cult Tradition," *VT* 15 (1965): 300–312; Weinfeld, *Deuteronomy and the Deuteronomic School*; Sweeney, "Deuteronomy," in *King Josiah*, 137–69.

9. Clements, "Deuteronomic Revision of Earlier Laws," in *Deuteronomy*, 24–27.

10. Weinfeld, "Treaty, Form, and Phraseology," in *Deuteronomy and the Deuteronomic School*, 59–178.

11. Sweeney, "Deuteronomy," in *King Josiah*, 37–69; Baruch Halpern, "Jerusalem and the Lineages in the Seventh Century BCE: Kinship and the Rise of Individual

Moral Liability," in *Law and Ideology in Monarchic Israel*, ed. B. Halpern and D. W. Hobson, JSOTSup 124 (Sheffield: Sheffield Academic Press, 1991), 11–107.

12. Carolyn Pressler, *The View of Women Found in Deuteronomic Family Laws*, BZAW 216 (Berlin and New York: Walter de Gruyter, 1993).

13. Campbell and O'Brien, *Unfolding the Deuteronomistic History*; Sweeney, "Deuteronomy," in *King Josiah*, 137–69.

14. Sweeney, *Reading the Hebrew Bible after the Shoah*.

15. Campbell and O'Brien, *Unfolding the Deuteronomistic History*, 39; Lundbom, *Deuteronomy*, 6–20.

16. Georg Braulik, "The Sequence of Laws in Deuteronomy 12–26 and in the Decalogue," in *A Song of Power and the Power of Song: Essays on the Book of Deuteronomy*, ed. D. L. Christensen (Winona Lake, IN: Eisenbrauns, 1993), 313–35.

17. The Hebrew expression is *lo' tirtsakh*, "you shall not murder," whereas "you shall not kill," would be *lo' tiqtol*. The instruction prohibits unjustifiable killing but not cases of justifiable killing, such as self-defense.

18. Wiseman, *The Vassal Treaties of Esarhaddon*; S. Parpola and K. Watanabe, *Neo-Assyrian Treaties and Loyalty Oaths*, SAS 2 (Helsinki: University of Helsinki, 1988).

19. McCarthy, *Old Testament Covenant*; Dennis J. McCarthy, *Treaty and Covenant: A Study in Form in the Ancient Oriental Documents and in the Old Testament* (Rome: Biblical Institute Press, 1978); Clements, *Deuteronomy*, 20–22.

20. Campbell and O'Brien, *Unfolding the Deuteronomistic History*, 39.

21. Levinson, *Deuteronomy and the Hermeneutics of Legal Innovation*.

22. Levinson, "The Innovation of Cult Centralization," in *Deuteronomy and the Hermeneutics of Legal Innovation*, 23–52.

23. Levinson, "The Transformation of Passover," in *Deuteronomy and the Hermeneutics of Legal Innovation*, 53–97.

24. Levinson, "The Transformation of Justice," in *Deuteronomy and the Hermeneutics of Legal Innovation*, 98–143.

25. Baden, *J, E, and the Redaction of the Pentateuch*, who argues that D knows the E and J strata of the Pentateuch.

26. Ibid.

27. Sweeney, *Reading the Hebrew Bible after the Shoah*.

28. E. F. Campbell, "Shechem," *NEAEHL*, 4:1345–54.

29. Jack Shechter, *The Land of Israel: The Theological Dimensions. A Study of a Promise and a Land's "Holiness"* (Lanham, MD: University Press of America, 2010), who demonstrates that Deuteronomy does not hold to a strictly conditional understanding of Israel's covenant with YHWH but envisions restoration following repentance in keeping with the unconditional nature of the covenant.

30. Lundbom, *Deuteronomy*, 852–57.

Conclusion

1. Joel Weinberg, *The Citizen-Temple Community*, JSOTSup 151 (Sheffield: JSOT Press, 1992).

2. "Community," *EncJud*, 5:808–29.

Glossary

apodictic law—a law form that categorically states legal principle concerning what one can or cannot do

Atrahasis—an Akkadian name of the Mesopotamian flood hero

BCE—Before Common Era, used in place of BC, Before Christ, to include Judaism in the chronology

case law—a law form that states the circumstances of a legal case followed by its resolution.

CE—Common Era, used in place of AD, Anno Domini, Year of Our L-rd, to include Judaism in the chronology

creatio ex nihilo—the principle of creation out of nothing

D source—the Deuteronomic source of the Pentateuch, named for Deuteronomy, which compromises most of the D source in the Pentateuch

Dead Sea Scrolls—ancient manuscripts of the Bible and other works written in Hebrew, Aramaic, and some Greek by a sect of Judaism that lived in Qumran during the late-Greco-Roman period, ca. second century BCE through the first century CE

Deir Alla Inscription—a late-ninth or early-eighth-century inscription found at a site called Deir Alla, southeast of the Sea of Galilee in modern Jordan; the inscription, written in a Semitic language akin to Hebrew, Aramaic, and perhaps Ammonite, which presents a vision of the Prophet, Balaam bar Beor

diachronic—a term used to describe the historical dimensions of literature, including both the time or setting of its composition or the historical process of its composition

DtrH, the Deuteronomistic History—a scholarly term used to describe the Former Prophets, viz., Joshua, Judges, Samuel, and Kings, which is believed by many scholars to be a history of Israel and Judah written on the basis of theological and literature perspectives from Deuteronomy

E source—the Elohistic or Ephraimite source of the Pentateuch, named for its use of Elohim, the generic term for G-d, until the time of Moses (Exod 3; 6) when YHWH was then employed

Gilgamesh—an early Mesopotamian King and Hero, who went on a quest to find immortality following the death of his friend, Enkidu

Hammurabi or Hammurapi—a major Amorite King of Babylon during the early-eighteenth century BCE known especially for his law code

Hathor, also known as Kadesha—an Egyptian and Canaanite goddess associated with life and death who apparently served as a model for the conceptualization of Eve

Ishtar—the Mesopatamian goddess of order and stability in creation, identified with the Morning Star or Venus, which is the first light to appear in the heavens each morning

J source—the Jahwist or Judean source of the Pentateuch, named for its use of the Divine Name, JHWH (German, for YHWH), throughout, and later named for Judah, where it was written

Kadesha, also known as Hathor—an Egyptian and Canaanite goddess associated with life and death who apparently served as a model for the conceptualization of Eve

lex talionis—the legal principle that the perpetrator of a crime should be punished with injury or loss equivalent to the crime (e.g., an eye for an eye)

Marduk—the city god of Babylon and chief god of the Babylonian pantheon

Masoretic Text—the Hebrew Text of the Bible prepared by Masorim, or Transmitters of the Hebrew text during the seventh through tenth centuries CE

Midian—the region of the northwest Arabian Peninsula, south and southeast of the land of Israel

In—an Egyptian god of fertility and life

P source—the Priestly source of the Pentateuch, named for the Priestly character of its material

Qumran—the name of small town on the northwest shore of the Dead Sea where ancient Jews wrote the Dead Sea Scrolls in the late-Hellenistic period, ca. second century BCE through the first century CE when the Romans destroyed the site

R. Abraham Ibn Ezra—Rabbi Abraham Ibn Ezra, 1089–1167, an important Rabbinic scholar from the Middle Ages, who wrote commentary on the Bible and the Talmudic literature, and played a role in laying the basis for modern critical scholarship

Radak—Rabbi David Kimkhi, 1160–1275 CE, a major Jewish scholar of the Middle Ages who wrote important commentaries on the Bible, foundational works on Hebrew grammar, and other works of Jewish scholarship

Resheph—an Egyptian god of plague and death

R. Saadia Gaon—Rabbi Saadia ben Joseph al-Fayumi, 892–942 CE, an early medieval Rabbi who wrote the first philosophy of Judaism, some of the first grammatical works on the Hebrew language, translated portions of the Bible into Judeo-Arabic, and set the order of the Jewish prayer book

Rashi—Rabbi Solomon ben Isaac, 1040–1105 CE, one of the most important Jewish commentators during the Middle Ages who wrote foundational commentary on the Bible and the Talmudic literature

Septuagint—the Greek translation of the Hebrew Bible, prepared initially according to tradition by seventy or seventy-two scholars working in Egypt during the second century BCE

Shabbat—Hebrew for the Sabbath

source—a discreet literary composition, such as J, E, D, or P, that was composed independently and later combined with the other sources of the Pentateuch

stratum—a layer of literary composition, such as J, E, D, or P, that was composed sequentially to expand and interpret the earlier layers of the composition of the Pentateuch

synchronic—the final, full, or present form of literature, apart from questions of its historical setting or the history of its composition

tefillin—phylacteries or small leather pouches containing quotations from the Torah that are tied to the head and army by Orthodox Jews when they pray

toledoth—Hebrew for *generations*

Torah—the Hebrew word for *instruction*, but often mistranslated as *law*. Torah refers to the Pentateuch, which instructs Jews in their early history, laws, and identity. It may also be used to refer to holy, Jewish instruction in general

Utnapishtim—one of the Akkadian names of the Mesopotramian flood hero

Ziusudra—the Sumerian name of the Mesopotamian flood hero

Selected Annotated Bibliography

General

Campbell, Antony F., and Mark A. O'Brien. *Sources of the Pentateuch: Texts, Introductions, Annotations.* Minneapolis: Fortress, 1993.

An authoritative source analysis of the Pentateuch, based on the foundational work of Martin Noth, that provides pertinent commentary to identify and interpret the major sources in the Pentateuchal narrative.

Baden, Joel S. *The Composition of the Pentateuch: Renewing the Documentary Hypothesis.* New Haven and London: Yale University Press, 2012.

A discussion of the contemporary understanding of source analysis that takes account of the advances in the field over the past century and provides analyses of selected texts to demonstrate how the method works.

Genesis

Arnold, Bill T. *Genesis.* New Cambridge Bible Commentary. Cambridge and New York: Cambridge University Press, 2008.

An up-to-date critical commentary on the book of Genesis that combines synchronic literary and diachronic historical reading strategies in interpreting the text.

Carr, David M. *Reading the Fractures of Genesis: Historical and Literary Approaches.* Louisville: Westminster John Knox, 1996.

A sophisticated redaction-critical analysis of the book of Genesis that identifies the final P edition of the book in relation to its underlying JE foundations.

Exodus

Meyers, Carol. *Exodus*. New Cambridge Bible Commentary. Cambridge and New York: Cambridge University Press, 2005.

An up-to-date critical commentary that combines literary, archeological, and social-scientific expertise in an analysis of the text that takes seriously the role of women, the presentation of ancient Judah's and Israel's priestly institutions, and the influence of mythology.

Stackert, Jeffrey. *A Prophet Like Moses: Prophecy, Law, and Israelite Religion*. Oxford and New York: Oxford University Press, 2014.

A well-conceived study that employs contemporary advances in source analysis to reconstruct the underlying interpretations of Moses as prophet and leader of Israel in the Pentateuchal narratives.

Leviticus

Milgrom, Jacob. *Leviticus*. Continental Commentary. Minneapolis: Fortress, 2004.

An authoritative and readable commentary that builds upon the author's earlier three-volume Anchor Bible commentary to present an analysis of the role of ritual, holiness, and ethical perspective in the book of Leviticus.

Knohl, Israel. *The Sanctuary of Silence: The Priestly Torah and the Holiness School*. Minneapolis: Fortress, 1995.

An innovative source-critical analysis of the book of Leviticus that distinguishes the earlier Priestly writings from the later Holiness school that played a key role in editing the entire Pentateuch.

Numbers

Milgrom, Jacob. *Numbers*. The JPS Torah Commentary. Philadelphia and New York: The Jewish Publication Society, 1990/5750.

A readable, critical commentary that combines insights from modern biblical scholarship and traditional Jewish Bible commentary in elucidating the text of the book of Numbers.

Roskop, Angela R. *The Wilderness Itineraries: Genre, Geography, and the Growth of Torah*. History, Archaeology, and Culture of the Levant 3. Winona Lake, IN: Eisenbrauns, 2011.

This ground-breaking study draws upon the use of itineraries in Egyptian and Assyrian scribal culture to re-envision the wilderness itineraries of the Pentateuch as a combined liturgical and military campaign to advance through the wilderness and to conquer the land of Canaan.

Deuteronomy

Nelson, Richard D. *Deuteronomy: A Commentary.* Old Testament Library. Louisville: Westminster John Knox, 2002.

A critical and literary commentary that draws upon ancient Assyrian treaty texts to identify Deuteronomy as a work designed to support the program of religious reform and national restoration initiated by King Josiah of Judah during the period of Assyria's decline.

Levinson, Bernard M. *Deuteronomy and the Hermeneutics of Legal Innovation.* Oxford and New York: Oxford University Press, 1997.

A ground-breaking analysis of the laws of Deuteronomy that demonstrates how they reworked earlier legal texts from the book of Exodus to update Israelite and Judean law during the late-monarchic period in Judah.

Author Index

Subject Index

CPSIA information can be obtained
at www.ICGtesting.com
Printed in the USA
LVOW07s2118190917
549321LV00002B/3/P

9 781426 765032